GET INTO MEDICAL SCHOOL

Write the Perfect Personal Statement

Effective techniques & over 100 examples of real successful personal statements

Olivier Picard, Dominique Pizzingrilli

Published by ISC Medical
97 Judd Street, London WC1H 9JG
Tel: 0845 226 9487

First Edition: May 2010
ISBN13: 978-1-905812-10-3
A catalogue record for this book is available from the British Library.
© Interview Skills Consulting Limited 2010. All rights reserved.

ISC Medical would like to thank all the medical students who have agreed to offer their personal statement for publication. The views presented in the personal statements contained within this book are those of their respective original authors and may differ from the views of this book's authors.

Printed in the United Kingdom by:
Purbrooks Ltd, Gresham Way, Wimbledon Park, London SW19 8ED

Preface

Many years ago, I was in the same position as you, the reader; I too was once a potential medical school applicant who was striving to make myself noticeable on the UCAS form. Now I help out and sit on interview panels that select these students.

Personal statements are one of the few times where the admission tutors can get an overview of the person applying. Whilst academic grades and references are used to ensure that the candidate meets basic eligibility criteria for an interview, it is the personal statement that can tip the balance on whether or not you get a medical school interview and a place.

Admission tutors face a daunting prospect picking the "right" person from a field of all equally brilliant and talented individuals. Competition is fierce, and there is no guarantee of a place. In 2009 there were 18,107 applicants for medical school, of which 7,977 were accepted. Anything that can help to distinguish you from the thousands of others who apply will be an advantage.

The personal statement allows you <u>one</u> page to showcase your talents and gives the admission tutors a glimpse of what motivates you, your personal experiences and anything else that makes you unique. This is your time to shine, display your own personal attributes and help your application to stand out from the crowd.

Back when I was writing my own personal statement, it felt like the most important piece of writing that I had ever written, and I took on outdated whispered advice from generations of students and doctors before me. The process was long and arduous, since there were neither sample statements nor up-to-date qualified advice from which I could draw upon.

This book, however, will help you make the most of your personal statement, providing you with all the high-quality information you need by showing you a sample of successful applicants' statements to help you build your own successful application for the medical schools that you wish to pursue.

Philip Xiu
5th Year Medical Student, Cambridge University

Contents table

1 Introduction

Competition for places at medical school is very high. Many prospective medical school applicants assume that getting as far as an interview is just down to sheer luck; that's far from being the case and there is a lot you can do to improve your chances of getting noticed, obtaining an interview and getting a place at medical school. It starts with your personal statement.

The personal statement is one of the few opportunities you will have to differentiate yourself from the thousands of other medical school applicants. Whilst your academic grades and references will demonstrate your basic eligibility for the course at your chosen medical school and entry exams will obviously influence the process, it is your personal statement that will tip the balance on whether or not you get an interview. This is particularly true when applying to medical schools where all candidates are likely to have good grades and where competition will be extremely fierce; some medical schools such as Bristol can have a ratio of applications to places as high as 17:1.

The space allowed for your personal statement on the UCAS application form is limited. Effectively, it relates to approximately one page of typed A4, in Arial font size 10. This is no mean feat since you probably won't have done much creative writing since your GCSEs, and, even if you have, writing about oneself concisely in a confident and mature manner is not something that most people are used to, or good at.

In addition, many excellent candidates fail to get shortlisted for interviews simply because they misunderstand what is required of the personal statement. They don't give enough thought to the information and skills they want to convey and consequently fail to produce a statement of a sufficiently high calibre.

This book will take you through the art of writing a personal statement, and provide you with structures and techniques that you can apply easily to find suitable content and write it up convincingly. We have also included over 100 examples of real personal statements from successful candidates in all UK medical schools so that you can visualise the different styles favoured by different admission tutors and develop your own unique and powerful personal statement.

2   How to use this book

Reflecting on and writing about yourself

This book contains all the information and advice you will need to write your own accomplished and successful personal statement. The first few chapters will help you understand what the admission tutors actually expect to see and suggest suitable content and structure. You will find comprehensive advice on how to tackle writing your personal statement, with examples of good and bad practice.

We have complemented this with over 100 examples of real personal statements, written by people who were successful in obtaining a place at medical school. These are intended to demonstrate the variety of styles and how differently people can write. They vary tremendously in style and content; some tell a story and others are more succinct and factual, but they are all successful personal statements.

As you read through the book and gain inspiration for your own personal statement, keep in mind that there are many ways to write a good statement. Everyone has their own style and it is important that you remain true to yourself. Whatever you write, make sure you don't lose your personality in the process or try to alter it in an effort to fit into a mould. This book contains techniques which you should use to reflect on what you have to offer and which you can then adapt to suit your own personal style.

Plagiarism / similarity detection

The examples provided in this book are a guide and for your reference only. They should in no way be copied either wholly or partially.

In the same way, be very careful when reading others' personal statements that you are not tempted to copy chunks of them into yours because you think it sounds really good. UCAS operates a Similarity Detection Service called Copycatch, which can identify statements that show similarity or have been plagiarised – plain copied!

The personal statement in each application is checked against a library of all personal statements previously submitted to UCAS and sample statements collected from a variety of websites and other sources. Each personal statement received at UCAS is added to the library after it has been processed.

Any personal statement showing a level of similarity of 10% or more will be reviewed by the UCAS Similarity Detection Service team and, if deemed necessary, the university you are applying to will be notified and will decide on the significance of the results and what action, if any, to take.

So, even if you get inspiration from looking at example personal statements and find it helps you structure and write your own, make sure it's all your own original work and don't be tempted to copy.

3 — What is a personal statement? What do admission tutors look for?

The personal statement

A personal statement is a brief résumé of your personal and academic achievements, as well as a description of your aspirations and objectives. It is intended to give you the opportunity to explain to the university or college to which you are applying about your suitability for the course you intend to study and about your enthusiasm and commitment for it.

The statement must be written in fewer than 4000 characters or 47 lines of text (based on the input system's definition of a line). It is deliberately designed to be brief; it is, after all, intended to be a résumé and not a full autobiography. It should also be tailored to the particular course you are applying for (bear this in mind if you are applying for more than one subject or if you applying to medical schools which place emphasis on different criteria).

It's all about you!

Before you get going, remember that this is a "personal" statement. It means that you are writing about you and not your best friend. It also means that it is not about writing a complete autobiography about what a fantastic person you are, because the admission tutors won't be interested in that as such. What they will want to know is why you, personally, want to do medicine, how you have demonstrated your interest for such a career and how you have demonstrated that you have the right attributes.

You are likely to receive questions about the content of your personal statement during your medical school interview. "Take me through your personal statement" is a common question asked, and you may be quizzed in more detail about some of the work experience you have mentioned, or particularly outstanding achievements. So it is essential that everything you write in your personal statement is a factual and truthful reflection of yourself and not someone else you know or an imaginary friend. If it is not, then inevitably this will become apparent in your interview.

What admission tutors are looking for

The admission tutors will be looking to see evidence of a number of specific criteria in your statement, such as:

- That you have demonstrated an interest and motivation for medicine.

- That you are well informed about the demanding nature and specific requirements for a successful career in medicine.

- That you can show compassion and commitment to helping and caring for people, through relevant work or personal experience.

- That you enjoy participating in a wide range of activities and interests.

- That you have actively contributed to a variety of school/college and community activities which demonstrate evidence of team working, leadership, communication skills and a willingness to accept responsibility.

- That you have accomplished a number of personal achievements, excluding exams, awards and other accreditations.

Your personal statement will be given a score based on the criteria set by the admissions team and this, together with your reference, will give an overall score for your personal attributes.

4   Starting work on your personal statement

Your personal statement may only be one page long, but it will take you more than an evening or even a weekend to compose it, fine-tune it and finalise it. Realistically, a winning personal statement that will guarantee you an invitation for interview will take much longer to develop than you think; you should therefore start thinking about it as early as possible and set aside enough time to formulate your content, write it, receive feedback on it and edit it several times before you have the final version. It will never be too soon to start working on your personal statement, but it could possibly be too late if you underestimate the amount of work involved and leave it until the last minute.

You can start thinking well in advance about the personal qualities that you will want to convey in your statement, perhaps over the summer holidays. Take the opportunity to ask your friends or maybe the people you are working with if they have any helpful observations about you that will help. You might want to ask them if they think you are a good team player, or whether you can listen, empathise and communicate well with others, and start thinking about situations where you have demonstrated those attributes. Getting someone else's viewpoint will help you formulate a truthful and credible personal statement which really will be about you.

As you start to think about the content of your personal statement, write down the ideas that come to you or that your friends, family and work colleagues give you. It doesn't have to be in much detail, just bullet points or headings will do, but enough to jog your memory when you come to sit down and start developing your personal statement.

A countdown for your personal statement

Applications for medical school through UCAS are usually open for a period of one month and ideally you should aim to submit your application as early as possible in the process, to allow for all eventualities and to avoid a last-minute panic. You might find the following suggested timetable useful to plan and write your personal statement.

Submission 'S' Day	Assumed first day of UCAS application submission for medical school. Your personal statement is finished and you've made the final checks of your application. Submit your application and wait for your interview date.
S - 5 days	Ask your friends, relatives and teachers for their final comments on your draft personal statement. Upload your personal statement into your UCAS application and do your final editing and proofreading, but don't send it yet.
S - 15 days	Give your draft personal statement to your friends, relatives and teachers for their comments. Continue to revise and edit your statement, taking into consideration the comments and advice you have received.
S - 20 days	Begin composing your first draft, reviewing and editing as you go along.
S - 30 days	Start brainstorming for ideas and look at different examples of personal statements.

By following this timetable, your application will be ready and submitted a month before the UCAS deadline for medical school applications. This will also give you a safe amount of contingency time, just in case something goes wrong and you're not ready to submit your application on the first day. This should not be an excuse to be complacent though. Time travels very quickly when you don't want it to!

Working back 30 days from the earliest possible submission day suggests you should consider starting to brainstorm for ideas during your summer holidays, but if you want to start earlier then don't let this stop you. Remember, the earlier the better in order to have time on your side.

5 Brainstorming your personal statement

A good way to start thinking about yourself, your experience and your personal attributes is with a blank piece of paper. You don't need to be too structured or worry too much about your style yet, because all you should be doing is brainstorming and jotting down a few thoughts and ideas that you can then go on to develop further.

As a starting point, here are some of the areas you should consider:

- Your motivation for a medical career.

- Specific aspects of the course that interest you.

- Examples of relevant work experience, such as voluntary work in hospitals or care homes, with St John Ambulance or the Red Cross. Also any community or charity work you may have done, what you learned from it and how it helped you decide to study medicine.

- Any experience of looking after others in a non-work related context, e.g. looking after an elderly relative or a sibling with a disability, helping out a local disabled child, giving lessons to children in a deprived area.

- Any experience which may have given an insight into a medical issue such as a relative with a particular condition (e.g. diabetes, dementia or other chronic illness or disability).

- Courses, conferences and exhibitions you have attended, or books and journals that you have read which can help demonstrate your commitment to study medicine.

- Details of any committees or other social or sporting clubs in which you have any kind of responsibility.

- Examples of helping out at school events and open days.

- Any awards, prizes or particular achievements of note, such as Duke of Edinburgh, sporting medals, etc., and what you've gained from these experiences.

- Details of what you do in your free time – sporting activities, playing musical instruments, amateur dramatics, etc., which demonstrate that you are sociable and proactive and enjoy doing things with other people.

- Interpersonal skills that you possess. If you are a graduate entry, transferable skills that you can bring from your previous degree or career.

- Languages that you speak.

- If you're planning to take a gap year then why, what do you plan to do and how may this relate to your decision to study medicine?

You should have listed quite a few thoughts by now. Don't worry if you don't seem to have too many from this list because you only need to concentrate on personal experiences or achievements which will show off your good qualities and sound reasons for studying medicine. It is the quality of those experiences and personal attributes that matters, not the quantity. You are not trying to prove to the admission tutors that you are superhuman!

Hopefully, your list, although still in a fairly crude and unfinished form, will include personal attributes that start to demonstrate you are enthusiastic and passionate about studying medicine and becoming a doctor. If you're struggling to come up with anything to show your commitment and drive to do medicine at this point, then it will be difficult for you to come across as genuine in your personal statement, so you will need to be absolutely sure that this is what you really want to do.

6   Structuring your personal statement

Personal statements are most often written in an essay format but you don't have to do this straight away; in fact using headings to structure your statement into distinct sections is a good way of helping you develop your ideas and provide a focus to the content. It will also prevent you from waffling or going off-topic, and will demonstrate an organised and logical way of thinking.

It is best not to use the headings in your personal statement though, because obviously you must remain mindful of the character and line limitations imposed by UCAS and including headings will waste valuable space. If your statement is well written, it should be obvious to the admission tutors that you have attempted to structure it in such a way, without having to actually spell it out to them in black and white. You could try following a simple and logical structure like this:

- **Section 1**: Introduction and why you want to study medicine.

- **Section 2**: Work experience, voluntary and community work.

- **Section 3**: Other achievements, experience and interests.

- **Section 4**: Closing statement.

In the remainder of this section, we describe in detail how to approach the above structure (which is the most common one). Other structures can be used following the same information and principles, though presented in a different order. You will see from the examples shown in this book how this common format was used successfully by many of the candidates, and how others tweaked it to produce a different type of statement.

6.1 Section 1 – Introduction & why you want to study medicine

The opening paragraph is crucial to the success of your personal statement. Not only will it grab the attention of the admission tutors reading it, it will also set the tone for everything else you write. Having said that, the introduction should not be overpowering and must be in balance with the tone and style of the rest of your statement; otherwise it will seem completely out of place.

Your introductory paragraph is the most appropriate area for you to explain why you want to study medicine. This may seem obvious to you, but it is not obvious to the admission tutors who know nothing about you, your background and your personal circumstances; so this will be your opportunity to tell them why you want to be a doctor. There's no right or wrong answer here because everyone is different and there will be a variety of different factors that will have influenced your decision. For example, you could have had certain personal experiences which have drawn you to a career in medicine, there may be other family members in the medical profession, or your work and voluntary experience may have given you valuable insight into working as a doctor.

A simple opening statement would look like this:

"I want to dedicate my life to a profession I would feel passionate about. I have always been interested in the science of the human body, and as such would find the medical profession stimulating and rewarding. It is a profession that presents endless opportunity for growth, both intellectually and personally, as a human being."

"I have always wanted to make a real difference to people's lives and my ensuing interest in medicine has been further fuelled by my strong academic record and my extensive voluntary work. Through my choices of A level subjects, I have developed a strong interest in the complexities of the human body and my results have shown my ability to work to a high level across the board."

Such opening statements may appear slightly contrived because they tend to state the obvious, and you can guarantee that the words "rewarding", "enriching", "fascinating", and "interesting" will appear within the statement in

15

different combinations (see section on clichés on page 45). However, if you are short on ideas, though they may not create a wow factor, standard opening statements will provide a decent introduction. They have certainly been successful for many candidates.

Alternatively, if you are in a position to do so, you could mix in some personal experience, as follows:

Example using personal illness:
"From an early age I developed a deep appreciation of the life-changing qualities of the medical profession. Suffering from Cleft Palate in early childhood, I came into contact with several surgeons who all contributed in improving my quality of life. Their dedication and empathy helped me deal with the psychological consequences of my disability and restored my self-esteem and confidence, whilst the combined skills of a team of dedicated professionals working together guided me through corrective surgery, which improved my physical disability. This complicated situation stimulated my desire to pursue a medical career."

Example using family experience:
"I cannot think of anything more gratifying than saving lives, alleviating pain and improving or restoring people's health. I was exposed to the world of medicine from an early age at my mother's GP surgery where I learnt about the importance of treating people as humans rather than cases. My father's heart attack four years ago, his subsequent treatment and recovery also helped me realise how teamwork, fast thinking, knowledge and interpersonal skills can result in what many people would regard as pure miracle."

Example using personal observations:
"My desire to study medicine originated from the miseries that I witnessed as a child in Bangladesh, where a simple sand fly bite could cause black fever and gradually lead to silent death. Thousands of people die every year of this curable parasitic disease, not helped by the poor infrastructure and shortage of doctors. Although I may not find the answer to this particular problem, I know that I can help people in many other ways and that a career as a doctor will be both worthwhile to others and rewarding for myself."

These statements usually make more interesting introductions, particularly if the story you have to tell gave you a genuine insight into the medical world and goes beyond the obvious and non-credible experience such as "I broke my leg when I was three years old and therefore I want to be a doctor" or "I gained a good insight into medicine when I took my mum to the GP". If you intend to use a personal experience as an introduction, don't limit yourself to naming the experience you had; try to give some detail about the parts of the experience which informed your decision the most.

You might prefer a more informative introduction, providing a taste of what is coming up in the rest of the statement, as follows:

> *"I graduated from Birmingham University with a First Class degree in Biomedical Sciences. After doing some volunteer work in an orphanage in Sri Lanka for 6 months, I returned to the UK to work for the Christian Aid Foundation. I have considered my career aspirations and personal ambitions and believe that a career in medicine will provide me with the challenges and rewards that I am seeking, whilst allowing me to make full use of the experience I gained when studying for my first degree and in my charity work."*

This introduction is almost a contents table for the statement as a whole. Although it provides only basic information, it gives a clear indication of what is to come. Its downside is that it doesn't leave much opportunity for the candidate to surprise.

Finally, you may decide to go for a more memorable and powerful introduction by adopting a more direct approach. An example of this would be as follows:

> *"At some stage, everyone becomes ill, requires medical treatment and relies on the knowledge, skills, hard work and dedication of healthcare professionals. I am determined to play a central role in society as a doctor, working hard to benefit others through the knowledge and skills that I will have gained through medical school and my future career."*

6.2 Section 2 – Work experience, voluntary and community work

Why do you need work experience?

Work experience is an opportunity to gain a valuable insight into what will ultimately become your lifelong profession and to help you make an informed career choice.

By organising work experience placements and by being able to discuss what you gained from them, you will be demonstrating a serious interest in medicine which will make your application more attractive. To put it bluntly, we have only ever known of one person who managed to get into medical school without any work experience; so it is pretty much an essential requirement.

Medical schools expect applicants to be able to demonstrate <u>relevant</u> work experience and preferably some participatory hands-on work in a caring role. For the admission tutors, this will show that you have an awareness of what a career in caring for people may involve and that, through your own first-hand observations and experiences, you are realistic in your understanding of the attractive but also the less glamorous aspects of working as a doctor.

If you plan to study medicine, then obtaining relevant work experience is particularly useful for two main reasons:

1. You will be expected to demonstrate that you have a good understanding of the nature and demands of the medical profession. After all, medicine is a vocation to which you will commit to a lifetime of continuous training and development, and such a commitment should not be undertaken lightly. Your work experience, providing it is relevant to a career in medicine, should have given you a realistic insight into the challenges and rewards of a life in medicine.

2. Work experience is also an important way to help you develop and mature and to demonstrate that you have the relevant skills and qualities to become a good doctor.

How will your work experience be judged?

Work experience is variably judged by the admission tutors of the different medical schools, but, generally speaking, they will expect you to demonstrate that you have acquired or improved some key personal qualities through the outline of your work experience in your personal statement.

Some of the personal qualities they will specifically look for from your work experience include:

- Good communication skills including empathy, listening skills and an ability to express yourself clearly.
- Good team playing abilities, in particular demonstrating experience of working with diverse groups and recognising their associated cultural, social or religious needs.
- Enthusiasm, energy and perseverance through your work experience endeavours.
- Reliability both at an individual level and as a team member, as well as willingness to take responsibility and show initiative.
- A sense of service to the community.
- Initiative and problem solving skills.

Make your work experience count

All your hard work in obtaining work experience shadowing a doctor in hospital or accompanying a GP on home visits will be pointless unless you can effectively articulate this, and reflect upon what you have learnt, in your personal statement. You will not get much credit if you simply describe your work experience without providing details of what you have learnt and of your reflection on it.

Remember, you are trying to demonstrate to the admission tutors that you have acquired insight into life as a doctor and this will be your opportunity to do this. Within the statement it is therefore crucial that you define what the admission tutors should take on board from your experience and why it matters to your application.

What type of work experience is best?

Many prospective medical school applicants make the mistake of thinking that work experience must include either working with a doctor in a hospital or shadowing their local GP, but this is not strictly true.

This type of work experience is not always available and it is not easy to find work placements in a medical environment. The availability of volunteer placements in hospitals, general practices and other clinical settings is often limited due to worries about confidentiality issues. So don't worry if you have not been lucky enough to shadow a GP or come into contact with patients on a hospital ward; there are plenty of other areas related to medicine in which you can demonstrate that you have gained worthwhile experience.

Some of these are described below, together with some examples from real-life personal statements to show how you can reflect on your work experiences and use them to demonstrate your understanding of working in the medical profession. All examples are extracts taken from real-life successful personal statements,

Shadowing a doctor in a hospital

This is one of the most sought-after forms of work experience but finding a placement in a hospital setting can be quite difficult to organise as places are very limited. Some applicants are lucky enough to be able to organise work experience shadowing doctors from different specialities on several wards. If you are fortunate to have found a placement shadowing a doctor on the wards, you will experience first-hand how multidisciplinary teams work together in caring for the complex needs of patients.

Teamwork and communication skills will be amongst your key learning points and you may witness how deeply sensitive and delicate issues are dealt with by the healthcare team such as breaking bad news, which may affect not only the patient and their relatives, but also the doctor delivering the news. It is important to reflect on these aspects of your time and experiences in shadowing doctors in a hospital in your personal statement, to demonstrate your understanding and knowledge of these issues.

"My commitment to study medicine was reinforced by a work experience placement which provided a valuable perspective on the challenges of the profession. As I spent time in the A&E

20

department shadowing the doctors in minors, majors and resuscitation, I gained valuable insight into the roles of both junior doctors and senior consultants. As well as helping me to appreciate the emotional and physical stresses doctors are faced with daily, I saw the rewards of being able to have such a significant impact on patients' lives."

"Through shadowing doctors in four specialities at a Sheffield Hospital, I developed an awareness of the realities of being a doctor in the modern NHS. I considered a patient's distress when their condition could not be treated and a doctor's frustration when he was unable to help his patient to be amongst the difficulties of the job."

Shadowing a GP in a practice

As with work experience placements in a hospital setting, gaining work experience in primary care can be difficult to achieve mainly due to possible issues of patient confidentiality, particularly if you are trying to get work experience in a GP surgery in your local area.

You will find that aspects of the doctor-patient relationship are significantly different in general practice to those in a hospital setting. Consultations take place on a one-to-one basis and, over time, a GP will develop a more personal relationship and rapport with their patients.

Although a multidisciplinary team does not function in quite the same way in a GP surgery as it does within a hospital environment, you will see how various healthcare professionals work and interact within general practice to provide a diverse range of medical services such as therapy clinics, physiotherapy, counselling services, minor surgery, immunisation and so on.

GP surgeries operate like small businesses and employ a number of non-clinical staff such as a practice manager, a receptionist and a telephonist who all play a crucial role in the running of the practice and the ultimate provision of general medical services to the public. You may be fortunate enough to sit in on a number of practice or management meetings and gain first-hand experience of the operational side of general practice, which to some prospective medical school applications may appear to be the less glamorous side of being a GP.

The diversity and range of experiences you will gain from your time in general practice will enrich your personal statement enormously and you should try, as much as possible, to include comprehensive details of what you have seen and your reflections on this.

> *"I was eager to see the primary care side of medicine and arranged placements at two surgeries. I had the opportunity to see all the different aspects of a working practice, including going out on visits and attending a monthly meeting to discuss arising issues. Seeing doctors put their sometimes hesitant patients at ease I saw the need to be patient and understanding."*

> *"I undertook a work experience placement in a GP practice. I observed clinics with the doctors and spent time with the practice nurse, the health visitor and the reception team. This helped me to appreciate the importance of utilising and valuing the particular skills each member brings to a healthcare team. Whilst I found the detective-like nature of diagnosis appealing, what I enjoyed most was seeing the fine-tuning involved in managing the medication of patients with several chronic conditions."*

> *"Volunteering weekly as a GP's receptionist for a year revealed the holistic approach and continuity of care provided at a community practice. I learnt about record-keeping, ethics and striking rapport with patients."*

Working with other associated healthcare professionals
A doctor is just one member of a multidisciplinary team and work experience with other members of the team will also provide you with valuable insight which you will be able to demonstrate in your personal statement. For example, in a hospital you could try working with biomedical scientists, haematologists, nursing staff and healthcare assistants on the wards.

Even volunteer work, being responsible for the tea and coffee trolley round, taking time to talk to patients and their relatives and trying to make their time in hospital less worrying, will give you an excellent understanding of how patients feel and respond to their care. Within a GP surgery, you may be able to work with the practice nurse running an asthma or diabetes clinic for example. You may find it easier to obtain work experience in a GP surgery reception, but try to make sure you gain sufficient insight into life as a doctor and don't just end up pushing paper, filing or photocopying.

Working in residential or care homes and hospices

There are other caring environments in which you can gain work experience which will help you demonstrate that you have an understanding of the needs of different groups: for example, helping out in a residential or care home, hospice or similar centre, either on a paid or voluntary basis. You will be likely to come into contact with doctors visiting residents of these establishments and see how they adapt their consultation and communication techniques depending on the severity of the patient's condition. Spending time in care homes and hospices can be a deeply moving experience and, for many, this can prove a real turning point in their decision to pursue a vocation in the medical profession.

> *"Working enthusiastically as a Healthcare Assistant on a surgical ward, I enjoyed patient interaction and the provision of care, expanded my understanding of hospital procedures and also recognised the importance of interdisciplinary communication."*

Volunteering

This is a popular form of work experience which is relatively easy to organise. It could include:

- Working with the elderly in the community. There are many ways in which you can help elderly members of the community with shopping, cleaning, entertainment and basic hygiene tasks, again on either a paid or voluntary basis with charitable organisations. Such experience could take place in care homes, or working with charities that organise visits or meals for the elderly.

- Working in youth centres, schools or summer camps. It is useful to demonstrate an aptitude to work with a diverse age group and working with young children in a youth centre, school or perhaps at a summer camp is also a popular form of relevant work experience. This could also entail getting involved in supporting a child with learning difficulties or regularly caring for children with a particular condition (e.g. autism).

- Working in other care centres. There is a plethora of other care centres available in which to gain work experience. These could involve working with physically or mentally disabled people and disadvantaged groups of all ages. You may also like to consider involvement in local community or church volunteer schemes, which also count as relevant work experience as does working with disadvantaged groups such as the disabled or homeless.

"I have been a volunteer at the League of Friends' tea bar at Wythenshawe Hospital. This has given me experience in communicating with a range of people, including patients and visitors."

"What spurs me on is the challenge to understand and relate to different people as individuals. I discovered this in my weekly nursing home volunteering. Patience is essential; working with each person as a whole, seeing not just their ailment and listening out for things unsaid, is also vital. Building trust and understanding their eating and behavioural habits is extremely satisfying and the personal reward when I successfully get someone to eat a full meal or to have a conversation – no matter how brief – is enormous."

"At a hospice I do a Sunday tea time duty: serving dinners and taking the opportunity to chat with patients. Although at times I find this work heartrending, I also see how much difference this social interaction can make to their day."

"Every Friday night I am a volunteer at a nursing home. My work includes exercises to stimulate the residents' memories, encouraging conversation and discussion. I enjoy the work immensely and get great satisfaction out of making a small difference to their lives. It is great to see a reclusive old man suffering from dementia suddenly brighten up and actively engage in conversation."

"My weekly voluntary work at 'Kids Can Achieve', a centre for children with autism, ADHD and schizophrenia, allows me to interact with disadvantaged members of the community and help them to develop social skills. The variety of ages, temperaments and personalities means having to adjust to suit the needs of each individual child."

"Being a mentor to inner city primary school children contrasted with being a Form Prefect in our junior school. This has given me practical experience in dealing with people from all walks and stages of life, supporting them with patience and respect."

First aid

Volunteering for St John Ambulance and the Red Cross is an extremely popular form of work experience which many prospective medical school students consider. First aid is also a useful skill to acquire regardless of your intentions to study medicine or not and will teach you some basic life-saving and triage techniques.

"I have been working with St John's Ambulance for over a year now and have learnt how to confidently put my first aid to practice. The care I have provided has been rudimentary, and funnily enough, during the summer holidays, I was even asked to guard a puddle of vomit from unwitting members of the public! My time at St John's, however, has been a valuable lesson in teamwork."

Charity and fundraising work

This may sound like unlikely relevant work experience potential, but providing you can explain the relevance of this to your application for medical school, it can sound as interesting as shadowing a doctor. If you want to mention charity and fundraising activities as relevant work experience to give you an insight into the medical world, make sure that you show the link to your motivation.

For example, collecting money at a train station for a charity would not, by itself, constitute a strong motivation factor unless you had previously been given the chance to meet some of the beneficiaries of the charity or felt particularly strongly about the lack of care these people received. In that case the motivation factor for medicine would be the awareness that you had developed of the fact that some members of society are less catered for than others.

If all you gained from your charity work are generic skills, then that experience may fit better in section 3 of your personal statement.

"I have been involved in fundraising events for the MS Society and met many MS sufferers with differing levels of disability. This highlighted the fact that some diseases have varying levels of severity and therefore the need for healthcare solutions to be structured around the individual."

Medicine awareness activities

In section 2 of your statement, you may also wish to mention some of the activities that you have undertaken to demonstrate an interest in medicine. This could include:

- Attending some medical awareness courses or conferences (whether commercial, or organised by various medical schools or not-for-profit organisations).

- Reading scientific or medically-related papers or books (such as *Student BMJ, The Lancet* or *New Scientist*).

- Attending open days.

Such activities may have heightened your awareness of medicine and the attributes required. As such they may have contributed further to your decision to study medicine and are worthy of mention.

"My interests in the subject further developed after I attended an 'Exploring Healthcare' spring school and a recent Medsim conference. From lectures to laboratory work, and from clinical practice to participation in PBL, I found the course an invaluable learning experience. I especially enjoyed wearing surgical scrubs and putting my manual dexterity to the test whilst performing a simulation of keyhole surgery. Although I was initially apprehensive about being observed by practitioners during this procedure, this challenging clinical task gave me a sense of the pressures encountered by surgeons on a daily basis."

Too much work experience to mention?

If you find yourself in the very fortunate position of having numerous examples of relevant work experience then you will need to ensure that you do your experience justice. Always remember that it is the quality of the examples that will matter more than the quantity. As such you may want to take out some of the experiences from which you did not gain much. Resist the temptation to list all your experiences. You will not get any extra marks for something like this:

> *"Last summer I worked in a GP surgery and sat in on some consultations with patients. At Easter I worked in a local care home. I spent a week doing deliveries for Meals on Wheels and I help out at the local Riding for Disabled club at weekends."*

This just reels off a list of activities but we don't learn anything about the candidate, their skills, their motivation or their personality. However, something like the following will demonstrate more relevant and impressive examples of work experience which show that you recognise the key attributes of being a doctor and feel passionate about it:

> *"I was fortunate to spend time shadowing a GP whilst working in a GP surgery over the summer. I found the experience extremely rewarding and it gave me great insight into the need to show empathy and remain calm and patient, which I was able to put to more use when I later worked with dementia sufferers for two weeks in a local care home."*

Another way of dealing with the problem is to categorise your various experiences by type. For example, one group of experiences may be more focused on your demonstration of empathy and listening skills, whereas another group of experiences may reflect more on your organisation skills, your teamworking abilities, your initiative and leadership qualities. This approach will enable you to list everything that appears relevant whilst at the same time bringing appropriate reflection into the answer.

6.3 Section 3 – Other achievements, experiences & interests

The third section of your personal statement provides an opportunity to discuss the personal attributes and skills that you have developed through various life and work experiences which you think are relevant to a career in medicine, but may not necessarily be in a medical field.

Doctors must be able to communicate effectively on a variety of levels with patients and their relatives, colleagues, medical students and NHS managers. Not only does it mean that you should be able to talk to others, it also means that you should be able to listen effectively, empathise and to receive and provide feedback. Your personal statement will receive particular credit if you are able to demonstrate experience in communicating with different groups and even better if these have involved any barriers to communication.

Working in medicine also involves a high level of teamwork. You should be able to demonstrate in your personal statement not only that you can work in a team, but also that you are a reliable and responsible individual who can actively contribute significantly to it; that you are able to support and respect others and that you understand the impact that your actions have on others. You can give examples of teamwork from experiences both in and out of school/college, or university/current career if you are a graduate applicant.

Other personal attributes that could be demonstrated here include your leadership skills, particularly by mentioning any positions of responsibility you may have held. Coupled with this, you could go on to demonstrate examples of your organisational skills and instances where you have shown initiative.

As you are under no particular obligation to pursue personal hobbies and interests, mentioning them presents you with an ideal opportunity to explain how these activities demonstrate your own personal drive, ambition and desire to achieve. You can then reflect on how this is relevant to your application to study medicine and a career as a doctor.

Finally, from your research and understanding of the requirements of a career in medicine, you will hopefully have gained an appreciation of the extreme demands and pressures encountered by doctors and the need to counter the stresses experienced with other activities and interests. You would be well placed here to describe how you currently cope with your work-life balance and how you would propose to tackle this in your time in medical school and after graduation. Reflect upon ways in which you relax and release pressure so that the admission tutors can see that you will be able to cope with the pressures and strains of what is to come.

Suitable examples

You can mention pretty much anything provided the examples you give help you demonstrate some personal attribute. This could include the following:

Achievements at school

There are countless examples that could be mentioned here which demonstrate your willingness to take responsibility and provide leadership, such as becoming Head Boy or Head Girl, or a Prefect. You could also include occasions where you have represented your school in interschool competitions.

"At the annual school presentations, I have been awarded subject prizes for music, science and resistant materials in recognition of my hard work. I have also been awarded the tutor prize twice and the Head of Year's award for consistent achievement and involvement in extracurricular activities."

"As Deputy Head Girl, my responsibilities include initiating an academic mentoring system, helping students understand their learning types, public speaking, coordinating meetings between pupils and teachers and helping at school events. This role has not only furthered my sense of responsibility but enhanced crucial organisational skills."

"Competitively, I have captained my school's Chemistry team to victory in the National RSC Top of the Bench competition. I feel that I was an effective leader for the team, as I was able to coordinate our efforts to complete the range of challenges as well as maintaining morale."

"As House Captain, I organise many events which involve working with a number of people in order to prepare and lead teams. This has developed my organisational skills and has increased my ability to motivate others."

Hobbies, personal interests and group activities

There are many activities that can be included here such as sport (either individual or team sports), hiking, drama groups, learning to play a musical instrument or playing in an orchestra, or participating in investment clubs. These will be activities in which you can demonstrate an ongoing commitment and a motivation to achieve. Group activities, as the name would suggest, highlight your teamworking abilities as well as your willingness to take responsibility through leadership and initiative.

"Two years ago I began weightlifting; I hope to excel in the forthcoming British Junior championships, as my understanding of the science behind this sport has been supplemented by commitment and hard work."

"My good time management and organisation have enabled me to relax while enjoying a range of social activities. I have practised Tae-Kwon-Do for seven years, gaining the red belt. I also like practical work and am a keen cross-stitcher. I intend to continue with these activities as I recognise that, for a doctor, work-life balance is important."

"I am well aware that the ability to cope with pressures of student life is essential and so I enjoy playing badminton on a weekly basis and train in Indian classical dance, both of which help me to relax and keep fit."

"For the past seven years I have been a keen horse rider and through perseverance and determination I have become an advanced rider and have competed successfully."

"For the past two years I have enjoyed taking a course in metalwork and jewellery-making in which I have developed new skills relating to precise hand-eye coordination."

"Sport plays a very important part in my life and requires good time management to fit it in alongside all my school activities. I represent the school at rugby (captained the sevens team), football, golf and badminton. I play tennis to a national level and, in order to put something back into the tennis community, I qualified as a coach and regularly assist the Scottish National coach with junior squads. Being involved in the development of

people has given me great satisfaction and I would relish the opportunity to further this in a career within medicine."

"I am a member of a Youth Orchestra, a Philharmonic Youth Orchestra and two string quartets. Music and medicine require teamwork and integration of mind with body, intellect with emotion and communication ability with commitment. I hope that I can use these skills learned from music in medicine."

Clubs and societies

Participation and membership of clubs and groups is an excellent way to demonstrate your continued enthusiasm and commitment, and also shows that you are a well-rounded individual who is able to apply themselves to activities outside academia.

"Outside of school, 13 years' membership of the Girls' Brigade has given me opportunities to take part in a variety of activities and recently I was able to complete an Emergency Life Support course."

"I am a member of the publicity team of an active Science Society, responsible for producing a fortnightly newsletter and I am thoroughly enjoying the research and exploration involved in this project. In addition, being appointed Secretary of the Asian Society has taught me to be self-reliant and cultivate my organisational and time management skills."

"Being a member of the debating society and representing the school in public speaking competitions has greatly developed my fluency and articulacy, which has developed my ability to work under pressure."

Community, charity or religious activities

This could include your active participation in community groups, charity work or religious activities such as Sunday school.

"Community service was and remains an important focus of my extracurricular activities. To raise money for my school's charity club, I set up a 'Monday Muffins' programme and was in charge of the annual raffle. I also worked as part of a team on a

steering committee for a charity fundraising scheme, helping students to arrange a day of paid work with their wages being donated to charity."

"I currently volunteer at a social gathering for the elderly at my local church, which has been a great opportunity to serve the elderly members. Befriending them and ensuring they have a good time is very rewarding."

"I worked in a Polish Saturday School, supervising four- to seven-year-old pupils. I feel that working there, along with performing the roles of a senior prefect at my school, helped increase my maturity and allowed me to gain valuable communication and organisation skills."

"I have worked at an Oxfam charity shop for two years and successfully completed my Millennium Volunteer Award, doing over 200 hours of community work. This has allowed me to have fun while also working towards a worthwhile achievement."

"My Catholic faith is a very prominent aspect of my life and I currently lead the children's liturgy at my local parish church. This has made me a more confident and outgoing person, yet also more considerate and caring."

Technological projects

If you have set up your own website you can use this in your personal statement whether it was done for personal, educational or business purposes. You may have also been involved in, or initiated, other technological projects.

"I have good IT skills and learned to use video editing software. I videoed my Silver and Gold expedition teams, edited and produced our DVD diaries and DVDs of several school concerts."

"Aside from my academic interests, I also enjoy designing and programming websites, something which I self-taught. At the age of 16 I started my own design and print business and, since establishing it, I now have over 15 contracts with companies

who regularly come back to me. Meeting clients and being able to gain their trust is, by far, the most rewarding aspect of my business, even more than earning the money."

Character-building or simulation exercises

Involvement in activities such as the Duke of Edinburgh's Award or Young Enterprise schemes are commonly mentioned and demonstrate initiative, organisational and leadership skills. A useful point to mention here is that you will get more credit for your achievements if you give examples of how you demonstrated these personal attributes, than by simply saying something like "through good teamwork, management and leadership, my team and I completed the expedition safely". In other words, describe what you actually contributed personally.

"I enjoy working with people and have developed my teamwork and leadership skills through my involvement in the Duke of Edinburgh Award Scheme. I have completed Bronze and Silver and aim to complete the Gold Award. I attended a First Aid course in preparation for the Gold expedition, which helped me to deal with a panic attack experienced by a team member. I also took a lead role in organising route plans and spreadsheets and delegated responsibilities to team members."

"Participating in a Young Enterprise Company, making and selling scarves, helped to develop my team working ability but also concentrate on time and money management skills. Involvement in a debating society has helped me to argue my own opinion but to also consider the views of others."

Gap years

You can exploit these not only for all the planning and preparatory work that you have invested (including raising funds, organising travel and work placements) but also for the actual experience, particularly if you have done a bit more than lying on a beach for 12 months.

"I am currently learning Spanish in order to prepare for my gap year placement in Peru. For a period of five weeks I will be volunteering at the hospital in Cuzco and helping doctors in remote jungle locations, after which I will spend three weeks travelling around the Andes, following in the footsteps of the

Inca people. I intend to use my gap year to gain as much experience as possible in a medical and caring environment."

"In my gap year, my outgoing personality secured me a job as a customer service officer for Lloyds TSB, from which I was able to finance a very rewarding chapter of my life. For four months I travelled around the South Pacific and South East Asia. The trip not only afforded me many valuable life experiences, but built my confidence in dealing with a wide range of social situations."

Travel

You can differentiate this from any travels you may have done, or are preparing to do during your gap year: for example, many candidates may have travelled extensively due to family or parental work commitments and so have been exposed to different societies and cultures which have provided them with valuable life experiences.

"Travelling widely in India has been a great experience of life beyond my immediate environment. I attended an international boarding school for 3 years, which enabled me to experience a diverse range of cultures and develop independence and responsibility."

"In response to the Kashmir earthquake, I volunteered and travelled to the affected area where I was involved with hospital fund-raising, counselling and emotional support for a month. This experience helped me to comprehend the various traumas people can experience."

"Moving around the world made mine an unpredictable childhood and taught me to adapt quickly to new situations. I became accustomed to change and my international upbringing has allowed me the flexibility to be an independent student."

Work experience outside a medically-related environment

You could include any work that you do which is not directly related to the healthcare profession such as working at the customer service desk of a retail store or the delicatessen counter of a local supermarket. This type of work experience can also be used to demonstrate your ability to communicate with various social groups and members of the public, your willingness to take responsibility and your reliability.

> *"I have been employed part-time in a busy high street fashion store, working closely and constantly with the general public. My experience on customer services has shown the variety of approaches that different members of society use and I now appreciate that it is very important to listen, confirm and resolve any issue as calmly as possible. The demands of a vibrant retail environment have required me to be flexible and adaptable and not to expect to leave work on time!"*

> *"Outside school, my work in Waitrose enables me to engage with a variety of people and has taught me to handle stressful situations using effective communication skills combined with self-confidence."*

Personal achievement

Here you could describe how you have had to fund your studies or a lifetime ambition by working every weekend, having to study through an illness or whilst looking after a disabled parent or sibling (note that, in this case, what you would be describing is the resilience that you demonstrated in juggling your various responsibilities rather than the medical awareness gained from caring for the relative in question). Alternatively, you could describe a personal achievement that has rewarded you with a great sense of satisfaction.

> *"One of my proudest personal achievements was to lose 6 stone in weight in a bid to raise awareness of diabetes within the South Asian ethnic community."*

Making the most of achievements, experiences & interests

To optimise the impact of such activities, you should stick to a few and explain how they demonstrate that you possess the key skills and attributes required in medicine. Generally speaking, it is best to mention the more recent activities. There is a benefit in mentioning older interests only if you can demonstrate their value to your application as of today. For example, having attended drama classes at the age of six is not that interesting but if you have been obtaining music prizes since the age of six, then this demonstrates consistency, hard work, resilience and passion. Here, it is not the fact that you play music that matters, but the constant achievement.

If you are planning to take a gap year, then give details of what you intend to do. You could at least mention some of the preparation that you have already undertaken. Relate your proposed activities to your desire to study medicine, to demonstrate your continued enthusiasm and commitment to further your work and personal experience and to acquire further understanding and insight into a career in medicine.

"I have worked at a hospice as a Father Christmas, dishwasher and decorator and led music and furniture restoration workshops at the Meath Epilepsy Trust. I am a volunteer at Cancer Research sorting clothes and manning the till every week as well as working on the meat and fish counter at Waitrose. Juggling these commitments alongside studying and socialising has honed my time management skills and made me much more confident in communicating with a wide range of people. Waitrose in particular has given me good teamwork skills, having to work with others to strict standards."

"In school, I created and managed 'GreenSoc', an environmental society formed to raise awareness and sell recycled stationery. Trying to motivate a team of volunteers with no incentive to perform was very challenging and helped me develop some strong managerial and influencing skills. Through this work I also discovered a natural ability to motivate others and to communicate with people at all levels on sometimes complex issues. Trying to make children understand the complexities of global warming was a real test of my teaching abilities and proved an immensely rewarding experience, with feedback far exceeding my expectations."

6.4 Section 4 – Closing statement

Once you have explained your motivation for medicine, your work experience and the array of relevant skills and personal attributes that you possess, you should give a conclusion that summarises your personal statement and ends it on a positive note.

Bear in mind that, by this point, the admission tutors may already have formed their opinion on your application and, if they consider you a borderline applicant, your concluding statement may just tip the balance into being put forward for an automatic interview, or being relegated to the "on hold" pile. Try to keep your conclusion short, punchy and attention grabbing because it is this that will leave a lasting impression.

The easiest way of finishing a personal statement (providing you have not used this technique in your introduction) is to relate briefly all the experiences mentioned in your statement or the skills you demonstrated to the field of medicine in an upbeat manner which demonstrates enthusiasm and an aptitude for your future career.

For example:

"I have thoroughly researched what will be required of me as a doctor and gained relevant work experience, which has given me an even greater insight into what will be involved. I believe that working in the medical profession will give me the personal and intellectual challenges that I enjoy and provide me with a challenging and rewarding career."

"My A levels and my experience in observing medical practice have increased my motivation and determination to read medicine. Although demanding, medicine is immensely rewarding and offers vast opportunities for further study and specialisation. It is also an ever-changing field with new techniques being developed almost daily. By pursuing a career in medicine I will be proud to become part of a rapidly advancing profession, which will allow me to receive intellectual stimulation and to provide compassionate care."

"I work hard and feel I can balance my extracurricular, social and academic activities to meet the challenge of studying medicine. At the core of medicine is the ultimate aim of a physician to enhance quality of life. I would truly love to be a part of this process and look forward to a lifelong learning curve in that vast arena of health professionals."

"These positive steps have strengthened my desire to become a doctor and fuelled my ambition further. I now have a focused direction, about which I am passionate, and a career aim that will complement my academic ability and existing skills. I am fully committed and determined to achieve, as illustrated by my paid, voluntary and academic work. With my relevant life experience, I believe I am the perfect age to embark on my studies as I have maturity and the advantage of having many years to commit to medicine."

If you started your personal statement with a story, it often looks very powerful to finish with the same story. For example, you may have started your personal statement by talking about a little boy called Jason whom you cared for as part of your voluntary involvement and through whom you discovered the joys of caring for others, the importance of patience and empathy, and the personal reward that you gained from your altruistic involvement. You could then finish with a statement such as:

"I am looking forward to a career in medicine to satisfy my hunger for constant learning and for the challenge that it will offer on a daily basis. More importantly, I want to feel proud to work in an environment where I feel I can make a real difference to children like Jason and their parents."

Spend as much time as you can on the start and finish of your personal statement. An interesting start will grab the admission tutors' attention and encourage them to read your statement thoroughly rather than just skim read it. The introduction is a good opportunity for you to convey something special about yourself which you can then elaborate on further. A good ending will make your personal statement memorable, help it stand out from the crowd and will hopefully result in a recommendation for interview.

6.5 Is it different for graduate entrants or Oxbridge applicants?

Graduate entrants

There is no particular reason why graduate-entry personal statements should differ widely from A-level entrants' personal statements if only the fact that admission tutors would be expecting a more mature approach based on further experience gained prior to the application. Indeed, graduate entrants will be expected to detail:

- Their motivation for medicine.
- How they have demonstrated their interest through their work experience, their degree, and/or prior career.
- If they are joining much later in life, how their prior career led to medicine and/or what transferable skills they possess.
- The extent of their personal attributes.
- Personal and other interests.

Candidates with degrees or prior careers relating to medicine will obviously find it easier to describe their path towards medicine; however, those with degrees and careers which appear unrelated (i.e. journalism, retail, politics, etc.) are equally successful provided they can provide a sensible reason for their switch of career and are able to elaborate on their transferable skills.

Oxbridge applicants

Oxbridge applicants will also be applying to other medical schools and, as such, the same rules apply. However, to enhance your chances of getting into Oxbridge, you should bear in mind that many of the personal statements produced by those who are shortlisted at Cambridge or Oxford contain a number of distinguishing features:

- Many have strong scientific content, either because the candidate has been involved in some form of research, or often because they explain in more detail their understanding of topics they have come across during work experience or their reading. The extensive detail helps increase credibility.

- Candidates have extensive work experience covering a wide range of areas. They have also often attended various courses and read relevant books or journals.

- The statements contain a strong paragraph on leadership, with candidates presenting an array of areas where they have taken responsibility. The statements also contain references to personal achievements rather than simply an involvement.

- Candidates emphasise personal interests considerably in an effort to demonstrate a work hard/play hard attitude.

7 Refining your personal statement

Once you have put together a first draft of your statement, the hard work really starts. Leave it aside for a few hours or overnight, and reread it with fresh eyes. Does it make sense? Does it flow well? Is it too boring? Would some paragraphs read better if they were fleshed out with examples? Are some paragraphs too lengthy or too short in relation to others? Does the statement contain enough personal information or is just a succession of statements? Is the content okay but you still feel that it can be tightened?

In this section we present a number of tips that you can follow in order to improve the statement.

Writing a story

Personal statements usually look standard because they are lacking the personal touch. That personal touch can often be added through the use of stories. Stories can be used in two different places:

- In the introduction: "Meeting Jason, an 8-year-old autistic boy was one of the most frightening but also enlightening experiences of my life". This guarantees an entrance with a bang!

- In the description of your work experience: for example, when you describe your experience of reading books to elderly people in a local hospice, you can go further than the usual "It really showed me the importance of listening and caring" by talking about a particular patient who really made an impression on you.

This approach doesn't suit everyone, but it is one of the best ways of writing a personal statement. It feels different and potentially far more powerful.

The story may revolve around an experience or an observation that has unearthed a personal goal or objective and could serve as evidence of your insight into a career in medicine. It doesn't need to be a tear-jerker or a comedy, but rather something poignant and, above all, truthful. If you decide to include a story in your personal statement make sure it's not fiction but something you have experienced first-hand. Don't forget that, if your wonderfully creative personal statement does the job and you get an invitation for interview, you may be asked to elaborate on your story, so it needs to be your own.

Writing a good story will certainly hold the attention of the admission tutors, but be careful not to get too carried away with it and forget to include other important attributes which they will be expecting to see. They will still expect you to demonstrate an aptitude and commitment for studying medicine, relevant work experience and personal attributes which show that you are a well-rounded individual, not just that you can write a good story!

There are a number of examples of personal statements in this book where effective story-telling techniques have been used.

The words aren't coming?

Creative writing comes much easier to some than others. Even if you have had a productive brainstorming session and have lots of ideas for what you want to put in your personal statement, you may be completely stuck when it comes to knowing how to make it read well.

If you find yourself in this position and just can't get started or find yourself drying up with writer's block, one of the best ways to get ideas to help you move forward is to look at examples of other personal statements. You will find a large variety of personal statements in this book, all written in different styles. Your school or college may have some personal statements to show you from former students.

Reading other personal statements will give you an idea of how others tackled the job of explaining why they wanted to study the course they did. You will see how they described their own interests and abilities and how they weaved these into their application. You will also get a feel for the different kinds of structure that others have followed and the language used. By language we mean the style adopted – brief, succinct, eloquent, flowery, simple, descriptive, plain – rather than the actual language, because, of course, your UCAS application should be in English!

After reading other personal statements, you will be able to judge for yourself which ones you think are good and bad and will find particular explanations and descriptions that others have used that you like or dislike and, before you know it, you will find that you know exactly what you want to say and how to say it.

But remember the caveat here. Even though it may help to read others' personal statements, you must not copy someone else's work. Feel free to gain inspiration from them, but never to plagiarise.

Creating your own content, language and style

As you start to compose your personal statement you will need to consider the style of writing and the language and tone you want to use. This may not happen immediately and you may only start to develop this after a few drafts. In fact, your first draft may read like an incoherent mix of styles and tones and you won't be able to develop a consistent language until you have been through the fine-tuning and editing process. But here are a few hints and tips for turning your brainstormed ideas into the most effective and persuasive language and style of writing:

- Try to compose your personal statement while you're in an enthusiastic mood, because you will find that this translates into a positive image on the page.

- Use your best English and check spelling, punctuation and grammar. A personal statement full of errors will give a negative impression of the amount of effort you are prepared to put in to your studies. If you want to make reference to medical specialties in your personal statement, such as orthopaedics, paediatrics or gynaecology, then make sure you have spelt them correctly and use the English spelling (paediatrics and ophthalmology are often misspelt!)

- Avoid the use of "SMS" language and abbreviated words.

- Try to avoid using elaborate language. Keep it simple. If you're not usually confident in using long or fancy words, then don't even try using them in your personal statement because it will show.

- Use positive language and always try to emphasise the positive side of things.

- Every word needs to be relevant to your personal statement. If a word is superfluous or doesn't add any value, then don't use it. Remember your space is very limited, so don't waste it. Be concise.

- Try not to sound arrogant or pretentious. You want to try to make sure that you come across as sincere. You have to be particularly careful when you describe work experience that relates to people from a different cultural or socio-economic background to yours. You want to avoid words such as "poor people", but talk instead of "populations living in deprived areas" or "people with limited resources". No one likes a judgemental doctor and, even if you did not mean it in that way, writing it down always makes it sound harsher.

- Don't lie or exaggerate. Remember, you will be questioned about the content of your personal statement in your interview and you will be caught out if you're asked to elaborate on some interesting fact in it.

- Don't waffle about things that aren't relevant to your application. If you feel like you're beginning to go off-topic then stop, take a break and come back to it when you're feeling more focused.

- Avoid the use of humour to try to make your personal statement stand out. Remember, the admission tutors may not share your sense of humour.

- Keep your sentences short. Your average sentence length should be 15 to 20 words. This doesn't mean that you need to make each sentence the same length. Be punchy because it makes an impression. You should vary your writing style by mixing shorter sentences (like the last one) with slightly longer ones (like this one) because this engages the reader and makes your writing more interesting. Stick to delivering one main piece of information per sentence for more impact.

Write in the active voice

Like it or not, unless you have a flair for creative writing and do it all the time, you will find yourself reverting, almost subconsciously, to writing in the passive voice. This is all very well and you are unlikely to even realise that you are doing it, but what this means is that your sentences will be more wordy, less interesting and lack the punch they would have if you had written them in the active voice.

For example:

Passive voice
"I feel that the extent of my work experience gave me a good insight into the world of medicine."

Active voice
"Through my extensive work experience, I acquired a good insight into the world of medicine."

You can easily recognise when you are writing in the passive voice, because you will use a lot of the form of the word "to be", such as "was" or "were".

A helpful tip in minimising your use of the passive voice and to give your writing more style and creativity is to arm your vocabulary with some "power verbs". You will find a list of suggested power verbs at the end of this book. Reread your draft personal statement now and rewrite some of the sentences that you find in the passive voice, using some of the power verbs from the list to give it more impact.

It is of course acceptable to have some sentences in the passive voice because it provides some variety in the style, but you have to make sure that there is a good balance between the two styles. The best statements tend to contain far more active sentences than passive sentences.

Avoid clichés

A cliché is a phrase or expression that has been used so many times, it has become commonplace. The problem with using clichés is that the admission tutors will invariably have seen them before, time and time again. If you are trying to create an original and memorable personal statement, then the use of clichés really won't help.

If you say something like "Ever since I was young, I wanted to be a doctor so that I can help people", it doesn't really say much about you because, invariably, this is a cliché (two clichés in fact) which will have been said many times before and isn't unique to you. Notice how general and vague it is with no concrete details and no examples of why you want to help people, why you

45

like to help people and what kind of people you want to help. It also goes without saying that doctors want to help people, so it's nothing new either! Clichés like these will always seem worn out, old, predictable and too familiar. The admission tutors reading this will quickly tune out and it will be difficult to get their attention back at this point.

Many clichés tend to be overgeneralisations and don't say very much at all or add value, so you should avoid using them if you want to make every single word in your personal statement count.

Some of the more popular clichés appear over and over again in medical school personal statements, such as:

- I am fascinated by the workings of the human brain.
- I am fascinated by the workings of the human body.
- I have a fascination in science and with how the human body works.
- The functioning of the human body holds a particular fascination for me.
- The study of science is fascinating to me, particularly with regards to the human body.
- I have been fascinated by the complexities of the human body.
- I am fascinated by the workings of life and the complexities of the human body.
- The complexities of the human body never cease to amaze me.
- Science and the human body have always fascinated me.
- I am fascinated by science.
- My interest in science has led me towards a career in medicine.
- Studying medicine will provide me with a challenge.
- I have an enthusiasm and passion for science.
- I am hard working and often burn the candle at both ends.
- I like to do things by the book.
- My work has never given cause for complaint.
- I'm excited by the changing face of medicine.
- Studying medicine is a once in a lifetime opportunity.
- Getting a place in medical school will make my day.
- I hit the ground running when I set up a community kids club.
- I can really make a difference.
- I get on well with people.
- I have always been a good communicator.
- My desire to study medicine stems from my childhood.

- I have always wanted to be a doctor.
- I like caring for people.
- I like working under pressure.
- I love helping people.
- I want to save lives.
- I want to make a difference in the world.
- I was a good science student.
- Medicine runs in the family.

Put yourself in the shoes of the admission tutors for one minute and imagine reading several hundred personal statements, of which a large number include a worn-out cliché in their introductory paragraphs, such as these. Would you be inclined to think "Wow! I can tell this candidate is really passionate about wanting to study medicine ... let me read on" or "I've heard this all before, now tell me something new"?

What creates a cliché is the fact that you make a statement without backing it up with examples. So, for example, saying "I have an interest in science" does not convey much until you start explaining that you enjoy reading certain publications, that you have enjoyed certain activities at school such as dissection, etc. Similarly, "I have always been fascinated by medicine" means little until you start explaining that you volunteered from an early age to work in a hospice or that you trained as a Red Cross volunteer.

Conclusion: only use such standard statements if they are backed up with examples. If you do intend to use them on a stand-alone basis, then they would fit best as part of a short and sharp conclusion to the personal statement:

> *"Throughout the past 10 years I have demonstrated a strong interest in science and in caring for others through the array of personal and work experience in which I participated. As a colleague and a friend, people describe me as someone who is hardworking, professional, but also approachable and supportive. As such I feel that I will make a good doctor."*

Such a statement would look trite within a personal statement itself but would work well as a conclusion which builds on all the examples provided.

47

Use power words

"Words are, of course, the most powerful drug used by mankind" Rudyard Kipling [1835-1936]

The use of power words and action verbs will greatly enhance the impression given by your personal statement. Using action verbs will also help your writing style assume an "active voice" instead of a "passive voice" as described previously, and this, in turn, conveys a stronger message with more impact.

The effective use of power words will make a big difference to the way in which your personal statement is perceived by the admission tutors and could make all the difference in whether they are left with a favourable opinion of you.

One of the most uninspiring introductions to a personal statement must be: "I would very much like to study medicine because I enjoy science and want to care for people." This could so easily be turned into a stronger, more powerful introduction to really make an impression, such as:

> *"My interest in medicine developed at an early age when I was given my first model laboratory and test tube kit. It took me little time to realise this was my passion and my desire to seek ways of helping the sick has grown ever since".*

What a difference the use of action verbs like "developed", "given" and "grown" makes, coupled with more creative words like "desire" and "passion", without going completely over the top and sounding artificial.

The clever use of power words turns a sentence like: "I worked as part of a team with other pupils to organise the school summer ball", into "I worked closely with other pupils to secure sponsorship to the tune of £2,000 from local firms, for the school summer ball". Again, you can see what a difference this makes and how much more impressive your achievements appear.

There are lots of other power words which give more assertive and powerful ways for you to describe yourself and provide real impact, such as:

- I have <u>developed a strong interest</u> in understanding the possible causes of dementia.

- I am <u>very keen</u> in pursuing my interest in a surgical career.

- I <u>played a key role</u> in organising a charitable disco for the local community centre.

Be careful though; overusing power words and action verbs may make your personal statement seem fake and unnatural. Remember the other golden rule of not using words with which you are unfamiliar, because you may have difficulty in making them sound correct in context.

A list of 500 power words and action verbs can be found in Chapter 13. You should be comfortable in incorporating these throughout your personal statement to help maximise impact.

8   Making the personal statement fit

You should hopefully now be at a stage where you have a first draft of your personal statement. Don't worry if it's too long because it's easy to edit it down. It's much harder to increase the length of a short personal statement than trim down a long one. Incidentally, if your personal statement is a little short, but you're sure you've included everything in it, then don't panic. There is no requirement to fill the allocated space and it's better to have a short and well-written, succinct statement, than a long, waffly and irrelevant one.

Be mindful of your character limit. UCAS set a limit for a reason and this is so that you can demonstrate your ability to explain your reasons for wanting to study medicine clearly and succinctly. The art is in being able to tell the admission tutors everything they need to know about your desire and motivation for a career in medicine without writing a book about it!

The space allowed for your personal statement is up to 4,000 characters (including spaces), or 47 lines of text (including blank lines), whichever comes first. If you come in under 4,000 characters but exceed the line limit, then your application will be rejected.

If your personal statement is too long, look for ways of editing out unnecessary, repetitive or irrelevant words and phrases. You can easily check whether or not you're within the 4,000 character limit by using the 'word count' in your word processing package. Just remember that your statement may fall within the character limit, but still exceed the 47-line limit which would result in automatic rejection, so bear this in mind as you put the finishing touches to it.

Here are a few ways of reducing the number of characters:

- Try to avoid a long list of hobbies and interests just to fill space, unless you can show their relevance to your application.

- Don't repeat facts that are already on your UCAS form, such as your academic qualifications or anything which may be contained in your reference.

- Unless you have lots of space left, avoid using headings. Although this may look well structured and logical, it's also a waste of space and may make your statement appear too regimented.

Also take a moment to look at the layout of what you've prepared. A well-presented and organised personal statement will give a stronger impression than one where little thought has been put into how it appears. Try to make sure you haven't compromised the readability of your statement by trying to cram everything in without paragraphs and spaces in the appropriate place. Make sure also that your paragraphs are well balanced. In particular, you should aim to make the paragraph on work experience of equal length to the paragraph on personal skills, achievements and interests.

Finally, don't bother with any fancy formatting by underlining key words, putting them in bold or using colours to try to reinforce what you're trying to say. The UCAS online application system doesn't pick up formatting, so your efforts are wasted. Your words really should speak for themselves.

Bear in mind also that the UCAS system can't process text with foreign characters such as accents. Worth remembering if you have done lots of work experience abroad perhaps or want to use words like "cliché".

9 Editing & checking your personal statement

Once you have put together a good first draft, the next thing you should do is read your statement out loud and slowly. This will help highlight any areas which sound disjointed or if you've missed anything out. You will also spot if something doesn't read very well or sounds confusing, because if you find yourself confused about something you read in your personal statement, then it's likely that anyone else reading it will do too. By reading your personal statement out loud, you will also discover if your sentences are too long because you will run out of breath!

Don't rely on automatic spell check

It's highly likely that the word processing program you will be using to draft your personal statement will come equipped with a spell check function. By all means use this and, in fact, you should. But don't rely on it completely because it is not 100% foolproof.

For example, a spell checker will only detect if words are spelt correctly (or incorrectly), but not if they have been used correctly. There are a number of commonly misused words that many spell checkers will not detect, such as advice/advise, their/there, to/too, whether/weather, practice/practise, cite/sight and so on. Take a look at this sentence and spot how many correctly spelt, but incorrectly used words there are.

"I to developed a better understanding by listening to the advise the consultant gave too all there patience."

Correctly spelt, this sentence should read as follows:

"I too developed a better understanding by listening to the advice the consultant gave to all their patients."

The spell check may also try to correct words which are already correctly spelt and used, for example 'my self discipline' may be corrected to 'myself discipline' which of course, is completely wrong in this context.

Your spell checker will only be as accurate as the language you have selected for your word processing package. One of the most common spelling errors encountered is the use of American spelling for certain popular words such as:

- customize (UK English prefers customise)
- realize (realise)
- specialize (specialise)
- organize (organise)
- recognize (recognise)
- materialize (materialise)
- behaviour (behaviour)
- color (colour)
- pediatrics (paediatrics)
- gynecology (gynaecology)
- anesthesiology (anaesthetics)
- fulfill (fulfil)
- skeptical (sceptical)

So, although a spell checker is a handy tool, and you may like to use it for your first stab at editing and checking your personal statement, it's no replacement for good old-fashioned proofreading.

Ask for opinions

Getting multiple opinions from others is also very useful, as it's hard to spot errors in your own writing because you're so close to the content. Ask family, friends or teachers to give you an opinion. Career advisers are also useful people to read through your statement because they will have seen many in the past and will have a good idea what it should contain, but don't leave it until the last minute because they will be very busy at this time of year.

Whoever you ask for an opinion, ask them to consider the following specific points as they read your draft personal statement:

- Is the introduction engaging and attention grabbing?
- Do I give a plausible and genuine reason for wanting to study medicine?
- Do the descriptions of my work experience and voluntary work support my desire to go into medicine?

- Does it all make sense?
- Have I waffled or am I too wordy?
- Does it all flow logically or are there areas which seem disjointed?
- Have I included anything that seems irrelevant?
- Is every single sentence crucial to my personal statement?
- Have I used unnecessary clichés?
- Are there any spelling mistakes or grammatical errors?
- Am I using the active voice and power verbs to make my point?
- Are my sentences the right length and easy to read?
- Is my conclusion memorable and does it provide closure?
- Are there any weak areas?
- Are there any parts that need more detail or which don't seem clear?

And ask them directly: "Can you describe what you think this personal statement says about my personality?"

By now, you will have read and reread your personal statement several times and will have input from anyone else you may have shown it to, so you will have quite a few changes and amendments to make to it. Before you go ahead and start rewriting the bits you're not happy with, make sure you save a copy of the original statement because you may want to refer back to it. After you've made your changes then repeat the process of reading the statement to yourself and showing it to others for comment. Each time you go back and make more changes, save the previous version of the statement so that you keep a copy of each one for reference.

The final golden rule is to read and reread your personal statement as many times as possible, to check there are no typos. Don't forget that spell check isn't foolproof and you will already have seen instances where this can go wrong on previous pages, so you would be well advised at this point to revert to traditional proofreading techniques. If necessary, ask your friends, family or school teachers to read it and check the spelling for you, because this is vitally important. There is no point in presenting a beautifully worded and structured personal statement if it is littered with spelling mistakes and errors.

Now, your personal statement reads well, it looks good, is well presented and contains no spelling, punctuation or grammatical errors. You're happy with it, so now you're ready to upload it into your UCAS application.

10 Personal statements critiqued (A Level and Graduate entrants)

In this chapter, we present and critique personal statements from candidates who have been successful at entering medical school, including Oxbridge, after their A levels or as graduate entrants from different walks of life and with a variety of prior experience. All statements were provided by candidates who were successful not only at obtaining interviews but also at getting into medical school.

Although we have occasionally modified some of the names or dates mentioned within the statements in order to protect the identity of some of the candidates, all statements are real and are presented in their unedited form.

After each statement we give a balanced critique so that you can identify the good and bad points, and take on board some of those points when writing your own statement.

Note on the personal statements shown in this book

For each of the personal statements in this and the following chapter, we have indicated the medical schools for which the candidate was successful at being shortlisted. This means the following:

- For medical schools that have an interview process, the candidate was invited to attend an interview, whether they attended the interview or not, and, if they attended, whether they were successful or not.

- For the medical schools that don't offer an interview (e.g. Southampton), the candidate was made an offer based solely on their application, including the personal statement.

10.1 Personal statement 1 (A level)

Personal statement successful for: Imperial College, King's College, St George's

Personal statement

The large number of specialities and things to learn in medicine make it one of the most diverse subjects. I found this out personally on numerous hospital visits for a variety of reasons ranging from chicken pox to eye tests. During these visits I also saw many medical teams working in harmony for long hours in an attempt to help patients to overcome illness, malfunctions and suffering. The diversity of the job and the constant learning about the way that the body malfunctions appeals to me.

As a St John's Ambulance cadet, I have learnt a wide variety of skills. For example, leadership among panicked people and how to put into practice basic medical knowledge effectively. I have also found that teamwork and communication are extremely important. I feel that these experiences will put me in a strong position when I enter the medical field.

I attended the 'Introduction to Healthcare' course at Charing Cross hospital last year. It provided me with insight into the role of doctors within the medical team, highlighting the importance of good communication, teamwork skills and also opened my eyes to the large number of careers open to a doctor.

Shadowing my uncle, who is a consultant orthopaedic surgeon in Hong Kong, provided insight into the life of a doctor, I was surprised to find that he spent little time in surgery and often spent large amounts of his time in clinical work, talking with the patients and discussing each case with doctors and the patients themselves.

I spent one month of my summer in India dividing my time between: trekking in the Himalayas, sightseeing and helping with a community project at a local school in Baragram. At the school, for the children of that town and the surrounding area, a team of us went out to repaint the interior of the building and to do some maintenance work. Many of the children there were keen to help, sanding down the walls and painting. The classrooms contained only rugs for the children to sit on, a blackboard and a desk for the teacher. This showed me the dedication that some of the children put into their education to make it into secondary school, working in classes of between 40 and 50 children. My share of the cost for this expedition was raised by giving music lessons in piano and I feel that I learnt a lot about time management and communication. The job taught me to divide my time between study and work and about communication with people of a variety of ages.

I have also achieved grade 8 in both clarinet and piano and I am currently working towards grade 7 on the organ. My self-discipline has been tested by having to divide my time between work, School Orchestra, Concert Band and School Choir, with which I have taken part in several concert tours to Europe. I also play the organ at Sunday Mass in my parish. Learning a martial art, Wing Chun, has also helped to develop these skills.

I look forward to the diversity of opportunities that life at medical school will offer and the chance to become a doctor, working in a team to serve the community.

Critique

Good points

- Good range of personal and work experiences, from observation (consultant orthopaedics) to personal participation (St John Ambulance and helping at the school).

- Good effort demonstrated to find out about the medical environment through the attendance of courses.

- Good effort to reflect on the experience.

- Good highlight of personal skills (particularly at the end of the paragraph on the school in the Himalayas).

- The statement conveys strongly that the candidate is someone who is proactive, takes initiative and is able to plan well.

- All sentences apart from two (end of first and fifth paragraphs) are active sentences. This helps give pace to the statement and increases the feeling of proactivity and initiative.

Points that could be improved

- The statement is structured around the different work and personal experiences of the candidate. This makes it very "listy", and sometimes causes confusion. For example, the first paragraph talks about the diversity of options in medicine, a theme which comes back in the paragraph on the "Introduction to Healthcare" course. Similarly the theme of teamwork is addressed in the first, second, and third paragraphs. These repetitions suggest that the statement should be structured in a different way.

- Some of the experiences are not fully exploited. The statement places a lot of emphasis on organisation skills, but there is little about listening, communication and empathy. These themes could have been addressed in the paragraph about the Himalayan school (communication quickly mentioned briefly at the end but as something important rather than a personal experience).

- Similarly the teamwork theme is underexploited. The candidate talks about the importance of teamwork with St John Ambulance, at the "Introduction to Healthcare" course, or when shadowing his uncle, but not about his own experience of working in a team. More could be written about it, particularly within the Himalayan experience where the candidate missed an opportunity to discuss how he worked with the teachers to motivate the children and to organise other activities. The teamwork theme could also have been raised when mentioning the school orchestra, concert band and school choir. So basically it would better to have less about observed teamwork and more about the candidate's own demonstration of teamwork.

- Parts of the statement are not that relevant, for example the following paragraph, however interesting, adds little value to the candidate's application as it describes a situation rather than the candidate's own role in the situation: "Many of the children there were keen to help, sanding down the walls and painting. The classrooms contained only rugs for the children to sit on, a blackboard and a desk for the teacher. This showed me the dedication that some of the children put into their education to make it into secondary school, working in classes of between 40 and 50 children."

- Some of the wording could be tightened. The use of the word "things" in the very first sentence of the statement weakens its impact.

Similarly, the phrase "a team of us went out to repaint the interior of the building" sounds a little heavy. Finally, the candidate mentions "St John's Ambulance", whereas the real name is actually "St John Ambulance". It is unlikely to make much of a difference, but an astute admission tutor could be influenced by such lack of accuracy.

Overall comment

This statement is in line with the type of statement that most candidates would write, i.e. a statement which combines experience with skills, and shows the relationship to a career in medicine. With a bit more emphasis on the candidate's soft skills (communication and teamwork in particular), and with a stronger focus on his own experience rather than observations, the candidate would have presented a more balanced picture of what he has to offer.

These weaknesses are, however, compensated by the extent and variety of the experience as well as the strong feeling of proactivity that the statement generates.

10.2 Personal statement 2 (A level)

Personal statement successful for: Birmingham, Leeds, Nottingham, Sheffield

Personal statement

Science-based subjects and the human body have always interested me and over the last few years I have been drawn to a career as a doctor. I feel I have a caring personality and, as a result, I would like to help others and improve their quality of life.

Undertaking relevant work experience in working with people in a caring role has confirmed my interest in a career in medicine. Last year I spent 2 weeks at a school for physically disabled children where I learnt the importance of treating all people equally and how to work with vulnerable children. One thing that struck me was having to feed a student of my own age. However, I managed to complete the task whilst still being able to be empathetic, something which I feel a doctor needs to be able to do. Following my GCSE exams I arranged to spend 2 days a week for 5 weeks in a community hospital in various departments including Minor Injuries and Pharmacy, and visiting patients with the District Nurse and Occupational Therapist. During this time I learnt about different medical professions, how they work individually and the importance of working together to ensure the patient receives the best care possible. Over the past year, during my weekly free afternoon, I have been a volunteer on a surgical ward talking to patients and providing them with drinks. This has broadened my knowledge of an acute hospital environment. It has also taught me the importance of good communication with patients, and I now have more confidence in being able to talk and listen to patients.

Having passed Grade 7 with merit on the flute, I am currently working towards Grade 8; I have also passed Grade 5 Theory at distinction level. For the past 6 years I have been a member of the school orchestra and enjoy playing a key part in working as a team by helping younger students to participate. I have travelled to Belgium and Austria on tour with the orchestra. At the annual school presentations I have been awarded subject prizes for music, science and resistant materials in recognition of my hard work. I have also been awarded the tutor prize twice and the Head of Year's award for consistent achievement and involvement in extracurricular activities.

Outside of school, 13 years' membership of the Girls' Brigade has given me opportunities to take part in a variety of activities. Recently I was able to complete an Emergency Life Support course. I also thoroughly enjoyed the opportunity to undertake the Bronze and Silver Duke of Edinburgh's Award. This year I decided to start the Gold award which necessitated me finding a new group to work with. I have found it demanding both physically and mentally. As well as the specific skills needed for the expedition such as map reading, I have learnt about teamwork and how to cope in totally unfamiliar settings and under pressure. For the past 3 years, to complete the service part of the Award, I have voluntarily taken on a responsible role of teaching beginner swimmers at the club where I also swim and this enabled me to complete my ASA Level 1 Certificate for teaching aquatics.

I have also been a member of several Birmingham Schools' ensembles for 5 years including Flute Choir, Training Wind Orchestra and Concert Band and have recently joined the Wind Orchestra. With these ensembles I have participated in concerts in various venues in Birmingham including the Symphony Hall. For the past 6 years I have helped at our annual Church Holiday Club, increasingly taking on more responsibility beforehand and during the week, giving me more experience of working alongside a team.

I feel that I am suited to the course because I am hardworking, enthusiastic and have the ability to work both independently and as a team member. I am capable of managing time and always look for a challenge. Following my 6 years 100% attendance at school I feel that I am committed and dedicated to learning and look forward to the opportunity to fulfil my ambition to study medicine.

Critique

Good points
- The statement follows a clear format: relevant work experience, achievements, activities and teamwork, general skills. There is also a good variety of activities, from observation to personal involvement. Extracurricular activities range from simple team involvement to areas of responsibility.

- The description of the experience is very accurate: "Last year I spent 2 weeks ...", or "I arranged to spend 2 days a week for 5 weeks". This type of detail helps enhance credibility because it provides something concrete for the reader to hang on to. Saying "Last year I spent 10 days doing ..." would have a lower impact.

Points that could be improved
- The introduction is very standard and does not grab the attention. The candidate makes up for it through the extent of her experience and a good display of interpersonal skills thereafter.

- Some of the experiences mentioned don't seem to lead to a specific point. For example: "I have participated in concerts in various venues in Birmingham including the Symphony Hall." What is the candidate trying to say? That she works well in teams? That she has a good work-life balance? Earlier in the statement she had raised the issue of playing in an orchestra as being a team activity. The repetition of the experience in two separate parts of the statement is confusing.

- One of the sections is clearly about personal achievements (e.g. various prizes). The section is very relevant and well placed in the statement; however the candidate does not fully exploit its value. Is she trying to say that she always strives for the top? That she enjoys working hard and that this pays off? That she is organised and very good at handling pressure, which means she can balance and achieve in different fields? The lack of reflection on the experience weakens the statement somewhat.

- The candidate presents many of the skills and experience as a discovery journey ("I have learnt about teamwork and how to cope in totally unfamiliar settings and under pressure") rather than as a demonstration of her own skills.

Overall comment
The statement ticks all the boxes in terms of experience and skills, which is reflected in the fact that she received 3 interviews out of 4 applications. The statement would benefit from a bit more personal reflection and a bit more headlining within each section so that the reader is in no doubt as to what message she is trying to convey.

10.3 Personal statement 3 (A level)

Personal statement successful for: Cardiff, Leicester, Newcastle, Sheffield

Personal statement

From my early school years, I was inspired by the idea of a career in medicine. I therefore took the opportunity of my school Work Experience period last year to arrange a placement at St Peter's Hospital. This provided me with my first experience of the reality of working in healthcare. My week of shadowing nurses taught me a great deal about patient care, especially the importance of maintaining privacy, dignity and confidentiality. I also recognised the communication and empathy skills displayed by the team working with each patient, comprising doctors, nurses and physiotherapists (amongst others), who provide effective care, treatment and rehabilitation. Following this, a week-long course called 'An Introduction to the NHS', at the same hospital, gave me a chance to appreciate and understand further the different roles of those working within the NHS and the extent to which they are interdependent upon each other.

Also last year, I arranged to shadow an ophthalmologist at St Peter's Hospital for three days. I observed laser treatment for a patient with diabetic retinopathy and this allowed me to appreciate how such a disease can affect many areas of an individual's daily life. This year, I arranged to shadow a consultant psychiatrist for a week at Hillingdon Hospital and gained a greater understanding of mental illness. Working closely with patients, within a team, to achieve set goals, and applying up-to-date knowledge to diagnose and treat illnesses, is an ideal job description. However, I was glad to find that I was not put off by what I learnt to be the challenges of a career in medicine. Senior doctors and young medics were aware of the frustrations of having limited time and resources for individual patients, but I was impressed by the ability of healthcare teams to continuously aim to improve their services. In fact, this is something I am still seeing in action, working as a healthcare assistant on an orthopaedic ward at St Peter's Hospital during this gap year. From my first day at work in September, I saw new ideas and procedures being applied to allow nursing staff to spend more time with each patient and improve infection control. As my aim is to become a doctor myself, having the opportunity to observe how doctors work on the ward and at the fracture clinic has been particularly interesting.

Away from work, I volunteer at my old primary school, helping children with special needs. I work, in particular, with a girl of seven who has dyslexia. Last summer I gained my National Pool Lifeguard Qualification after learning how to swim within a year. I enjoy passing on the determination and perseverance I displayed at this time to children who face greater challenges with learning. My leadership and teamwork skills have been further developed through my weekly volunteering at a local Brownie pack, which I have done for almost eighteen months, supervising and running activities for twenty-five lively girls, and accompanying them on a weekend away in September.

While at school, I enjoyed and really benefited from the Bronze Duke of Edinburgh award, playing netball for my school team, taking part in House competitions, being a senior prefect and spending a month on an expedition to Northern Peru, which was both challenging and enlightening. Singing in my school choir, achieving a Grade 8 in LAMDA Public Speaking and playing the violin to Grade 5 gave me a chance to enjoy activities that contrasted with my school subjects. Currently, I enjoy running, swimming, reading and seeing friends in my spare time. The experience thus gained over this gap year has further fuelled and cemented my ambition to become a doctor. To this end, I look forward to continuing to make the most of every opportunity this gap year presents, in order to best prepare for every aspect of university life.

Critique

Good points
- The statement clearly shows the path that the candidate followed to acquaint herself with medicine. This reinforces the perception of commitment to medicine. The type of experience described is also varied, from observing and shadowing through to personal participation as a healthcare assistant.

- Half of the statement is spent on medically-related experience, with the other half being dedicated to personal interests and achievements. This provides a good balance.

- The statement is written in a very personal style, using a lot of active sentences. Many of the activities described by the candidate offer opportunities to demonstrate good communication skills, empathy, teamwork and initiative, though these are not always explicit and are often inferred. Overall the candidate comes across as someone who is well balanced and friendly.

Points that could be improved
- The major point of improvement in this statement is on the reflection of the experience. The candidate barely reflects on her own experience, preferring to focus on what she has observed rather than the skills she demonstrated. For example, the whole of the paragraph on last year talks about teamwork observed and how this was also further observed when she worked as a healthcare assistant. The candidate could have made more of her own involvement as a healthcare assistant and how she coordinated her own work with that of others in the team to ensure patients received the best care. The experience as a healthcare assistant would also have enabled her to demonstrate her empathy and communication skills, none of which is mentioned in that paragraph.

- When the candidate does mention her own skills in the second half of the statement, they are simply stated but not elaborated on. For example, the sentence "My leadership and teamwork skills have been further developed through my weekly volunteering at a local Brownie pack" does not really explain anything about the skills. We know from the second half of the sentence that the girls were lively but how does that relate to teamwork and leadership? More work would be needed to make a clear connection between the skills and the context in which they are demonstrated.

- Similarly, there is quite a lot of information in this sentence: "I enjoyed and really benefited from the Bronze Duke of Edinburgh's award, playing netball for my school team, taking part in House competitions, being a senior prefect and spending a month on an expedition to Northern Peru, which was both challenging and enlightening." But no reflection. Why was the expedition challenging and enlightening? How did the candidate benefit from the Duke of Edinburgh's Award? Some of these activities present an opportunity to demonstrate initiative and leadership, whilst others can be used to demonstrate organisational skills and a supportive attitude, or an ability to deal with stress. The Peru expedition is almost being wasted by being simply listed.

Overall comment
The statement is good from a content point of view and the candidate is able to present herself as a good all-rounder, using a very structured approach. However, the lack of reflection means that there are many missed opportunities to sell the full package, which could cause problems with some of the more selective schools.

In all fairness the candidate was offered interviews at all four medical schools to which she applied, though this is most likely due to the fact that some of those particular schools place a greater emphasis on the amount and type of work experience than on the skills exhibited. The interview itself would then focus more heavily on interpersonal skills. Other schools may take a different view.

With different schools looking for different features, it can be difficult to write a statement that caters for the needs of all four schools applied for. Consequently, the statement should be as comprehensive as possible both from the content and the reflection point of view. Once you have written a first draft, you should reread the statement to spot any imbalances and adjust the statement accordingly. This is the part of the process that can take a long time and you may need to go through several drafts to achieve the desired effect (hence the need to start early).

Many times, as is the case in this statement, all the elements are there, waiting to be exploited. Candidates often miss those opportunities because they are so engrossed with the statement that they often cannot spot them. Leaving the statement to one side for a few days and reading it again later with fresh eyes can help.

10.4 Personal statement 4 (A level)

Personal statement successful for: Belfast, Glasgow, Liverpool

Personal statement

Medicine is a challenging, demanding and rewarding area of study, and is of vital importance to all members of society. My intellectual interest for the biological sciences and my desire to work directly with people are the initial reasons for my desire to study Medicine.

I have gained insight into the work of a doctor through four varied work experience opportunities, totalling fourteen days at several hospitals which treated numerous specialities. In a Neurology Department I shadowed a Neurological Consultant, and observed him discussing with patients the symptoms of conditions such as Epilepsy and Alzheimer's disease. This experience reinforced for me that it is not always possible for a doctor to 'cure' a condition, but to help the patient learn to control and live with their disease. I was impressed with the way the Consultant treated each patient as an individual and not just as a person with a disease. In a Cardiac Department, I observed and spoke with patients undergoing procedures such as ultrasound and ECG. This showed me how information is gathered to aid in the diagnosis and treatment of various heart conditions, such as Coronary Thrombosis and Angina. In a Brain Injury Unit I accompanied different members of a multidisciplinary team, giving me insight into the value of various professionals working together to meet the needs of patients and demonstrating the pivotal role of the doctor in the team. While accompanying a Resuscitation Officer, I gained knowledge of life-saving techniques by participating in an Immediate Life Support course for newly qualified doctors.

Through these work experiences, I had the opportunity to explore what it is like to be a medical student, for example, by attending a tutorial at which a Consultant discussed heart-related case studies. I discovered that I could communicate well with the patients I was given the opportunity to talk to – I was involved in discussions with patients who had brain injuries heightening my awareness of the distinctive needs of different patients. This experience highlighted the importance of good communication skills. In addition, I work as a volunteer with children who have learning and physical disabilities under the auspices of Barnardos. I enjoy communicating with the children at their level and pace.

I have several achievements which demonstrate my intellectual suitability for a career in medicine. I gained third place in Northern Ireland in GCSE English Literature, won a School prize for overall GCSE results, a two-year school Scholarship for Outstanding Achievement, and an academic prize in every school year. I have achieved Grade 5 in alto saxophone and am working towards Grade 7 in clarinet, and I play these instruments in the award-winning school Orchestra, Jazz Band, and Saxophone Quartet. I represented my school in a 'Paperclip Physics' competition as part of a small team. I am a Senior School Prefect and the Deputy Head Librarian in the Careers Library. I have gained certificates in First Aid and the European Computer Driving Licence. These academic and extracurricular achievements demonstrate my abilities and interests; also I have learnt how to operate as a member of a team and how to undertake organisational and leadership tasks efficiently. I have benefited from the opportunities provided by this range of activities and responsibilities. For relaxation, I am interested in photography and art, and was awarded a prize for the best final Art and Design examination piece in the school.

My academic record, coupled with my extracurricular activities, would provide a positive basis for a career in Medicine. My work experience has developed my insight into the practice of Medicine. I appreciate that this career means a dedication to lifelong learning as the boundaries of medical knowledge and treatment are continuously expanding. I feel ready to meet the challenges of being a medical student and subsequently having a career as a doctor.

Critique

Good points
- The experience is clearly signposted by statements such as "I have several achievements which demonstrate my intellectual suitability for a career in medicine" or "I have gained insight into the work of a doctor through four varied work experience opportunities". Although this can be cumbersome to read if overused, it does convey a good sense of structure. The reader knows what to expect and admission tutors will be left in no doubt as to which boxes they need to tick.

- There is a good balance between what the candidate observed and what he experienced personally, for example "I discovered that I could communicate well with the patients I was given the opportunity to talk to – I was involved in discussions with patients who had brain injuries heightening my awareness of the distinctive needs of different patients."

- The statement is full of active sentences, using phrases such as "I observed and spoke", "I accompanied", and "I represented".

Points that could be improved
- The introductions and conclusions are both pretty standard. In this particular statement, the candidate could have cut out most of the introduction and gone straight to the heart of the matter with a sentence such as "Shadowing a neurologist managing epilepsy patients was an experience I will never forget, etc." This would give the start more impact. The information provided in the introduction could then be placed in the conclusion, where it would sound less contrived.

- Because the candidate adopted a format of the type (i) headline statement and (ii) list the achievements, the statement might appear a bit of a list. That list portrays the candidate in a good light but, at the same time, stops him from going into much detail about each of the experiences. This is particularly the case in the penultimate paragraph on personal achievements, in which the candidate reflects less than in the others. One theme, which is particularly underdeveloped, is teamwork, which is never really mentioned other than as an observed skill.

Overall comment
The statement is very systematic and comes across as a good and "safe" statement, the word "safe" being used in a good sense. After reading it, we know everything there is to know about the candidate, who comes across as an achiever and a good academic with a caring nature. The only real downside is the quasi-absence of teamwork, which could easily be resolved by reflecting a bit more on a couple of his achievements in the penultimate paragraph.

10.5 Personal statement 5 (A level)

Personal statement successful for: Birmingham, Cambridge, Manchester, Nottingham

Personal statement

The complexity of the human body never fails to amaze me. Specifically in young children, understanding how the body functions, poses a challenge in itself as they are still growing, much like our knowledge of human biology. It is this intermingling of constant change and the multitudinous possibilities for advancement that I believe makes medicine, and paediatrics in particular, a stimulating field to be involved in.

In the further pursuit of this interest, I shadowed a paediatric surgeon at Singapore's National University Hospital. My time here taught me the importance of good beside manners and the need to show empathy when reassuring young patients. While observing surgical procedures, I realised that surgeons had to be patient and possess mental and manual dexterity as one error of judgement could impair a life forever. A particular case which interested me during ward rounds was a liver transplant patient who suffered tissue rejection, post-surgery, requiring immediate remedial intervention. This made me realise the uncertainties permeating medical procedures. I began to appreciate the value of making a personal connection with patients while volunteering at a hospital. A simple act of engaging the patients in entertaining conversations could distract them from their discomfort which I found very fulfilling.

In July, I was employed as a Patient Service Assistant at Raffles Hospital where I was required to interact with patients from diverse ethnic backgrounds. Overcoming language barriers to communicate effectively helped me develop my interpersonal skills and gain a deeper respect of cultural diversity and needs. I also assisted in the hospital's Annual Scientific Symposium where specialists presented papers on medical advancements. I was especially impressed by technological developments such as the 64-slice CT scan, which are reducing the need for invasive diagnostic procedures, thereby increasing the comfort of patients and the ease of diagnosis.

Academically, I aim to achieve the best I am capable of. This year, I was honoured with an academic scholarship from the Government of Singapore. Beyond textbooks, I am an avid reader of scientific journals like the Biological Sciences Review, New Scientist and others. I also regularly participate in the informal debates held in school as I enjoy the thrill of spontaneous repartee. Last year, I participated in a Model United Nations Conference where thought-provoking socio-political issues were debated. For this, I was commended with an award for Best Presentation. As for my abilities in the leadership arena, I was the class Vice Chairperson in secondary school and the current Publicity Secretary of the students' committee. Executing successful school events with both committees has taught me invaluable lessons in teamwork and dedication. Regular meditation and jogging helps me relieve stress and keep fit mentally and physically.

Through my extensive work experiences, I have a realistic idea of the challenges and rewards of studying medicine. I believe the demands of this course require maturity, which academic rote learning alone cannot provide. Hence, I am deferring entry to university by a year, to volunteer in hospitals in Asia with the company, 'Projects Abroad'. While engaging in meaningful humanitarian efforts, I intend to expose myself to the varied practice of medicine around the world. Additionally, I hope to seek placements in biomedical research firms to gain insights into this developing field. I believe that these exposures will prepare me for the rigours of a medical course and hold me in good stead for my future endeavours.

Critique

Good points
- The statement is very clearly structured and laid out, starting with work experience, academic achievements and interests and a conclusion discussing the benefits of deferred entry.

- The second paragraph discusses the candidate's work experience from a personal perspective. The candidate's use of an example such as the liver transplant patient gives a different dimension to the statement, different from the often seen "and I learnt a lot from this experience". An effort is made to explain what was actually learnt.

- The candidate has written the statement in a way designed to tick a number of boxes. The third paragraph concentrates on communication skills, whilst the fourth focuses on initiative and leadership. This would make it easier for a tutor to tick the boxes.

<u>Points that could be improved</u>
- The introduction starts with a cliché, though luckily the candidate then seeks to qualify the statement made at the outset by talking about children.

- More could be done to emphasise the candidate's interpersonal skills. Much of the statement focuses on the candidate's achievements and his understanding of the world of medicine. Though the third paragraph does mention communication skills this could be elaborated upon further and there would also be value in bringing more aspects of teamwork into the answer (a skill only briefly mentioned at the end of the penultimate paragraph when he talks about organising school events).

<u>Overall comment</u>
Aside from the slightly clichéd start, the statement sets out clearly what the candidate has to offer. As is often the case for candidates with a strong academic background and strong leadership skills, teamwork and communication skills are often reduced to a simple mention, without being elaborated upon.

His chances of success were nevertheless not impaired by it since he obtained four interviews at some of the most prominent universities, suggesting that, on balance, tutors are far more likely to be influenced by the extent and type of experience gained than by the reflection, provided that experience is well described.

10.6 Personal statement 6 (A level)

Personal statement successful for: Newcastle, Oxford, Sheffield

Personal statement

When I first discovered how the solar system was made up, over a decade ago, I naturally assumed I would be an astronaut. As I matured I did consider going into nuclear or particle physics research before settling on becoming an industrial chemist. I was inspired by the way molecules interacted; I took part in a 'changing perceptions of industry' scheme; I organised work experience in an industrial testing laboratory and I was accepted to the Sutton Trust chemistry summer school at the University of Oxford. These experiences have only heightened my interest in science and broadened my practical skills.

Despite my interest in chemistry I could not ignore the colossal urge I felt to help those around me. I no longer want to improve the yield of an industrial process to make money for huge companies. I want to give something back to my community, just as my faith has always encouraged me to do, and I have therefore settled on a career in medicine. I believe this desire is the only thing that can satisfy both my love of all things scientific and my deep religious conviction to help improve the lives of others.

In order to be sure that medicine is the right career choice for me I have attended a work experience programme at my local hospital, which gave me an insight into how an NHS hospital works. I was also given the chance to practise clinical skills such as catheterisation and venepuncture. I also spoke to consultants from different areas of medicine. My time in the hospital only furthered my desire to become a doctor, despite many of the negatives explained to me by the staff. Also, my GP agreed to let me shadow her. She explained many of the workings of the surgery and how different medical conditions can affect different people. This allowed me to compare primary care to the specialist hospital services I had previously observed.

Volunteering at a local care home has allowed me to see how long-term illnesses can affect not only patients, but their families too. This setting allows me to speak to patients, get to know them and develop a rapport with them and their families. I have enhanced my communication and patient skills during my time there and I believe I have become more empathetic as a result.

I assist in the SEN department of my school, helping with homework and providing advice, guidance and comfort to those who need it. I also volunteer at a dyspraxia support group. Although I sometimes find it challenging to meet the needs of all the young people, I strive to be as helpful and as friendly as possible, being a supportive and playful companion.

I currently participate in first aid and life support training with the St John's Ambulance. This makes me one of the first contacts for medical assistance at many large events, improving both my patient care and decision making skills. My Catholic faith is a very prominent aspect of my life and I currently lead the children's liturgy at my local parish church. This has made me a more confident and outgoing person, yet also more considerate and caring. I am also about to train as a Eucharistic Minister, which will involve my delivering the sacrament to the sick and housebound of my parish.

Outside of academia I particularly enjoy classical music. I teach piano in a local primary school. I sing bass in my school chamber choir and I have also recently performed in two massed choir events, one of which was at The Sage, Gateshead. I have enjoyed working with members of the Tees Valley Youth Choir in workshops and had the privilege to take part in an opera workshop with two leading performers. Music allows me to relax and get away from everything in daily life and it is something that will stay with me throughout my life. I believe that I have the empathy, the enthusiasm and the excellence required to become a doctor and I truly believe becoming a doctor will allow me to help others in such an exciting and unique way. For that reason alone, I would relish the opportunity.

Critique

Good points
- The statement has a very different introduction to the majority of statements, with the candidate choosing to emphasise his interest in science in a very personal manner. This is likely to be in order to make a strong impression for Oxford (where he was shortlisted for interview) and works well generally because it is detailed and personal. The admission tutors would appreciate the change.

- The statement is well structured, with a logical progression, from the interest in science to the need to help others, work experience, volunteer work, other responsibilities and personal interests.

- The candidate offers a strong personal reflection on his experience and clearly highlights his interpersonal skills: "This has made me a more confident and outgoing person, yet also more considerate and caring" or "Although I sometimes find it challenging to meet the needs of all the young people, I strive to be as helpful and as friendly as possible, being a supportive and playful companion." This gives a very personal and genuine feel to the statement. Generally the whole statement presents the candidate as a strong team player and a caring and empathic person.

Points that could be improved
- Although the statement demonstrates a strong interest in science and an altruistic nature, it contains little about leadership. Indeed even the conclusion makes no mention of it. This could have been addressed by mentioning positions of responsibility, events organised or projects managed.

Overall comment
This statement stands out for its unusual science-based introduction and its strong emphasis on soft skills (when most statements would start with generalities on medicine and place an emphasis on organisational skills, teamwork and leadership. It is overall a very good statement, which could be improved further by the introduction of more leadership skills and experience. Some candidates may be wondering whether the mention of religious activities is appropriate or not. Generally, candidates should not feel that they should avoid anything religious provided it is mentioned within a relevant context, for example to illustrate empathy, a caring attitude or organisational skills (e.g. if a candidate is involved in organising religious activities).

10.7 Personal statement 7 (A level)

Personal statement successful for: Bristol, UCL

Personal statement

Witnessing a friend's fight against cancer was a turning point in my life which has driven my determination to pursue a career in medicine ever since. It is often observed that extreme circumstances bring out the best in people, and I enjoy facing the difficulties of a challenge as I work well, if not best, under pressure. I understand that as a doctor it is vital to uphold personal responsibilities as well as be an effective team member. It was the dedication of the team who treated this complex disease and the strength and perseverance of the doctor specifically which inspired me to follow a career in medicine. Competency in clinical expertise and emotional support are two different but essential aspects of becoming a doctor which I aspire to excel in.

Having the opportunity to shadow a Senior Registrar in Obstetrics and Gynaecology in Hillingdon Hospital was very beneficial to me as I was able to explore a range of science and medical-based departments; from pathology and microscopy, to gynaecology clinic, labour ward, and theatre. In the latter two I witnessed the demands of working successfully within a team and under pressure, where the complications of birth led to an epidural, attempts at an assisted delivery and a caesarean section. My understanding of the daily running of a hospital was developed through work experience in Northwick Park Hospital where I realised the invaluable role of nurses, especially in caring for the elderly.

Throughout my years of schooling the study of science has been continually fascinating to me, particularly in regards to the human body. Attending lectures and exhibitions has been enjoyable as it has allowed me to go beyond the curriculum and inspired my contribution to the school's Medical Newsletter. It was through an exhibition on malaria at the Royal Society's Summer Exhibition that I discovered a specific interest in infectious diseases and immunology, which I had the opportunity to develop during a week's work experience in the NIMR. Completing a genetics course run by the Institute of Education built on the laboratory techniques I learnt and broadened my mind through ethical discussions about genetic testing and doctor-patient confidentiality. Attending Medlink was a valuable experience as the lectures broadened my knowledge of specific aspects of medicine, and I gained a brief insight into student life which I look forward to experiencing fully.

While my main interests lie in science, I have equally enjoyed studying English Literature and Spanish, as these have opened many doors to a diverse range of cultures. These pursuits have led to visits to the theatre, taking a Spanish course in Barcelona and doing a Spanish exchange. Being a member of the debating society and representing the school in public speaking competitions has greatly developed my fluency and articulacy, which has developed my ability to work under pressure. Striving to raise over £3,000 pounds for World Challenge for our expedition to Argentina last year has made it vital that I manage time effectively in order to balance my employment with academic pursuits. Walking 60km and raising over £1,500 for Breakthrough Breast Cancer research was challenging and incredibly rewarding. This has inspired a particular empathy for cancer sufferers which I have followed by volunteering in a hospice for the past two years.

Belly dancing and lambada dancing are hobbies which I do purely for enjoyment. Playing in the school lacrosse team for six years and regular training at the gym has developed my perseverance as I have realised every challenge is a matter of mental strength.

Through my experiences I believe I have gained a realistic insight into the challenges of both studying medicine and becoming a doctor, challenges which have reinforced my dedication to medicine, a career in which I could never tire of striving to achieve my best.

Critique

Good points
- Starting with a story always pays off and grabs the attention. There is also a good natural link between the initial story and the work experience that follows.

- The statement is clearly set out, following the structure: work experience, awareness of medicine through other means, key achievements, and personal interests.

- The experiences described are very varied. The section on science is memorable because of the mention of the interest in infectious diseases and genetics, which is different. The section on personal achievements stands out because it is detailed and therefore credible.

Points that could be improved
- The statement contains too many passive sentences. For example, the phrase "having had the opportunity" does not convey anything about the effort the candidate put into organising it. Sentences such as "My understanding … was developed" presents the candidate as an observer, but does not convey anything active. Some passive sentences are acceptable and indeed can introduce variety in a personal statement, but overuse often leads to complex sentences which impair understanding and readability.

- The statement is very academic in that it mostly focuses on science and achievements. This gives a picture of a candidate who is driven, passionate and hardworking. However, interpersonal skills such as teamwork and communication/empathy barely feature. Teamwork is only mentioned as a skill observed in medical environments when the candidate could have used her experience of organising expeditions. Instead, she emphasised only her organisational skills. Empathy is mentioned in passing at the end of a paragraph, but without any explanation. More could have been done on that topic, for example by explaining how she supported her friend's fight against cancer. Furthermore, the link between raising funds for a cancer charity and empathy is not obvious, given that many people contribute to charities but have never necessarily met a sufferer. The candidate would have benefited from mentioning her own experience of meeting cancer sufferers to add weight to the statement.

Overall comment
The statement is good, packed with achievements which project the image of a candidate in control, with ambition, organisational skills and initiative to match. As is often the case for such candidates though, it neglects the interpersonal skills, reducing them to a mere mention. Presenting a more balanced statement may have endeared the candidate to schools that value interpersonal skills as much as academic achievement and drive.

10.8 Personal statement 8 (A level)

Personal statement successful for: St George's, Southampton,

Personal statement

As a child, I aspired to become a footballer. I was agile, quick and in my opinion crafty with the ball. However, living in Sierra Leone, a third world country with the world's highest infant mortality rate, I witnessed first-hand the trauma sick and vulnerable people faced. This is a country where a doctor's consultation exceeds the average monthly wage; people simply fell ill and died. It infuriated me that lives were valued according to the size of a person's wallet, and I knew from a very early age that I wanted to be part of a solution to resolve these injustices. I have since been driven by the ambition to be a Doctor.

To feed my interest in medicine, I organised work experience to ensure that I had made the right career choice by understanding the realities of being a doctor and to appreciate the challenges they face. I worked at a doctor's surgery where I learnt that confidentiality and interpersonal skills are fundamental in this profession. Every aspect of the experience further entrenched my ambition, but, more importantly, I realised that, aside from academic acumen, doctors need personal strengths to be successful. I believe I have these strengths.

I am extremely hardworking and work well under pressure. This can be verified by the fact that I arrived in the UK at the age of eleven, unable to speak English. I worked diligently to overcome this barrier. Adapting to change with ease is another attribute of mine which can be demonstrated by the transition of my studies from a comprehensive to a grammar school. I feel this quality is invaluable with an ever-changing NHS. Being a keen participant in school debates has helped me become a strong communicator who can listen to other people's perspectives, whilst being able to get my point across. It is also true that my organisational skills, reliability and confidence have enabled me to be chosen as prefect at Wilson's and as Deputy Head Boy at my previous school.

On a recent visit to Lebanon, I was fortunate to shadow a doctor. This experience strengthened my already solid desire to become a doctor and left me longing for the day I would be able to deal with the stress and pressure they face daily. I learnt that good medicine takes a holistic approach and is not just about diagnosing and treating patients. I saw how the patients who were properly informed and invited to ask questions became less nervous about their ailment. Although no statistical data was collated, I felt this approach yielded the best outcome. I understood this in greater detail when I was the chair of a fundraising committee for a charity specialising in youth homelessness. I saw how welfare issues combined with social ones led to good or bad health. My experience with the voluntary sector made me realise that we are fortunate to have a welfare state. It also enabled me to reflect on the actions of doctors in Sierra Leone who often seemed to turn their backs on the needy, in the absence of a welfare state. They had little choice.

I also volunteer at a Refugee Day Centre, where I am able to support people from various cultures and age groups. Being trilingual, fluent in both Krio and Arabic in addition to English, I help them overcome the language barrier.

I do my best to achieve a work-life balance, combining my studies, voluntary work and household chores with activities that I find personally stimulating such as tennis, swimming and cooking. I also thoroughly enjoy acting, particularly in comedy roles.

For many people the commitment that medicine requires is overwhelming, whereas, for me, it is one that I cannot wait to make. I feel that medicine offers me a career where I would get total job satisfaction, and combine this with my deep-rooted drive to contribute and serve the community. My dedication and desire to be part of a field where new discoveries are constantly being made can only be matched by a career as dynamic as medicine. Not even Roman Abramovich can tempt me otherwise.

Critique

Good points
- Very strong introduction which grabs the attention immediately. The statement is strengthened by a structure in which the different experiences are described and then recalled throughout the statement. The concluding sentence referring to Roman Abramovich cleverly closes the loop with the very first sentence. The way in which the Sierra Leone experience is first mentioned in the introduction and

then recalled at the end of the paragraph on Lebanon is particularly clever. It helps tie everything in and avoids making the statement too much of a list of experiences.

- The statement is signposted (or headlined) very clearly, i.e. more or less every paragraph starts with a message, which is then backed up by examples. For example: "To feed my interest in medicine…", "I am extremely hardworking and work well under pressure", "I do my best to achieve a work-life balance". Although this strategy can make a statement feel a bit "military", it does make the information stand out more.

- The candidate has undertaken a good range of work experience, with a good mix of observation and personal participation. Every part of the experience is reflected upon, and on occasions the candidate also explains how he has demonstrated the skills or attributes that he observed.

- The candidate uses the final paragraph rather than the first paragraph to explain why he wishes to study medicine. As mentioned in Chapter 7, page 45 – section on clichés), anything that is at risk of sounding "cheesy" is often best placed at the end as a conclusion to all the experience described previously, rather than at the beginning where, if unexplained, will sound very contrived. This strategy enables the candidate to give the statement a more punchy start and to create a stronger impression.

- The candidate has used a mix of story telling and facts, a strategy that makes the statement come to life. The reader can almost picture the candidate in action; this helps humanise the applicant.

- The statement contains a lot of active and power words such as "I volunteer", "I organised", "I do my best to achieve", with passive sentences being kept to a minimum: "It is also true that my organisational skills, reliability and confidence have enabled me to be chosen as prefect at Wilson's". Overall, the balance works well. On occasions, the candidate has mixed both the active and the passive style in the same sentence, a style which enriches the statement by providing variety, for example."Every aspect of the experience further entrenched my ambition, but, more importantly, I realised that, aside from academic acumen, doctors need personal strengths to be successful."

Points that could be improved

- The fifth paragraph on the refugee centre has not been fully exploited by the candidate. He makes a point of saying that he is able to support people of different cultures and age groups, before mentioning that his knowledge of three languages helps him translate. It is not clear as to whether his role is limited to translation or whether he offered any other types of help. Amongst other qualities, such an experience offered a good platform for the candidate to explain how he was able to empathise with people who were in vulnerable situations, and also how he gained an insight into how different cultural values can influence a person's thinking process. People will view medical care with different eyes depending on their cultural or religious values and the refugee experience would have been an excellent opportunity for the candidate to demonstrate a non-judgemental approach.

- The statement is a very "social" statement, which focuses a lot on the hardship of others. This makes it very human and the caring nature of the candidate really comes out. However, the statement contains virtually no academic element. This may have been introduced by talking about books or journals that he may have read. The statement also contains little on teamwork.

Overall comment

This statement reads well and really conveys the image of a candidate who is eloquent, a good communicator, but the academic and teamwork qualities are not sufficiently highlighted, which may be the reason why the candidate was interviewed and successful at St George's, a medical school reputed for its focus on the more caring side of things.

The other schools applied for would have wanted a better balance between the various interpersonal skills. So, although it reads well, more emphasis on teamwork and academia would have made it tick more boxes and would have ensured shortlisting to more interviews.

10.9 Personal statement 9 (A level)

Personal statement successful for: Brighton, Cardiff, Hull York, Peninsula

Personal statement

I have been told this is one of the hardest things I will ever write and as I have always wanted to be a doctor I can understand why. A career in medicine would encompass my enthusiasm for science and people, whilst making the most of my personal skills. My desire to pursue this career has been confirmed by my work experience placements; I have loved gaining an insight into the realities of the medical profession. After writing to countless GP surgeries I obtained a placement shadowing a practice nurse. I learned about the importance of the patient's right to confidentiality and how adopting a holistic approach allows better understanding and thus more effective treatment.

At Alderney Hospital in Poole, I spoke with patients who had suffered a stroke. At times this experience was extremely heart-wrenching, but seeing how their quality of life could be improved only served to strengthen my desire to embark on a medical career. Ward rounds and home visits with other members of the healthcare team highlighted how patient care depends on many individuals and requires efficient communication. A placement observing General and Orthopaedic Surgery at Bournemouth Hospital showed how an intimate understanding of the structure of the human body, as well as precision and skill, can improve lives.

I attended Medlink and Medsim courses and, following Medlink, undertook a pathology project researching embryonic stem cells, which passed with Merit. My interest in science often leads me to explore subjects further than required at AS level. I read medical articles and subscribe to 'Biological Review'. I will look forward to not only the five years' study at medical school, but the lifelong learning in this dynamic profession. I loved the practical aspects of the Medsim course such as keyhole surgery and the emergency call out. I also completed a rapid response life support certificate which strengthened my skills gained on a Red Cross first aid course.

Whilst working at a greengrocer's, in a theme park and currently as a cleaner I have developed an ability to engage with a diverse range of people and have been required to be hardworking, as well as demonstrating commitment and teamwork. As Head of Year 8 I lead the year 8 team and together we instigated a 'drop-in centre', allowing younger students to discuss problems. In addition I was a peer mentor in 'Drugs Squad'. These roles showed the importance of interpersonal communication skills, in particular the ability to sit and listen; they also taught me that if people see you as trustworthy they communicate more honestly. I am currently a Form Mentor.

Good time management skills have been necessary to balance study for my 5 AS levels with extracurricular activities including rowing, cycling and rock climbing. I am a qualified Explorer Scout Young Leader and for the past three years have helped lead a Beaver Scout group, which has required a sense of humour, patience and ability to think on my feet. Caring for a partially deaf Beaver has motivated me to enroll on a sign language course. I thrive on challenges and have completed my Bronze Duke of Edinburgh and Ten Tors; endeavours requiring great perseverance, focus and, most importantly of all, teamwork to achieve success. I have also completed the Moonwalk, a charity marathon. I frequently meet with the youth group from my church and help to run a soup kitchen for the homeless. The people attending often have drug and alcohol addictions or mental health problems. Talking with them and reflecting on why people become homeless helped me work in a less judgemental and more empathic manner. Participating in French and New Zealand exchanges has further increased my social awareness and respect for individuals from various backgrounds.

Although medicine is a demanding career, I am aware it is also one of the most satisfying. I remain determined to become a doctor and feel ready for this challenge. I can see myself in no other profession than medicine.

Critique

Good points
- The statement follows a clear structure with each paragraph designed to illustrate a different point or experience (medical experience, courses and journals, other experience and interpersonal skills).

- The candidate has demonstrated involvement in a wide range of experiences, both as an observer and an active participant. The statement conveys a strong sense of initiative and responsibility. The mention of the homeless group also helps the candidate convey a sense of social and personal responsibility and a degree of empathy.

- The introduction, though slightly unusual, brings an element of humour and irony; and grabs the attention of the reader. The rest of the statement is more conventional in its approach but this helps convey a sense of stability.

- The statement is effective at conveying a complete range of personal skills, from initiative to empathy. The mentoring experience, combined with the team sports, youth group and other activities, also introduces the candidate as a sociable individual and a good team player.

Points that could be improved
- The statement uses a passive style a lot, particularly in the first and second paragraphs; for example:

  - "my desire ... has been confirmed".
  - "seeing how their quality of life improved only served to strengthen my desire".
  - "a placement ... showed how an intimate understanding".
  - "ward rounds ... highlighted how patient care".

  This can make some of the paragraphs a little difficult to read as the reader's mind attempts to convert those sentences into active sentences.

Overall comment
This statement is very well balanced and ticks all the boxes. It is formatted in a conventional manner, with the unusual introduction providing an interesting start. The candidate clearly comes across as motivated and able to show initiative and resilience (note the comment on having had to write to countless GPs) as well as strong interpersonal skills. A more active style may have improved the reading flow; however, the extent of the candidate's experience and her reflection on his experience more than makes up for it as the reader's interest is maintained by the variety of the achievements. This explains why she was offered medical interviews at all the schools she applied for.

10.10 Personal statement 10 (A level)

Personal statement successful for: Brighton, Hull York, Peninsula

Personal statement

Moving around the world made mine an unpredictable childhood, and taught me to adapt quickly to new situations. I became accustomed to change, and my international upbringing has allowed me the flexibility to be an independent student. My drive to study medicine stems not only from my interest in human biology, but also from its sheer diversity as a discipline and career. Both a science and an art, medicine remains an inimitable area of knowledge. It is precisely this that attracts me to the course, while my drive to become a doctor has always been rooted in the prospect of caring for others. As a re-applicant, I have had the opportunity to carefully reconsider and better familiarise myself with the career through further work experience. As a result, my desire to become a doctor has only been reinforced.

Last year I had the opportunity to carry out research in an Extended Essay, in which I tested the antibacterial properties of five herbs. Writing the essay developed my keen interest in complementary medicine and the impact of nutrition on health. Curious to learn more about life as a medical researcher, I arranged to shadow an onco-haematology researcher at a lab where dendritic vaccines were being tested. Her intense patience epitomised the dedication required in medicine, and seeing biology theory being put into practice was especially intriguing. A biology module on neurology later inspired me to read 'Phantoms in the Brain'. The innovative methodology described made me realise just how important creativity is to medical research, while the analyses reminded me of how truly complex the human body is.

Human psychology has always been another subject of interest, and reading 'Social Intelligence' has made me all the more aware of the emotional impact every interaction can have on a person. I saw the importance of this in medicine when I spent two weeks at a dermatology clinic in Hamburg, where the doctor's calm, confident and even witty behaviour helped to put the patients at ease. Her fast-paced day also introduced me to the sometimes stressful reality of the career, which I again met with during my week at a London hospital. Having just faced the challenge of speaking a foreign language in a clinical setting, I came to really appreciate the value of adept communication skills in medicine. Most notably, the placement taught me the value of a patient's own understanding; I realised that 'not knowing' can be the most terrifying aspect of a prognosis, and saw how key a doctor's didactic role is to the patient's peace of mind.

Community service was and remains an important focus of my extracurricular activities. To raise money for my school's charity club, I set up a 'Monday Muffins' programme and was in charge of the annual raffle. I also worked as part of a team on a steering committee for a charity fundraising scheme, helping students to arrange a day of paid work with their wages being donated to charity. I now look forward to an eventful gap year, which will begin with more hands-on work experience at a German cancer clinic. During times of stress I find cooking very relaxing, and am now saving for a culinary and language course in Florence next spring. I hope to later be able to fund more travelling as well as voluntary work abroad.

Medicine as a subject area has long sparked my curiosity, not only because of its uniqueness, but because of both the logical and yet innovative thinking it encompasses. What set the clinical environment apart from the research lab during my work placements was the patient contact; it is what attracts me to the career, and witnessing it has cemented my desire to become a doctor. I believe my persistence and motivation will always fuel my drive to continue learning, and hope that my patience will help me to one day become a good doctor.

Critique

Good points
- The statement has a catchy start which focuses on the candidate's ability to adapt to change, a quality that she links to her ability to become an independent student.

- The candidate is bold enough to mention that she is a re-applicant and uses it as a strength, showing that she has taken the opportunity to utilise the time efficiently to enhance her experience.

- The statement is clearly structured, with a first half focusing on her academic background, and a second half focusing on leadership and other personal skills. The conclusion cleverly brings everything together by contrasting the research experience with the patient contact.

Points that can be improved
- Although the candidate states in her introduction that her "drive to become a doctor has always been rooted in the prospect of caring for others", there is nothing about caring in any of the experiences described. Indeed, even when there was an opportunity to raise caring and empathy in the fourth paragraph when describing the community service experience, the candidate chose to highlight the fact that she was part of fundraising and on a steering committee. The emphasis is therefore on initiative, leadership and responsibility (which is good!), but not the softer skills. This experience could also have been used to highlight teamwork.

- Generally speaking the statement contains little on communication and teamwork. Even the hobbies mentioned (cooking and travelling) don't help in removing the uncertainty.

Overall comment
The candidate comes across as a highly motivated, self-driven, enthusiastic and capable achiever, with a strong scientific interest and appetite for learning.

The main concern is the lack of emphasis on any personal skills other than leadership and an ability to take responsibility, which maintain an ambiguity as to the candidate's ability to care for and work with others. This is not to say that the candidate does not have those skills (and indeed she would have successfully been assessed on these at the interview), but that they are not demonstrated in the statement. There were missed opportunities to bring those skills into the statement such as the shadowing or the community service experience.

Overall this is a good statement that would have pleased those schools which choose to focus more on personal achievement. The candidate may have benefited from a better balance between the different skills tested and particularly teamwork.

10.11 Personal statement 11 (A level)

Personal statement successful for: Cambridge, Cardiff

Personal statement

Joe took his hands off his ears and smiled. For weeks he had remained withdrawn, physically blocking out a scary world with his hands. This was the first step in my building a relationship with this severely autistic boy. Joe can now look me in the eye and his confidence is rapidly growing at the Horizons swimming club where I work with him. To me, Medicine is about using my skills to benefit people like Joe.

Working with disabled people at Horizons and Maplewood Special Needs Sixth Form inspired me to explore the causes and effects of disease to better understand the challenges people face. I know from attending Medlink that practising Medicine requires continuous learning. I particularly enjoyed the chance in my Biology course to study polio in detail, which taught me much about the science of the human body, and I am an avid reader of the 'Student BMJ'. I know that science is key to Medicine; when I spent a day in the Paediatric ICU at the John Radcliffe Hospital, I was struck by the fact that the science of the life-support machines was the only thing keeping these acutely ill children alive.

I first knew I wanted to be a doctor after a week's work experience at a GP surgery where I observed the doctors and nurses in different clinics. I was impressed by their dedication and the compassion they displayed in putting each individual patient at their ease. I improved my own communication skills by volunteering at a day centre for adults with learning difficulties. Their lives improved dramatically when we helped them learn the practical skills needed to buy milk, catch a bus, or cook a meal. My job at the Shelburne Hospital, which involves serving meals to patients and cleaning the ward, has taught me that every member of the medical team is important in providing care.

When I shadowed a Gastroenterologist at my local District General Hospital for a week I was able to join ward rounds and watch endoscopies, as well as talk to the junior doctors about their experiences – this really strengthened my resolve to follow them in my future career. I enjoyed this experience so much that I joined a Radiologist in Great Ormond Street Hospital where I was impressed by his sensitivity in caring for the children and their parents. This experience was both exciting and challenging for me, as I saw some children recover and go home, and others be diagnosed with serious life-threatening conditions. This, and my time on the Paediatric ICU, has encouraged me to consider becoming a Paediatrician.

I feel I have a good work-life balance as I have many different interests. I play the flute and piano, both to Grade 8 level, and I take part in the school Orchestra and auditioned Chamber Choir. I enjoy swimming and trampolining, and I have recently qualified as a scuba diver. In the kayaking expedition for my Gold Duke of Edinburgh's Award, I learned personal stamina and the flexibility to work well in a team. I have also developed leadership skills; as a Tutor Assistant I have led lessons in drugs education and used my First Aid training to teach CPR to younger pupils. My self-confidence has really been increased by the Youth Leadership at Sea Scheme, which led to me directing thirty adults to set the main sail of a tall ship in rough conditions on the Irish Sea.

Until recently, Joe would have been misunderstood and isolated. Now, with new medical understanding of autism, he is included and has the chance to develop with his peers. I want to study medicine as it is not only intellectually challenging, but gives people like Joe the opportunity to live the best life possible.

Critique

Good points
- The statement has a personal style which is engaging, particularly with the use of a real-life story based on a specific individual, Joe. The use of the story both in the introduction and the conclusion helps maintain the statement's cohesion. That cohesion is also maintained through the mention of the ICU experience in two relevant places.

- The statement is clearly structured, first discussing the candidate's interest in medicine, followed by caring-related work experience, procedure-based work experience, and personal interests.

- The statement contains a wide range of experiences, from reading to volunteering, presenting the candidate as an all-rounder. The medical work experience is by itself also varied, covering both primary and secondary care, with a mix of observation and personal experience.

- The candidate offers some insight as to his possible career options, with a statement heavily focused on children and the mention that he is considering becoming a paediatrician. This helps position him as an individual and gives a statement which is more credible.

- The candidate offers good reflection on his own experiences, with enough detail to make his statement credible.

- There is a strong paragraph on personal interest, combining sport and music, both as a participant and a trainer, which Cambridge tutors would (and obviously did) love!

Points that could be improved
- In the second paragraph the sentence, "I know that science is key to Medicine" is linked to an observation that life-support machines were the only thing keeping the children alive. This does not add much about the candidate himself and would only be of value if the candidate then concluded he had a strong interest in research which would enable him to contribute towards medical advancement.

- There is little mention of teamwork anywhere in the statement, other than as an observed skill or briefly during the Duke of Edinburgh's Award. The candidate may have benefited from examples where he supported others.

Overall comment
The statement is highly effective and the high emphasis on achievement and science, balanced by the demonstration of a caring nature, makes it an ideal statement for Oxbridge. A better demonstration of teamwork may have led to a more balanced statement.

10.12 Personal statement 12 (A level)

Personal statement successful for: Cambridge, Newcastle, Sheffield, Southampton

Personal statement

I have wanted to be a doctor for many years. Having medical parents meant that I grew up seeing the demands of medicine, but greater insight began with my friend's father's terminal pancreatic cancer. Diagnosis was difficult, his end-of-life care demanding. I supported her throughout, and was moved by the skill and compassion of the healthcare team and the importance of personalised care, and intrigued by the intellectual quest for a diagnosis. During work experience in hospital and primary care I shadowed doctors and practice staff from many disciplines and began to appreciate the breadth of the doctor's role. I worked with disabled adults as a Millennium Volunteer. I now teach dinghy sailing to physically and mentally disabled teenagers and adults. Their resilience and adaptability is impressive. One sailor is autistic, leading me to explore more about the autistic spectrum disorders.

I have many of the attributes doctors need: interpersonal and communication skills, leadership, teamwork, compassion, determination, intellectual curiosity, adaptability and integrity. I enjoy problem solving and new challenges. I can thrive on the demanding academic course. Awarded an academic scholarship at 11, I am a member of NAGTY, and have achieved gold, silver and 'best in school' awards in UKMT Maths Challenges. My GCSE PE mark was among the top five in the country. I relish the power of language, have won national prizes for public speaking and story writing, regional prizes for prose reading and poetry speaking, and achieved Distinction in Advanced Speech (LAMDA Grade 6).

I get on well with people from all walks of life. Elected Head Girl by both staff and pupils, I lead a team of officials, liaise with the Headmistress, organise and manage a wide range of publications, committees and events, and represent the school at external functions. I set and achieve consistently high standards, honing my ability to prioritise and delegate. Nominated Managing Director for our Young Enterprise photography company 'Shooting Stars', I dealt with clients, resolved problems and developed a strong team that won 'best stand' and 'best report'. RYA dinghy instructor training taught me adult learning styles: I 'delivered the best session of the week' (examiner). I mentor a younger class in school, provide individual and group support, encourage them to reflect and work through problems to achievable solutions. I have completed the Duke of Edinburgh Gold Award and am Assistant Leader for the scheme.

I enjoy a wide range of extracurricular activities, from team sports to music. I have good IT skills and learned to use video editing software. I videoed my Silver and Gold expedition teams, edited and produced our DVD diaries and DVDs of several school concerts. I play piano and tuba (Grade VIII Distinction, and perform in brass and wind bands, ensembles, and National Children's Wind Orchestra. An experienced mountaineer, rock climber and skier, I am used to assessing both hard and soft evidence, considering my own and others' competence, making difficult decisions and quickly adapting to situations. I swim and sail competitively, and am a qualified Coastal Skipper. Sailing requires self-reliance, motivation, discipline, cooperation and determination, and I am an experienced fleet and team racer, becoming Under 18 Firefly National Champion and winning CCF National Schools Regatta.

I want to and can be a well-rounded doctor, able to contribute to patients' physical and mental wellbeing. I can balance work and social activities and manage my time well, as shown by my significant academic and school workload alongside many extracurricular activities. I would love to take up this challenge and believe I have the necessary insights, intelligence, skills and motivation to succeed.

Critique

Good points
- This statement clearly conveys that the candidate is an achiever and is able to take responsibility, a common thread in statements written by candidates accepted at Oxbridge.

- The structure is very clear: motivation for medicine, achievements, responsibilities, other interests. The experience acquired by the candidate also covers a good range, from organisational to altruistic and empathic.

- The paragraph on extracurricular activities is very strong, a characteristic of many Oxbridge applicants.

- The use of a personal story is effective in the introduction. The story itself has two facets (the father's illness and the friend in need of support), both of which are highlighted.

- The statement is full of active words, which emphasises the applicant's determination, drive, enthusiasm and leadership: "I mentor", "I lead", "I play", "I set and achieve".

Points that could be improved
- Like all statements that focus on responsibilities, initiative, drive and leadership, the accumulation of achievements can make the person appear slightly overwhelming. In some cases, this can be to the detriment of the softer skills such as teamwork and communication skills. Some of those skills (interpersonal and communication skills, teamwork) are mentioned at the start of the second paragraph, but are not backed up by examples.

- Softer skills such as listening, empathy and teamwork could have been highlighted better using the experience of working with disabled children mentioned in the first paragraph, where, as well as mentioning the dedication of the staff, the candidate could have mentioned her own empathy skills. Instead the candidate preferred to mention that it gave her an impetus to learn about autism. This was a good move but could have been pushed further.

Overall comment
The statement is excellent in many respects and clearly shows the reader that the candidate is an achiever and will do well in an environment which is competitive and requires stamina. The candidate also demonstrates strong reliability and a wide range of interests, which makes the application attractive. A better reflection on interpersonal skills would have improved the statement but this clearly did the candidate no disservice as she was invited to four interviews and received four offers.

10.13 Personal statement 13 (A level)

Personal statement successful for: Cambridge, Imperial College, King's College

Personal statement

As a child I learnt to speak later than usual, as a consequence of continual illnesses, and even had a device invented specifically for me – the Bell-Herold device – as I had difficulties producing certain sounds. I think that my interest in medicine began with my curiosity into these difficulties, and I have always had a fascination with language, whether spoken, signed, or 'mentalese', the language of thought. I enjoy reading books about linguistics, in particular Steven Pinker's *The Language Instinct.* I have also found that the degeneration of language is often discussed in articles considering major health issues of the future, such as Alzheimer's disease or strokes.

I have spent three weeks in local hospitals, spending time on ward rounds, in meetings and in theatre. During ward rounds I recognised the importance of clarity and the patience needed by the consultants. I was also attracted by the teamwork involved. In a video meeting I saw the importance of good communication not only within hospitals but also between them. I was also lucky enough to attend theatre, seeing both a hip replacement and cardiac catheterisation, which I found exciting and stimulating. After seeing patients with various autistic spectrum disorders, I wrote an article on Rett syndrome, a rare pervasive developmental disorder. I have also won prizes for an article on Progeria, an extremely rare growth disorder, and for another on the possible causes of left- and right-handedness.

Last year I enjoyed developing relationships in a Day Centre, which I visited for two hours a week, and was amused to see how bingo became so competitive. As a member of the school Social Services committee I arrange similar weekly visits for those in the Sixth Form, and I am volunteering at a local Oxfam shop for two hours a week for the next year. I am also a member of the school Action Committee, which organises charity events throughout the year, including a charity day in September which often raises £25,000 or more. During my holidays I volunteer for the trolley service at my local hospital. Although I play a fairly minor role, it allows me an insight into the basic minute-by-minute workings of a hospital. After talking to patients I often see the importance of the idea of "continuation of care". This made me question the viability of proposed polyclinics, which will most probably remove this important one-to-one relationship.

I enjoy sports, and play for the badminton 1st VIII and tennis 1st VI. I also play the piano and take music theory lessons, in which I am working towards diploma and grade 8 qualifications respectively. I find both of these allow me time to relax from the daily stresses of life. I have read Oliver Sacks' *Musicophilia*, and enjoyed reading his tales of the power of music, though I found it frustratingly limited in explanations for certain conditions. Last year I was part of a group which won the national CIMA management award, and I was Finance Director of 'Divine Taste', a student-run catering company. These were both superb team-building experiences: the former was a tough academic challenge and the latter a big responsibility and great fun, with the occasional awkward customer keeping us on our toes. Finally, although not the greatest long-distance runner in the world, I ran the Windsor Half Marathon in September in a time of 1 hour 43 minutes and raised over £200 for the Sussex Air Ambulance charity.

After spending significant time in medical environments I am convinced that I am suited to a medical career. I am attracted by the way in which doctors are always learning and constantly have to be alert, whilst making challenging moral decisions. I know that my interest will be sufficient to sustain me through what is unquestionably a demanding career with a lengthy qualification time. Music and sports will provide a balance to my academic life, and I am very excited by the prospect of studying medicine.

Critique

Good points
- The statement offers a good balance of points, with a candidate coming across as scientific but also equipped with a good array of interpersonal skills. All this is complemented by a wide range of personal interests and achievements, which, again, is representative of Oxbridge applicants.

- The strength of the statement lies in its clear structure and the systematic detailing of each experience, though bringing into play a number of anecdotes and thoughts which reflect an element of both humour and maturity. For example, the anecdote on bingo and comments such as "although not the greatest long-distance runner", which may look out of place to some, are good at lightening the mood and demonstrating a degree of humility and personality. The comment on polyclinics is particularly pertinent in the current political climate and clearly demonstrates that the candidate is following current issues (much better than simply saying "I follow current issues").

- The statement is filled with power words such as "I learnt", "I saw", "I wrote", and "I am volunteering", which help convey that the candidate takes charge.

- The candidate conveys all the attributes that would be required of a doctor without any contrived references to "having wanted to do medicine for a long time" or "finding medicine fascinating". Even the conclusion, where he deals with his motivation for medicine, manages to deal with the topic without sounding trite.

Points that could be improved
- The concept of teamwork could be expanded slightly. In the penultimate paragraph, the candidate mentions that running a catering company is a "superb team-building experience" but leaves it to the reader to define what this may be.

Overall comment
Overall this is an excellent personal statement with very little that could be improved. The statement is very eloquent, steers clear of clichés, and presents the candidate as a well-rounded individual with a dynamic yet caring attitude, with a strong interest for science, personal development and caring for others.

10.14 Personal statement 14 (Graduate)

Personal statement successful for: Imperial College, King's College, Warwick

Personal statement

Pursuing my passion for science in an altruistic environment with intellectual and practical challenges enticed me to Medicine. Coupled with reading Biochemistry and work experience over the past 3 years, my enthusiasm has transpired into a mature determination to become a doctor.

Volunteering weekly as a GP's receptionist for a year revealed the holistic approach and continuity of care provided at a community practice. I learnt about record-keeping, ethics and striking rapport with patients. Arranging multi-weeks at University College London Hospital and St George's Hospital presented the realities in specialties such as cardiology, paediatrics and A&E. The synergy within multidisciplinary teams despite stressful conditions and tough expectations was inspiring to view. I was intrigued by the competence and dexterity of physicians using in-depth knowledge and judgement to diagnose, treat and also counsel patients to alleviate anxieties. A consultant impressed on me his duties as a clinician as well as in research, teaching and management. Attending seminars and talking to junior medics clarified the commitment required to reach these roles, yet this only affirmed my resolve for such a varied profession embracing lifelong learning. Spending 3 months befriending patients with neurological damage at the Royal Hospital for Neuro-Disability was humbling and at times disheartening. However, listening attentively to their concerns and showing empathy, veracity and support I felt I made a difference at a personal level. This stimulated my reading on neurodegenerative diseases. Voluntary work for 4 months at an elderly home involved helping residents with tasks whilst appreciating the need for clear communication, patience and integrity. As well as supporting paramedics as a first aider at events, I have cared for people when most vulnerable which has amplified my desire for a humane vocation in Medicine.

My degree has let me explore my fascination of the molecular basis of life whilst developing skills of critical appraisal, time management and self-directed, lecture and group learning. I won the 2007 BBSRC scholarship, awarded to one student from KCL, for an 8-week project at the MRC-Asthma UK Centre in Allergic Mechanisms of Asthma. Applying the scientific method and using immunological techniques and rigorous data analysis, I wrote a report of a novel finding I made on IL-10-Treg cells. I hope to contribute to the advancement of Medicine in the future.

At university I am President of the Snooker Society which requires me to multitask and use tact to negotiate with third parties, delegate tasks and raise funding. Selected as a Widening Participation Student Ambassador, my role has ranged from tutoring teenagers to delivering presentations at events of up to 150 people. Along with writing news articles published in the 'GKT Gazette', I have built extensive communication skills. In an initiative with Aim Higher as a debating coach, I work in a team to develop confidence and creativity in children, which is fulfilling as I see their evolving progress and learn much myself. I also regularly organise charity football with a team, which entails sharing ideas at meetings whilst respecting and adapting to views different to my own. In my spare time I love playing competitive tennis and football, which demands resilience and focus. Planning a year for my Duke of Edinburgh Award included leading a 30 mile hike in which some of my peers struggled with fitness. By being confident and decisive whilst remaining calm and approachable, I motivated everyone to finish.

Observing the dynamic nature of Medicine and feeling the thrill from ensuring the physical, psychological and social health of others has driven me to become a doctor. I believe my curiosity of how disease affects the body and psyche, along with my skills from academia and extracurricular activities, will equip me to grow and succeed in the career I truly aspire to.

Critique

Good points
- The statement is clearly structured starting with work experience, the candidate's degree and his personal interests, achievements and responsibilities, with highlights of personal attributes.

- The candidate has clearly explained the relevance of his degree, emphasising the research skills acquired, linking them to a possible future involvement in research.

- The work experience is suitably varied, ranging from primary to secondary care and, more importantly, has both observational and hands-on experience (e.g. by befriending patients and supporting paramedics at events).

- The section on personal interests and achievements presents a candidate who volunteers to take responsibility, has good organisational skills but can also work well in a team. The concept of teamwork, which is often missing from statements that focus on achievements, is highlighted through the description of how the candidate runs meetings and supports others.

Points that can be improved
- The paragraph on work experience is very lengthy in relation to the others. The candidate may have preferred to split it into two smaller paragraphs dealing with two types of experiences, for example observed v. personal involvement. In addition, as is often the case, the work experience paragraph contains a lot of passive sentences such as "A consultant impressed on me" or "Attending seminars … clarified the commitment", which makes comprehension harder.

Overall comment
The statement is very comprehensive, with the important elements being clearly highlighted. The section on personal achievements is particularly strong, ticking all the personal attribute boxes, and balances well with a heavier work experience section.

Overall, the candidate comes across as well balanced, a good team player and strong communicator, who is also driven, motivated and able to demonstrate initiative.

Although the introduction and conclusion play on the usual clichés, they work well because the statement itself provides sufficient explanations to make them credible.

10.15 Personal statement 15 (Graduate)

Personal statement successful for: UCL

Personal statement

"An individual has not started living until he can rise above the narrow confines of his individualistic concerns to the broader concerns of all humanity." Martin Luther King, Jr.

My undergraduate degree has made me realise that my passion and interests lie not only in the mechanisms of human development, but also in the people in which these processes take place. Research is too impersonal; I want a career that combines the excitement of scientific investigation with human contact. By completing a placement at Sheffield Fertility Clinic this summer, my perception of an embryo changed. I saw that the work done at the clinic was more significant than just whether an embryo was created; these tiny cells are the hope and fulfilment for so many couples whose whole reason for living is to have a child.

Over the past three years I have worked as an Auxiliary nurse. Duties require patience, a friendly and sympathetic manner, compassion and a mature attitude. Although hard work at times, the combined efforts of our multidisciplinary team made the satisfaction of it worthwhile. Much of my work has been on mental health wards: an area I find particularly rewarding especially now that I understand more about the factors underlying dementia. As a nurse I recognise my limitations. However, my enquiring mind means that I would thrive on the challenge of diagnosis and deciding what treatment should be given.

Spending time in general practice meant that I learnt the value of conversational skills used during a consultation. The way the doctor listens to his or her patient plays a crucial role in establishing a good rapport between them. Placement on a maternity ward showed me the excitement of birth, and reassured me that I'm not too squeamish at the sight of blood!

Being a doctor is not just about helping people, but being able to cope with unpleasant situations in everyday life. I have seen death as well as full recovery, and understand the range of emotions that are linked with people's suffering. My time in the NHS has given me the incentive to learn about current issues. Ethical dilemmas such as eugenics and euthanasia really concern me. Having given consideration to them, I realise that medicine is as much about the mind as it is about the body.

Over the past three years I have worked as a volunteer with Mencap. Working in a team taking care of a group of mentally handicapped adults proved to me the importance of good communication skills and patience. Voluntary work for St John's ambulance service, offering first aid to the public at large events, allowed me to show that I can act quickly under pressure in emergencies.

Music is a massive part of my life. I play piano, saxophone and sing. I have led many choir rehearsals, giving me the opportunity to practise leadership skills required to gain control and respect of a large group. I have been involved in regional choir competitions, annually entering festivals and winning trophies and certificates. I am a keen percussion player, spending hours immersed in the rhythm of UCL's bongo society.

I am heavily involved in the university rowing team. Last year I took on the role of UCL Women's Boat Club in which commitment, time management, and self-motivation were the essence of success. Winning several national events and being awarded Full Sports Colours taught me the importance of combining team spirit with individual effort. Whilst at UCL I have had the opportunity to raise money for charity. A crazy outdoor 48-hour Row-a-thon this February meant that we raised over £3000 for the British Heart Foundation.

This summer I spent six weeks travelling through South America. In a place where the focus of people's lives is so different, I evaluated my career options and decided what I really want from life. I know I have the compassion, skills and determination to become a doctor, not just as a career, but as a life commitment.

Critique

Good points
- The introduction is certainly attention grabbing. Using quotes can be very effective (and our experience shows that they are generally well received by tutors – indeed many doctors use them in presentations), but only to the extent that they are not used extensively by other candidates.

- The statement is well structured, starting from the degree, the current career as a nurse, work experience, volunteer work, personal interests and hobbies.

- The statement contains an element of reflection on the experience, which the candidate uses to illustrate some of the skills she possesses i.e. leadership, working under pressure.

- The candidate provides a credible explanation for his change of career, explaining his desire not to have a career which is too academic, whilst at the same time building on his experience as a nurse to explain his desire to take on a more diagnostic role.

Points that can be improved
- The candidate is a bit blunt in stating that research is too impersonal. Although many doctors may concur with that, the statement may be read by someone who is keen on research and may disagree. However, this is unlikely to cause great upset and, at worse, might lead to some quizzing on the topic at the interview.

- More could be made of the mental health experience to raise the issue of empathy. The candidate only uses that experience to highlight the work of the multidisciplinary team and her knowledge of dementia. This could then be linked directly to the Mencap experience. Also the communication skills and empathy could be emphasised by talking about the candidate's own experience of those skills rather than what she observed.

Overall comments
A good statement that provides a good overview of what the candidate has to offer, with a strong emphasis on work experience. Overall, the statement would benefit from greater reflection on the softer skills such as communication.

11 Personal statements from successful A level entrants

11.1 Personal statement 1 (A level)

Personal statement successful for: Imperial College, King's College, UCL

It was not an arbitrary decision to study medicine but an informed career choice. From an early age I have always been fascinated by science and I believe this to be the original building block to my current interest in medicine and the prospective career. I have chosen to study medicine because it combines both the theoretical side of science, as I study now, and the practical side, that I have experienced through work placements. I believe medicine will prove to be an incredibly varied, intellectually challenging and rewarding career and it will also develop my critical thinking as well as my social responsibility.

After completing my GCSEs, I spent a week working at Proctor and Gamble which gave me an insight into the research and product development procedures in a pharmaceutical company, ranging from clinical trials to batch production. I understood the importance of exhaustive testing and trials that have to be conducted prior to releasing a product.

During my two separate placements at St Peter's Hospital, I had the opportunity to explore various aspects of healthcare, beginning with shadowing a house officer in the gastroenterology and haematology department. Attending ward rounds allowed me to understand how important a methodical approach to writing up notes and good team management is to correctly diagnosing patients.

In the following placement in A&E I experienced my first 'difficult' patient, a body builder overdosed on opium, who had to be restrained by the police. The most moving encounter, also in A&E, was when a DOA patient was unable to be resuscitated having been rushed to hospital and I believe this to have been a true test of my resolve and motivation towards medicine. I also spent a day in theatre, where I was able to observe the entire procedure of keyhole surgery, from shadowing the anaesthetist to the actual removal of a gall bladder. This was my first experience. The time I spent at St Peter's was enormously rewarding. I had the opportunity to talk to the patients and, despite their predicament, they remained very positive and showed a great deal of confidence in the doctors.

At college I have many responsibilities; as an elected student representative to the College Board my primary role is to make sure new students feel comfortable on joining the college and, more importantly, they are able to voice their opinions to college faculty. I have also been elected form representative and fire marshal, because of my communication as well as organisational skills, in situations that require you to remain calm under pressure. I also have a seat on the student curriculum review board where I am able to openly debate with college governors and other members of teaching staff changes we believe to be beneficial to our own time at college.

Outside college I have kept myself involved in the local community by coaching badminton to a large group of primary school children varying in ability. I found this exceptionally challenging trying to keep children new to the sport interested and build their confidence whilst teaching them the rules of the game. By prioritising I have successfully balanced my academic and non-academic interests. I find time to take part in sports such as basketball, cricket, hockey and badminton. I captained the school's first team in badminton successfully winning the league trophy last year and because of my passion for badminton I have taken over the running of the badminton club at college. Parallel to my studies and other commitments, I also worked at David Clulow Opticians last year to finance the running of my car for the upcoming school year. I currently work in Superdrug on Saturdays.

I have seen and experienced at first hand the types of pressure facing doctors of today. However, this has only reinforced my conviction to study medicine, and, having over the last few years acquired the skills to pursue my career, I firmly believe that I will make an excellent student and a doctor.

11.2 Personal statement 2 (A level)

Personal statement successful for: Hull York, Leeds, Sheffield

I would very much like to study medicine as the knowledge that I have gained through my A level biology and chemistry courses, along with recent exposure to cutting-edge medical technologies, has been compelling. Last year, I particularly enjoyed attending the Exscitec Medicine and Biological Sciences MasterClass at Imperial College, London. Here I had the opportunity to participate in many lectures and practical investigations, the highlight of my time being the visit to the Pathology Museum at Charing Cross Hospital, where I was able to see how disease actually affects particular organs of the body. I also enjoyed my work experience at Ealing Hospital in the Urology and X-ray departments, which allowed me to take a closer look at the doctor-patient relationship and gain an understanding of the implications of being a doctor. I felt particularly privileged to be allowed into the operating theatre to watch cystoscopies and the removal of kidney stones using an ureteroscope and in one case, due to the location and size of the stone, using percutaneous nephrolithotomy. Being able to then watch the progress and recovery of these patients during daily ward rounds allowed me to gain an insight into how important a doctor's role is in postoperative care. I also attended a Hammersmith Hospitals NHS Trust Open Day, which was run by Professor Robert Winston, where I had the opportunity to perform an angioplasty on a prosthetic model and attend a conference, during which many ethical dilemmas concerning medical practice were raised.

Volunteer work at Meadow House, a local hospice, has given me a very different type of experience. Here, providing help for those who are terminally ill has reinforced my strong desire to study medicine. I believe that, in caring for those awaiting death, I have above all learnt the true meaning of empathy and concern for the suffering. Being bilingual in English and Polish and speaking French to a high level, I am now currently learning Spanish in order to prepare for my gap year placement in Peru (2 months). For a period of five weeks I will be volunteering at the hospital in Cuzco and helping doctors in remote jungle locations, after which I will spend three weeks travelling around the Andes, following in the footsteps of the Inca people. I intend to use my gap year to gain as much experience as possible in a medical and caring environment.

Studying five A level and one AS level subjects in the past two years meant I had to work conscientiously, prioritise and manage my time efficiently and effectively cope with the heavy workload. I also worked in the Ealing Polish Saturday School, supervising four- to seven-year-old pupils. I feel that working there, along with performing the roles of a senior prefect at my school, helped increase my maturity and allowed me to gain valuable communication and organisation skills.

In my spare time I enjoy playing the piano and violin and have achieved Grade 3 Music Theory. At school I sang in several choirs and took part in many drama productions. Performing with the Polish dancing group 'Mazury' for seven years has helped me keep in touch with my Polish roots and instil self-confidence. I also participate in a variety of sports such as skiing, sailing and hiking and I am a keen member of a rock-climbing club. Being a keen reader, I also like to read around my academic work; I have recently read Bill Bryson's "A Short History of Nearly Everything". I hope to continue with these extracurricular activities during university. Although I was very disappointed that I did not confirm a place for medicine last year, I am more determined than ever to be successful this year. I believe I have the ability, dedication and stamina to cope successfully with the challenges of a degree in medicine.

11.3 Personal statement 3 (A level)

Personal statement successful for: Birmingham, Cardiff, King's College, Sheffield

My interest in Human Biology over the past few years has steered me towards a career in medicine. I have an inquisitive mind and there is a satisfying degree of detective work involved in medicine. Where it's possible to solve a problem, and make a difference to someone with whom you have built up a relationship, it is even more gratifying. Many aspects of my life have contributed to my choosing a career in medicine. For example, I especially enjoy the human biology aspect of my present course, in particular the brain. My interest has been further developed by meeting Professor Steven Rose when he came to lecture here, as well as having read a few introductory books about the brain such as, "The User's Guide to the Brain" by John Ratey. I find the link between human biology and biochemistry helps me to learn and understand concepts more extensively in both areas. For example, in organic chemistry, the interrelatedness of geometric isomers when it comes to fatty acids lining the arteries is of great importance.

Helping out at the local primary school for the past three years and at a home for the elderly has confirmed my belief that I would like to work with a variety of people and being able to apply medical knowledge to do this would be fantastic. Talking both to children and to the elderly has taught me valuable communication skills vital for medicine. At a Medlink course at Nottingham University, the doctors talked honestly and enthusiastically about their work which really inspired me. During my work experience – a week at the Royal Free Hospital in Rheumatology and two weeks at Chelsea and Westminster Hospital, in Paediatric Surgery – I discovered how the medical profession really operates, and the commitment one must have. Spending time in a variety of different clinics, I saw the less glamorous side of medicine and learnt skills which will enable me to deal with the social aspects of medicine. I also saw how vital clear communication is, not just between healthcare professionals but between doctor and patient, especially if the patient is young or has English as a second language. I was very impressed by one of the paediatric surgeons I was working under as he was always at ease with people and he had an amazing manner when working with children.

At school I am a writer and editor of the school science magazine and have enjoyed writing articles on a variety of scientific issues. I help to run our Amnesty International group, organising fundraising events for the sixth form, such as the annual Valentine's Ball. I have been heavily involved in product management for the school's staff- and pupil-run farm. For example, within the management team we designed and produced the Christmas catalogue, processed the orders and started to design a website for it too. I have also participated in the building of a barn using traditional techniques with other students. Last year I took a course in complementary medicine which showed me some of the alternative ideas for dealing with medical problems and their variable usefulness. I lived in Zambia for a couple of years so I have had experience of other cultures and some of the problems they face, such as the growing pandemic of AIDS. Whilst in Zambia I helped to raise money for a local school by working with the children to make a calendar to sell at the monthly market.

For the past two years I have enjoyed taking a course in metalwork and jewellery-making in which I have developed new skills relating to precise hand-eye coordination. I take pleasure in playing the piano and have also been on a number of Outward Bound courses working in teams and doing activities such as trekking, canoeing and rock climbing.

11.4 Personal statement 4 (A level)

Personal statement successful for: Birmingham, Bristol, Cardiff, Nottingham

My grandfather has PSP, a terminal disease. Our GP has been a huge support with his authoritative advice and help, obvious concern and good humour. I don't know of any other job which gives this opportunity to make use of scientific knowledge to help people deal with serious problems, or which could be so rewarding to someone doing it well. That is why I want to become a doctor.

I am interested in all sciences, but mainly in human biology. While assisting in a university lab which researches pre-eclampsia, I dissected a placenta, learned about medical research and observed mitosis under a microscope. This experience gave me a real feel of what studying medicine would be like and confirmed my desire to learn from a clinical point of view – for example, not just mitosis, but the process of uncontrolled cell division in cancer and the treatments available.

A busy anaesthetist, whom I shadowed for a week, made time to communicate effectively with his patients and reassure them. This impressed me, as I find it easy to empathise with people and am a good listener. A number of my friends discuss their problems with me. My voluntary work this year in a nursing home has helped me develop this side of my character: I help out with activities such as bingo and quizzes and chat with the residents.

My experience of caring for terminally ill people in the St Frai Hospital in Lourdes this summer was most rewarding. I had never before been anywhere with such a good atmosphere, created by both carers and sick, and it helped me appreciate the psychology of medical care. A week in a GP's surgery showed me the self-discipline which a GP needs to cope with a long list. My job was to sort the patient index cards, and it made me realise how patient care depends on good administration. A Medicourse and a hospital training day showed me more of the life of a medical student and a hospital doctor, and increased further enthusiasm for it.

I have great respect for our GP. He has discussed with me at length the demands and rewards of medicine, not least the volume of work. However, that not does not frighten me as I am naturally self-disciplined, for example I find it easy to plan my own exam revision and complete it without last minute dramas.

All the medics I have met have enthused me with their dedication. In an ICU I observed a team of 14 doctors and nurses helping a man survive a crisis. I felt strongly how good it would be to be part of this effort. I enjoy teamwork, and, for example, was a member of a first aid team which came second in the national St John's competition. By making up for my size through determination and pace, I made the school 2nd XV at rugby in my lower sixth year. The enjoyment of the team's successes, and sharing of the odd failure, is a highlight of my school life. In a Young Enterprise company I had to push one flagging project through by my own efforts. We won an award, and I learned what is achievable through commitment.

I am a school prefect and head of the CCF RAF section. In these roles I have learned the importance of communicating the purpose of a task and a sense of shared responsibility for its success. I take part in debating and, for example, did a presentation on the death of JFK. My outside interests include the clarinet (I am in an orchestra and hope to play at university) and modern music. I read widely, such as biographies of Barack Obama and other politicians. At school I participate in many activities and try to maintain and encourage a high standard of personal behaviour, for example in mentoring junior pupils. At university I would do my best to be a valued member of the student community.

My ambition to study medicine is absolute. It is based on the belief that my interest in medical science, empathetic personality and capacity for work are well suited to life as a medic, and will give me a chance to achieve the high standards which I have witnessed in others.

11.5 Personal statement 5 (A level)

Personal statement successful for: Birmingham, Leeds, Liverpool

I have had a long time fascination in Science and in particular with how the human body works. This combined with my great interest in people has given me the desire to become a doctor and to help people in a practical way. My wish to be a doctor was further strengthened by attending Medlink where I learnt about the varied career opportunities in Medicine and an insight into life as a doctor.

To gain a realistic view of the challenges and rewards of a medical career, I organised work placements giving me an understanding of primary and secondary care. Work experience in a burns unit helped me understand the physical and emotional suffering that patients endure and the role of the medical team to help and heal on both these fronts. Observing junior doctors and consultants talking to patients highlighted the importance of interpersonal communication skills. By shadowing a GP for a week I learned about the social influences on patients' health and saw a wide spectrum of illnesses present in the community. Witnessing the breaking of bad news revealed the importance of being a good listener and being able to communicate clearly and sensitively. At the surgery I completed a research project, which involved interviewing patients on their opinions about hospital doctors and GPs. I discovered that continuity of care matters most to patients, as they develop trust in their GP, but they also regard hospital specialists highly.

I have been a volunteer at the League of Friends' tea bar at Wythenshawe Hospital. This has given me experience in communicating with a range of people, including patients and visitors. I have enjoyed helping and listening to the residents at a local nursing home for the past six months. This experience taught me the importance of empathy, and gave me the chance to build relationships and gain trust. For the last year, every Sunday, I have assisted disabled children and adults to swim at a local club. I am able to support them, as well as help develop their confidence and it is encouraging to see them improve.

My neuroscience project enabled me to interact with the general public as I explained reflex arcs in a way they could understand. My teaching skills have developed through my part-time job, tutoring maths and English for six years; I have also arranged revision sessions at school.

I enjoy working with people and have developed my teamwork and leadership skills through my involvement in the Duke of Edinburgh Award Scheme. I have completed Bronze and Silver and aim to complete the Gold Award. I attended a First Aid course in preparation for the Gold expedition, which helped me to deal with a panic attack experienced by a team member. I also took a lead role in organising route plans and spreadsheets and delegated responsibilities to team members. I have worked at an Oxfam charity shop for two years and successfully completed my Millennium Volunteer Award, doing over 200 hours of community work. This has allowed me to have fun while also working towards a worthwhile achievement.

I was a Prefect in Year 12 and an active member of the Charity Committee, which allowed me to contribute positively to my school life. My multilingual skills will be valuable while communicating with French and Asian communities and by achieving the ECDL I will be well equipped to work on electronic patient records.

My good time management and organisation have enabled me to relax while enjoying a range of social activities. I have practised Tae-Kwon-Do for seven years, gaining the red belt. I also like practical work and am a keen cross-stitcher. I intend to continue with these activities as I recognise that, for a doctor, work-life balance is important.

I understand that studying and practising medicine will be demanding. However, for me this is a profession in which I can make the most of my intellect, experience and personality while working with people to try and improve the quality of their lives.

11.6 | Personal statement 6 (A level)

Personal statement successful for: Aberdeen, Newcastle, Nottingham

What makes a seventeen year old decide he wants to do medicine? Is it just because his school says that he is a high achiever and that he should choose a career that needs hard work and conscientiousness? In my case, there has never been any doubt about my career choice. Since I was small, I have always been fascinated in what things really are and how they work, especially the most complex of all: the human body. I used to draw people from the inside out, showing their lungs, their brain, their stomach. I would draw these in place of the usual 'stick men' and loved looking things up in 'The way the body works' books that I accumulated. I marvelled at how all these complex structures fit together perfectly to function as one body. If my early fascination with the human body ignited it, then it is the last few years that have fuelled my determination to be a doctor.

Every Friday night I am a volunteer at a nursing home. My work includes exercises to stimulate the residents' memories, encouraging conversation and discussion. I enjoy the work immensely and get great satisfaction out of making a small difference to their lives. It is great to see a reclusive old man suffering from dementia suddenly brighten up and actively engage in conversation. I have been working with St John's Ambulance for over a year now, and have learnt how to confidently put my first aid into practice. The care I have provided has been rudimentary, and funnily enough, during the summer holidays, I was even asked to guard a puddle of vomit from unwitting members of the public! My time at St John's, however, has been a valuable lesson in teamwork, helping in big events such as the Humber Bridge marathon and Hull Fair. Being a mentor to inner city primary school children contrasted with being a Form Prefect in our junior school. This has given me practical experience in dealing with people from all walks and stages of life, supporting them with patience and respect.

My innate sense of curiosity and thirst for knowledge has meant that I have always enjoyed school. I chose to take both maths and further maths at A-level, so if I had cashed in the six maths modules I sat this summer, I would have achieved an A for A-level maths.

I play the clarinet for a wind band and two orchestras, including the Hull Philharmonic Youth Orchestra, aiming to take my Grade 8 exam at Easter. I love tennis and swimming, and regularly play for school teams, but I especially enjoy rowing and have been a member of the Ancholme Rowing Club for many years now, competing in regattas with other members of my club. I love nature, and built a nature pond last year. It produced lots of little frogs this year!

My four days at Medlink immersed me in the medical world, which I thoroughly enjoyed. Thereafter, my work experience in several different areas of the NHS revealed how difficult it can be to find and treat a problem effectively, despite medical advances. While shadowing a district nurse, I observed how important it is to improve a patient's quality of life. Most of the cases I saw were either chronic conditions like rheumatoid arthritis or terminal cases such as gastric cancer. I noticed how the district nurse was not there to simply cure, but to counsel and offer palliative care. I have also found it useful to spend a day with a PRHO during a week at Pinderfields Hospital, as it showed me the less glamorous aspects of being a doctor; medicine is not always action-packed. However, I witnessed several endoscopies and an arthroscopic subacromial decompression, which I found deeply fascinating.

I would feel honoured to be part of a profession that can use the scientific knowledge that I love so much, to help people in so many ways. I feel there is no better job satisfaction than this, and because every patient is an individual, every day will be different. That is why I want to be a doctor.

11.7 Personal statement 7 (A level)

Personal statement successful for: Bristol, St George's, UCL

Since an early age I have been fascinated by the workings of life and by the complexities of the human body. I have always wanted to know how things worked in life and an inquisitive nature led me to study the sciences in more depth at A-level.

When studying Biology I was introduced to some of the different ways in which our bodies are protected against diseases and infections, for example our ability to produce antibodies and memory cells to help prevent the recurrence of an infection. I was intrigued by the body's defence mechanism but was equally struck by the vulnerability of the body to diseases such as cholera, malaria and HIV. It made me value life even more and knowing that doctors worked to help improve such people's lives and dedicate a career to help people made me really appreciate their role in society. It is precisely this which has inspired me to pursue a career in medicine; the potential satisfaction I could gain by making such positive differences in people's lives is something which no other job can provide.

To gain an insight into a medical career I have been fortunate enough to have secured relevant work experience. In the summer, I carried out some voluntary work at my local nursing home for a five week period. In this role I gained invaluable experience in interacting with people, talking to them and developing my communication skills. This voluntary work was immensely satisfying and enabled me to fulfil my inner desire of helping people. It also allowed me to build my interpersonal skills. I further developed these skills whilst shadowing an SHO at Wexham Park Hospital. Here I was provided with the opportunity to attend ward rounds, talk to patients and shadow a hospital nurse.

Seeing doctors work in their occupational environment taught me a lot about the nature of their job. I came to appreciate that being a good doctor does not depend solely on academic excellence; rather a whole range of attributes are required, including the ability to work as a team, interact with people, effective time management and the capability of working under pressure. Attendance at the 'Medsim' workshop conference at Nottingham University over a three day period provided me with invaluable hands-on clinical experience in procedures such as suturing, X-rays, ultrasound, palpation, tracheotomy and keyhole surgery. The highlight of my experience was when I had to wake up in the middle of the night to be rushed to a simulated emergency situation in an ambulance. As part of a team I helped to save and rescue injured casualties. As team leader of the operation I was able to develop my leadership skills, make practical and pragmatic decisions, whilst remaining calm and composed at all times when under immense pressure.

Aside from my academic interests, I also enjoy designing and programming websites, something which I self-taught. At the age of 16 I started my own design and print business and, since establishing it, I now have over 15 contracts with companies who regularly come back to me. Meeting clients and being able to gain their trust is, by far, the most rewarding aspect of my business, even more than earning the money.

I have a strong interest in flying and hope that one day I could learn to fly. I enjoy playing cricket and tennis and I have won many trophies in both sports. I also enjoy expressing my views and opinions and have taken part in many discussions and debates relating to local community issues with local MPs and youth councillors.

Finally, ever since I determined that medicine was to be my career, I have been single minded in my focus towards this goal. My experience has shown my thirst for knowledge, ability to interact and empathise with people as well as a capability of working under pressure, all of which I hope to exercise as a medical student. I am dedicated in my studies evident by my achievement in getting one of the top 5 marks in the country for GCSE maths.

11.8 Personal statement 8 (A level)

Personal statement successful for: Barts, Manchester

For me, medicine will enable me to fuse my passion for science with my desire to contribute to society in a position of exceptional responsibility. I believe medicine will provide a dynamic and challenging working environment with continuous opportunities.

My extensive work experience has shown me that there is even more to the field of medicine than I originally thought. A doctor not only needs to provide medical expertise, but must also be an effective communicator with compassion for their patients. During my two weeks in Haematology at UHW, I attended daily ward rounds and outpatient clinics. I shadowed a radiologist undertaking routine X-rays and ultrasounds. Whilst at BUPA, I attended departments such as physiotherapy and theatre. During my work experience at a GP practice, I discovered the differences in the relationship between a GP and their patient compared to a hospital doctor and their patient. Most recently, I spent a week with a maxillofacial consultant, shadowing him in A&E and on his research projects. I have gained a good insight into many aspects of being a doctor, for example the importance of working with other health professionals as part of a team. On all occasions, doctors talked me through procedures, and made me aware of the importance of trust and confidentiality in the doctor-patient relationship. I observed the more negative aspects of medicine, such as the long hours and night shifts.

I have attended Medlink, Medsim and MedWales. All of these have confirmed my desire to study medicine, despite being called out in the middle of the night to a simulated emergency! I have also followed a course in Critical Thinking, which taught me decision making skills essential to a doctor. I have volunteered weekly in a nursing home for the last nine months, where I enjoy talking with residents, many of whom are blind, and take art and music sessions designed to stimulate them. This experience has shown me the importance of listening and empathising with people. Last Summer, after fundraising, I visited Australia with The Joshua Foundation: a charity that sends children with terminal cancer on once-in-a-lifetime experiences. Whilst there, we visited Sydney's Oncology Hospital, where we talked to teenage cancer sufferers. We also undertook conservation work in the forests. I have also volunteered for the WRVS, by carrying out a recruitment campaign:

delivering hundreds of flyers and signing-up new volunteers. Another exciting challenge was helping to create a sensory garden for the patients at the Ty George Thomas Hospice. I am involved in the Childline in Partnership with Schools scheme, where I advise younger pupils on problems that they may have. This gives me a position of responsibility and I have learned to communicate more effectively.

Over the last three years, I have taken part in the Duke of Edinburgh Award Scheme, and am completing the Gold award. I found the Gold Expedition physically, mentally and emotionally challenging, helping to develop my leadership skills. For pleasure and relaxation, I enjoy modern dance and regularly perform in shows. I take part in drama lessons, which have helped to increase my confidence. I also have a passion for music and am a committed member of school choirs performing in many concerts. I was Operations Director of a successful Young Enterprise company that held a fashion show, and reached the Welsh Final. I also organised our Year 11 School Ball. These successes have led me to being appointed Events Prefect.

I believe that the experiences I have gained both inside and outside school make me an ideal candidate for medicine. I have the dedication, motivation and ability to succeed. I look forward to meeting all the future demands of medicine.

11.9 Personal statement 9 (A level)

Personal statement successful for: Birmingham, Leeds, Liverpool

While studying Biology at A level I was fascinated to learn about the workings of the human body – from the dissection of a mammalian heart to the cutting-edge science of stem cell research – all of which has reaffirmed my desire to discover more about the use of Biological knowledge for diagnosis; in order to remain up to date with scientific advances, I regularly read the 'New Scientist'. I enjoy working with people as I can easily empathise with their problems, and by pursuing a career in medicine I hope to make a genuine contribution to people's lives in a scientific and rewarding way.

In order to gain an insight into the medical profession, I have undertaken various voluntary placements. I worked as a Ward Volunteer at the North London Hospice, where I learnt to take a sensitive approach to patients and gained experience of working as part of a team. I also regularly attend public events with the Red Cross to provide First Aid, which has improved my confidence and the way I interact with the public. Working as a Voluntary Befriender, I visited an elderly man who had cognitive difficulties and this made me aware of the importance of good communication skills, eye contact and reassurance.

This summer I worked at Camp Beaumont as a group leader where I was in charge of children from ages three to fifteen; this was a very important experience because I learnt about the significance of patience, organisation and leadership.

However, one of the most valuable experiences for my future career was the time I spent with the Red Cross in Mexico; where I was given the opportunity to work alongside doctors, nurses and paramedics. In the daytime I observed and assisted the medical staff with basic procedures such as stitches and injections, whilst at night I worked with the ambulance staff assisting at various emergency call-outs. The night shift was from 8pm to 8am so I have had a taste of long hours and working in stressful situations.

I am now taking a gap year. For the first part, I am working as a support worker, helping young participants with special needs to realise their potential in performance. I am also training to use the EMIS system as a medical notes summariser at a health centre; this is a useful experience as it gives me the opportunity to learn more about how the NHS works. At Christmas, I will be volunteering in various homeless shelters, giving out food and First Aid. In addition, I intend to volunteer in Barretstown, Ireland, to gain more understanding of paediatrics, whilst helping a good cause. Moreover, I shall continue providing First Aid at public events; I will also be attending courses such as 'Providing Emotional Support' and 'Child Protection' which will help me in improving patient interaction. I have also taken up volunteering at a day-care centre for those with dementia. These rewarding pursuits will allow me to further explore more facets of healthcare.

Whilst I take the academic side of my life very seriously, I am aware that Medicine is a demanding course and it is therefore essential to maintain a work-life balance. I have always participated in various sports and continue to pursue my interest in arts such as: graphics design, photography and music. I always endeavour to put my interests to good use; this year, I designed the advertising for a fundraising cabaret in aid of Lighthouse Ministries International.

I hope that I have demonstrated my sincere commitment to Medicine. I see my pursuit as a lifelong journey of learning and aiding others and I look forward to the challenges set ahead of me in the future.

11.10 Personal statement 10 (A level)

Personal statement successful for: Brighton, Cambridge, Imperial College, UCL

I like the idea of not knowing everything. I see medicine as a continuum of information, learning and experience and am not content with being happy to know only what is required. A recent case of injury at our local A&E led me to explore the domestic circumstances of the patient and see how they might impact on treatment and recovery. Regularly working there on a Friday afternoon has taught me to look beyond the obvious and treat each person as an individual.

Undertaking a work experience programme at another hospital involved me observing surgery, orthopaedic consultations and A&E. I was curious as to the role of the anaesthetist and fascinated by the interplay of all the different disciplines. Talking with the doctors there about how they deal with the more difficult aspects of the job gave me, what I believe to be, a more realistic view of medicine as a profession. I have observed the importance of doctor as educator at A&E and see myself fitting into this role. I'm good at explaining difficult concepts and would eventually like to teach medicine to new students. Maths has taught me that you only truly understand a concept when you've had to explain it and justify your reasoning to others.

Reading the Scientific American and Matt Ridley's 'Genome' has sparked my interest in the frontline of cancer treatment and the profound implications both physical and mental upon the patient. For example a friend recently undertook the BRCA1/2 genetic testing to determine her susceptibility to cancer. This raised issues of surgical intervention, possible inheritance and all-round stress. Her case made me consider whether such sensitive information is necessarily a good thing.

I have worked at Chase Hospice as Father Christmas, dishwasher and decorator and led music and furniture restoration workshops at the Meath Epilepsy Trust. I am a volunteer at Cancer Research sorting clothes and manning the till every week as well as working on the meat and fish counter at Waitrose. Juggling these commitments alongside studying and socialising has honed my time management skills and made me much more confident in communicating with a wide range of people. Waitrose in particular has given me good teamwork skills having to work with others to strict standards.

I play bass in a band who were selected to play at Guilfest last summer and undertook to organise the sale of tickets, press releases and photographs. This coincided with exams and involved much liaison with the festival organisers, bank and local media. This sharpened my leadership skills in organising the rest of the band and teamwork in liaising with the event organisers. Playing my bass is an important stress buster and creative outlet in my life. Food is another. I enjoy trading recipes with the locals at Waitrose and subsequently trying them out. My bronze Duke of Edinburgh award spurred me on to do Silver which I am due to complete in October. The award has challenged me and given me practice at making decisions under pressure, something which I am sure I will face in a future medical career. Most importantly it has been a source of great enjoyment and new friendships.

This past year has been exciting, challenging and satisfying. These are qualities I hope to find in the pursuit of a degree in medicine. My commitment to the study of medicine has been strengthened by recent participation in and work experience at our local hospitals and by the certainty that I can make a contribution.

11.11 Personal statement 11 (A level)

Personal statement successful for: Cardiff, Leicester, Peninsula

I am a dedicated and compassionate person, and am trying to gain as much relevant experience as possible to give me a good base from which to begin my career.

Having grown up within a medical family, I was always inquisitive about the trials and tribulations of a doctor. This curiosity led me to undertake work experience in the West Wales General Hospital last year, where I spent time in various departments, clinics and theatre. Here, I was able to observe doctors diagnose and treat patients, I learnt that confidentiality, honesty and trust between patient and doctor is of great importance in the medical profession, and that team work is also vital in order to achieve the correct diagnosis. The long working hours I merely view as an excellent personal challenge. I have also undertaken work experience in The Optic Shop in 2005, which also involved clinical observation. Here I observed the opticians diagnose several patients with various eye conditions and refer them as appropriate.

I attended the Medlink conference last year, which has given me an insight into what life is like as a university student and how lectures are delivered. The conference also gave me some idea of what life in medicine is like, the pressures, responsibility, team work, and quick decision making, all of which are very important factors in this profession. I attended the Medsim conference this year, which I found to be inspiring, and I was awarded a certification in basic life support as a result. During the simulated emergency in the Emergency callout night, I demonstrated quick thinking and level-headedness under stress.

I am currently a volunteer at a Red Cross charity shop where I help receive donations, organise the donated items and work as a cashier, which has developed my communication skills further. I participated in my school's Young Enterprise scheme working with 10 pupils. This has given me an insight into business management skills. It was through this highly enriching experience that I have developed further skills in team work, leadership, taking responsibility, and the need for commitment to quality, planning, financial control and communication. All these skills have helped my classmates and me to lead our business to success. I have completed the Duke of Edinburgh Bronze Award, undertaking various activities as well as a final expedition. The expedition was truly an arduous task; however, through good team work, management and leadership my team and I completed it safely and successfully. I currently attend regular first aid training classes with St John Ambulance, gaining further knowledge of life support skills, as well as assessing and responding immediately in an emergency situation. I am working as a volunteer at a nursing home where I tend to the elderly. This has given me skills working with the elderly and general patient contact, as well as improving my communication skills. In my spare time I read the New Scientist magazine and newspapers to gain knowledge about current affairs in politics, science and healthcare. I attend the gym in order to improve my physical and mental fitness. I enjoy regularly playing chess, taking part in karate, badminton and critical thinking classes, and listening to music. I am also intending to go to Bangladesh over Christmas to do voluntary work at rural clinics, help the poor and those that have been affected by severe floods and cyclones.

I believe that my academic standing, various work experiences and ethics have prepared me well to not only meet but exceed the demands of medicine. I would also embrace any opportunity to broaden my knowledge and skills in and after medical school in the hope of becoming a successful, qualified doctor.

11.12 Personal statement 12 (A level)

Personal statement successful for: Southampton, UCL

Personal experiences from a young age, strong academic interests in the sciences and the prospect of a challenging and fulfilling career have led to a passion to read medicine. I am fully aware that this will offer immense challenges not only in clinical settings but also in terms of keeping abreast of current medical research and technological advancements.

During the summer I spent a month of my holiday as a medical and community volunteer in Zambia. I worked in local clinics assisting nurses with 'vital signs', inoculations and baby weighing as well as visiting members of the community in their homes, providing palliative and preventative care. This was an amazing experience, though at times an eye-opening one, as human and medical resources were scarce. I also helped to develop a basic educational programme for adults regarding HIV/AIDS. This trip made me more aware of the enormous differences between healthcare in a Third World country and the UK.

Over the past year I have undertaken work experience at two contrasting hospitals. At a small post-operative geriatric hospital I spent time talking to patients on wards and in clinics, learnt about the many illnesses associated with the elderly, such as COPD, and witnessed the effects of the lack of funding facing PCTs. Whilst at UCH I was able to experience live theatre. It was particularly interesting to watch the extraction of a large facial tumour requiring extensive surgery. The consultant I shadowed is a leading expert on PDT, a new form of non-invasive cancer treatment. I have since researched this and other cancer treatments to draw comparisons. Work experience has made me aware that medicine involves long unsociable hours and high levels of stress and also that individuals have different needs and values that must be respected at all times.

I have attended Medlink and MEDSIM courses in Nottingham. Since MEDSIM I have developed an interest in emergency medicine having completed a rapid response course and participated in a mock emergency callout. At UCH I spent a morning in A&E and gained an insight into the variety of cases that may be seen. Due to my own recent medical problems, I have visited several consultants specialising in different branches of medicine giving me an insight into the various career paths available in the profession and the teamwork and communication required between these specialists and other departments. Both the courses and my experiences have confirmed that I would be willing to commit to the dedication required to study medicine.

My extracurricular activities are varied. For the past two years I have been a young leader for a local cubs pack, enabling me to improve my leadership skills and develop my ability to work as part of a team. I believe that I am able to communicate well with adults and children, a skill that is essential for a doctor, and one that has been enhanced by attending an Acorn listening course.

I am a music scholar at school and attend the Junior Guildhall School of Music and Drama in London, where I study trombone and am currently working towards grade 8. I have performed with the Guildhall Brass Band and Symphony Orchestra at a variety of venues including the Edinburgh Fringe, Symphony Hall in Birmingham and St John's, Smith Square. Prior to this I was a member of the National Children's Orchestra for 3 years. I am goal-keeper for my school's 1st X1 Boys Hockey Team as well as a keen player of squash and badminton and have obtained my advanced PADI Scuba Diving qualification. I am an active member of my school's MUN (Model United Nations) team, most notably participating in an international conference at UNESCO in Paris. MUN has greatly improved my confidence levels, inter-personal and teamwork skills and my ability to communicate with others.

I see medicine as a unique and evolving profession and I believe that I have the commitment, enthusiasm and personality required to become a successful doctor.

11.13 Personal statement 13 (A level)

Personal statement successful for: Birmingham, King's College, Oxford, UCL

Perseverance, enthusiasm and dedication are three qualities which I believe will allow me to succeed while studying medicine. As a student of the International Baccalaureate, I have demonstrated these traits effectively, as the course has given me the opportunity to consider notions beyond the curriculum and to work independently to solve problems. Taking such a diverse range of subjects requires me to complete tasks promptly whilst maintaining a high standard, and although I have focused my attention on the sciences, I continue to develop my language and communication skills. Writing my extended essay in French on the subject of organ donation and transplantation has also enabled me to consider the social and ethical issues involved in medicine.

My weekly voluntary work at 'Kids Can Achieve', a centre for children with autism, ADHD and schizophrenia, allows me to interact with disadvantaged members of the community and help them to develop social skills. The variety of ages, temperaments and personalities means having to adjust to suit the needs of each individual child. However, it was only after completing work experience in both a GP's surgery and a hospital that I was able to understand the commitment involved in the medical profession. From operating on a sick child, to working continuously for a twenty-four hour shift, the practice of medicine is both strenuous and demanding. After reading Atul Gawande's 'Complications', I have realised how much stamina is needed to study medicine owing to its unpredictable and variable nature. Nevertheless, I was delighted to diagnose molluscum contagiosum correctly in a toddler while working at the hospital.

My studies of Biology and Chemistry have given me a better understanding of scientific theories. I believe that these two subjects complement each other perfectly: the study of biochemistry this year has added a new dimension to my knowledge of human physiology, as it explains the metabolic processes which generate the energy needed by organisms. Further reading in this area has taught me about the biochemical mechanisms used by humans to survive in conditions to which they are not accustomed. These concepts are described in 'Life at the Extremes' by Frances Ashcroft, which conveys the vulnerability of the human body to disease.

I have also channelled my passion for science into my role as vice-chair of Science Society, a position that requires both teamwork and efficiency to organise activities for science club each week for the younger years and to arrange speakers who appeal to older students. Last year I founded the school science newsletter, of which I am editor. Producing an edition each month requires much energy and creativity, characteristics which I think will prove invaluable while studying medicine.

This summer I was awarded a Nuffield bursary to work in the division of Molecular Immunology at the National Institute for Medical Research, hence I read 'Biomedicine and the Human Condition' by Michael Sargent to familiarise myself with terms such as histocompatibility, cell apoptosis and autoimmunity. During my four weeks at NIMR, I studied the T-lymphocytes of mouse mutants, and the use of techniques such as fluorescence-activated cell sorting and enzyme-linked immuno-sorbent assay highlighted the importance of molecular immunology in medicine, as both of these techniques can be used to test for HIV in patients. After spending a month investigating disease and the human body's reaction to infection, I would now like to study its counterpart, the cure for disease: medicine. I look forward to the challenge of studying medicine at university; I believe that my love for science and my compassionate nature will enable me to succeed.

11.14 Personal statement 14 (A level)

Personal statement successful for: Imperial College, King's College, UCL

Medicine is a career that requires compassion, communication and teamwork and, moreover, the quest for knowledge. As a medical candidate, I believe I have these qualities intrinsically within me. Furthermore I am extremely fascinated by the speed at which modern medicine is progressing; new cancer treatments and the potential of stem cells research are such examples.

My interest in medicine was strengthened by attending the Medlink conference; participants were given opportunities to talk to undergraduate students which allowed me to envisage life as a medical student and newly qualified doctor. In addition to this I attended practical workshops to learn uses of a stethoscope and the sounds of the lungs. This summer I was fortunate enough to gain valuable work experience in Pakistan, a third world country. I worked at two different hospitals: 'The Tabba Heart Institute', a privately funded brand-new hospital, and 'the Sindh Institute of Urology and Transplantation', a charity-based hospital dedicated to free medical treatment to all patients. During these experiences I was able to observe a triple heart bypass surgery and a kidney transplant from within the operating theatre. I was able to shadow top consultants and learn about procedures I previously knew very little about such as Lithotripsy. My interest in medicine pressed me into reading a special report in 'Scientific American' called 'The Future of Stem Cells' and the book 'The Rise and Fall of Modern Medicine' by James le Fanu.

I am currently studying science-based subjects, with biology and chemistry being the main interests as they provide stimulating information relating to the human body and the world around us. These subjects and their links to medicine further strengthen my desire to read medicine. My interest in these subjects prompted me to subscribe to both 'Chemistry Review' and 'Biological Sciences Review' magazines; they provide me with additional knowledge in these subjects. Maths as a subject has allowed me to develop problem solving techniques that are vital in the field of medicine. Economics has taught me to be analytical and careful when considering the outcome of different possibilities which is vital in medicine when deciding on a patient's course of treatment.

There are also many other interests in my life. I play for the school cricket 1st XI and have played for Stanmore cricket club up to under 17 level. In addition I have represented the school in rugby, my house in rugby, cricket and basketball. I feel that the tense situations that can arise in sports can teach you to operate under pressure. Being a member of Amnesty International and the Iraqi fundraising trust within school has also taught me the concept of team work. As a result of my commitment to the school I was chosen as a senior school prefect, a role that includes the daily running of the school in many areas. It is important to be able to communicate between the prefect body and the younger students to ensure the smooth running of the school. Furthermore I was made my House's charities officer, teaching me leadership in organising a fundraising charity event. I am also a peer mentor to a year 9 form which allowed me to help these students with problems regarding their school and home life. I have passed LAMDA public speaking awards up to a Gold level, further improving my ability to communicate confidently. Within the school I am a member of our Islamic society, leading people in prayers, and it has provided me with the chance to befriend those in younger years and act as a role model.

My academic, extracurricular activities and my thirst for challenges make me a well-rounded candidate to study medicine, a subject that defies candidates to rise to their potential.

11.15 Personal statement 15 (A level)

Personal statement successful for: Leeds, Manchester, Newcastle, Sheffield

I have always had the desire to study medicine and explore its potential for increasing and enhancing life.

My passion for medicine was confirmed during a placement at the University Hospital of Durham which offered the fantastic opportunity to gain knowledge of the varied careers in medicine, talk to doctors and experience patient contact. I was able to practise skills such as taking blood and suturing a dummy and observe fascinating procedures including nerve testing for Carpal Tunnel Syndrome, ultrasounds and an endoscopy on a man with a suspected stomach ulcer. I met an inspiring man who had survived bowel and lung cancer and saw how vital family support was in battling against his disease. In contrast, I saw a woman who was told there was no cure for her condition: witnessing her tears was difficult but an important experience for me, helping me to understand that even less serious medical problems may still affect a patient's life. Spending a week in a GP's surgery allowed me to see a variety of medical problems. Time spent with the GP and nurses showed the value of each team member in maintaining a successful surgery. As a volunteer in a nursing home, painting patients' nails and listening to their stories, I learnt it only takes a little time to keep someone company but it is a sacrifice that is greatly appreciated. Helping children with dyslexia has been extremely rewarding, providing me with the chance to communicate with people of all age groups. Attending a PreMed course allowed me to hear from doctors in different specialities and learn how they cope with the demands of practising medicine. I have also recently gained my St. John's Ambulance First Aid qualification.

My work experience has given me an idea of what medicine entails and has made me more determined to achieve my goal. Another hospital placement in March will help me learn more about aspects of medicine.

My love of science led me to read 'Human Instinct' by Lord Robert Winston, which investigates the influence of instincts on our actions. Studying medical ethics in R.E. has made me aware of the problems facing the NHS such as the allocation of resources: should they be focused on research or the alleviation of suffering at a more commonly experienced level? I was fascinated by the series 'Trauma': revealing the reality of critical care today and providing an incredible insight and understanding to the service doctors provide.

As House Captain, I organise many events which involve working with a number of people in order to prepare and lead teams. This has developed my organisation skills and has increased my ability to motivate others. As a member of Amnesty International, I often take part in activities to show support for those suffering from the breach of human rights. Writing for the school newsletter has helped me to identify key information – a transferable skill useful in medicine to aid a diagnosis. Participating in a Young Enterprise Company, making and selling scarves, helped to develop my team work ability but also concentrate on time and money management skills. Involvement in a debating society has helped me to argue my own opinion but to also consider the views of others.

I enjoy playing a variety of sport such as rowing and tennis. I play netball and rounders for the school, having captained the netball team, and I help to umpire younger girls. My sporting abilities will allow me to relax and keep a healthy balance, leaving the stressful demands of being a doctor behind. I have gained my Silver Duke of Edinburgh's Award. Having a part-time job has enabled me to manage my own money and deal with difficult situations using my own judgement, making me more confident and independent.

I look forward to the challenge and commitment that both university life and a medical career will involve. My ultimate goal is to turn my desires into reality through being given the opportunity to develop further and extend my knowledge of medicine.

11.16 Personal statement 16 (A level)

Personal statement successful for: Aberdeen, Dundee, Glasgow, St Andrews

Throughout my life, I have been determined to succeed in every challenge that I face and the strong sense of vocation I feel towards helping people is what drives my ambition to become a doctor. Reading Lance Armstrong's autobiography, 'It's Not About The Bike', touched me emotionally and intrigued me academically, prompting me to investigate testicular cancer and advances in its treatment. His emotive account confirmed my desire to strive for success in medicine and to use that expertise to care for people with compassion and professionalism.

To gain a greater understanding of the medical field as a whole I have been reading relevant newspaper articles as well as more focused articles in the Student BMJ. I also organised work experience at Meeks Road General Practice in Falkirk, where I gained valuable insight into the running of a practice, and Stirling Royal Infirmary Respiratory Medicine Department where shadowing an FY2 doctor gave me a first-hand account of the duties of a junior physician. I arranged another inspiring placement in the ENT department in Leeds General Infirmary. I attended out-patient clinics and operating theatres where, in one, I witnessed a fascinating neck dissection. My experiences and discussions with medical professionals have allowed me to grasp the highs and lows of medicine and appreciate the vast amount of teamwork and communication involved in such an interpersonal career, cementing my ambition to become a doctor.

As Deputy Head Boy of my school, my commitments are shared between my drive to succeed academically and leading my school by example. I have competed annually in the Scottish Mathematical Challenge, gaining four gold awards, and each year I have been awarded Overall Academic Excellence for my achievements in school. My interest in the sciences has grown throughout my school years. Chemistry was my most absorbing Higher and I was selected for my school's Extreme Hydrogen Challenge team. This required an investigation into hydrogen as a renewable source of energy. My fascination with chemistry has prompted me to study the subject at Advanced Higher. My academic achievements highlight my thirst for knowledge and my drive to attain the best possible outcome to the challenges I face. My enthusiasm for working towards a common goal is highlighted by my participation in the school show in which, in recent years, I have held a principal part leading to the award of Repeat Full Colours in Drama. For the last year I have taken part in twice weekly paired reading sessions with children who require additional support to improve their literacy.

I am a fan of all sports and enjoy their competitive nature. I play golf regularly in the junior medal and have reduced my handicap from 36 to 22 over the last three years. Tennis, being one of my strongest sports, has seen me selected for the Central Scotland Squad. This along with competing for my school's rugby and football teams for the last two years has strengthened my skills in teamwork and has allowed me to appreciate the rewarding results obtained from a hardworking unit. This year, as part of a Sports Leader course, I am organising and delivering coaching to younger pupils in various sporting activities. I am currently undertaking my gold Duke of Edinburgh Award through which I have received my emergency first aid certificate. For the past two years I have been working part-time in a small accountancy firm where I am responsible for the accurate recording of financial data. Volunteering in the local nursing home has also given me experience of working as part of a team in patient care.

Medical professionals are held in high regard, with trust and all-round appreciation for the difference they make to people's lives. The prospect of contributing to society in this invaluable way along with involvement in an ever-advancing and most gratifying field fills me with immense excitement. I would relish the opportunity to be part of this profession.

11.17 Personal statement 17 (A level)

Personal statement successful for: Leeds, Leicester, Liverpool, Sheffield

Since my early days at secondary school, I have had a great interest in human science. I am a sociable person and I enjoy talking with people and helping in whatever way I can. A career in medicine would enable me to combine my interest in people and science. It will provide me with the opportunity to research, investigate, treat diseases and help others achieve a healthy body and mind.

Work experience in a cardiac ward for a week impressed me and provided an insight into the challenges faced by doctors, such as time constraints, workload and the sometimes difficult patients. Observing a pre-op clinic and daily ward activities highlighted the importance of clear communication, the need for prioritisation of work and the development of a trusting relationship between patients and doctors. I was also impressed by the dedication of medical and nursing staff. Assisting a radiographer, I recognised the importance of appropriate explanations pitched at the correct level and using accessible vocabulary. Shadowing a GP for a week highlighted the different roles they undertake as clinicians, manager and team leader. I also appreciated how social factors influence health and the need for preventative medicine. I witnessed doctors dealing with sensitive issues with empathy when having to transfer an elderly patient to a residential home. It was informative to attend a PCT meeting, about child vaccinations and problems associated with targets. I assisted in an immunisation clinic and enjoyed working with the children and their parents.

Over the last year, at a local residential home, I have been involved in helping and listening to the elderly residents, and have built up good relationships with them. Volunteering at the League of Friends tea bar allowed me to improve my communication skills through my dealings with staff and visitors. I completed my Millennium Volunteer Award by working with various charities, such as Oxfam, for more than 200 hours. Every Sunday for the past year, I help disabled adults become more confident swimmers.

As a part-time job, for 5 years, I have helped very young children to overcome their difficulties with maths and I have also organised and run science revision classes for pupils at my school. A neuroscience project at Manchester

Museum allowed me to explain about the 'sense of hearing' to the public. To keep up to date with developments I read Student BMJ and A-Z of Medicine Research, and have attended talks such as Lord Winston's on fertilisation. Obtaining ECDL has given me the necessary skills needed for ICT in the healthcare system. My ability to speak French and Urdu will be useful in helping these communities.

I love challenges and have participated in the Mock Trial Competition, the European Maths Challenge, and the Physics Paperclip Competition. These opportunities have improved my ability to prioritise and solve problems under pressure.

I have led my school's Charity Committee and organised a talent show delegating tasks to committee members. I am a motivated person and am currently working towards my Duke of Edinburgh Gold Award, having completed Bronze and Silver. I was the leader in the organisation of the gold expedition routes and a team player during the activities. Having completed a first aid course I was able to deal with minor injuries that occurred during the expedition.

For relaxation I enjoy playing the keyboard and doing craftwork. Practising Tae-Kwon-Do for 8 years, has taught me self-control and self-reliance whilst enabling me to keep physically fit. I am currently working towards my black tag. These activities allow me to develop time management skills.

I am a hardworking, reliable, and caring person who has the dedication, enthusiasm and commitment needed to be a good doctor. Practising medicine will be demanding and challenging; however, I am confident that I will be able to meet this challenge and also maintain an appropriate work-life balance.

11.18 Personal statement 18 (A level)

Personal statement successful for: Newcastle, Southampton, UCL

I believe that I am well suited to the demands and rigours of being a doctor. I have a strong interest in a wide range of scientific topics and, of late, I have developed a particular focus on Genetics. As a result of this, I joined a small Genetic Research project attempting to determine the function of two genes located within the plant 'Arabidopsis Thaliana'. In working as part of this team over the past 14 months I have developed many skills invaluable to a doctor: teamwork, problem solving, stamina and dedication. The success of our project thus far was recognised by an invitation to address a national conference, Showcase Science. I enjoyed the challenge of presenting and defending original research to a large and knowledgeable audience.

In order to gain a greater understanding of a medical career, I have organised a number of different types of work experience in medical-related environments. Firstly, I spent four days at Worcestershire General Hospital. During this time, I shadowed a variety of specialist consultants on ward rounds, observed the delicate and precise work of surgeons, spent a day in Accident and Emergency and worked with nursing staff. Doing this particular work experience made me realise the importance of teamwork in the medical profession, the difficulties and pressures of working in Casualty and the extremely understated yet valuable work of nurses. Having grown up in Hong Kong and Singapore, I sought to understand the practice of Medicine in different cultures. To that end, I spent one week at Eli Lilly Clinical Trials Singapore and one week at the National University Hospital in Singapore. During this time, I learnt that certain diseases such as Diabetes are more prolific in certain ethnic groups. I also attended a MEDLINK conference at Nottingham University: a course that has allowed me to build an appreciation for the huge variety of medical specialties. I have spent time helping in both homes and day care centres for the aged, developing my ability to empathise and communicate with the elderly. Above all else, my experience has taught me the importance of patience, compassion and maintaining the dignity of the patient. Furthermore, I spent one week on a MENCAP holiday working in a voluntary capacity helping a group of children with a variety of learning and physical disabilities. Although at times my work experience has been challenging, the clinical experience has simply re-affirmed my desire to pursue a career in medicine.

From speaking to doctors and medical students, it has been stressed to me the importance of maintaining interests outside the curriculum. Having been privileged enough to be in an environment where many opportunities are offered, I believe that I have fully involved myself in a variety of activities. I have enjoyed the challenge of the Duke of Edinburgh schemes, completing the Bronze, Silver and Gold awards as a group-leader. I am a committed member of the Combined Cadet Force and, as an NCO Platoon Commander, I am responsible for leading and tutoring cadets: a challenge that I find both rewarding and exciting. As President of the School's Medical Society, I have the responsibility of organising and introducing talks from medical experts. I am a keen, if somewhat modest, sportsman, and I also enjoy drama and music. Balancing these activities with the demands of my curriculum has required commitment and effective time-management. I have a tenacious attitude to my academic work and am very proud to have received a number of School prizes and awards in recognition of my achievements.

Through my study and work experience, I believe that I have gained a substantial insight into the medical profession. To stress the above, I believe I would be capable and suited to a career in Medicine and look forward to the challenges and new experiences offered at university.

11.19 Personal statement 19 (A level)

Personal statement successful for: Brighton, Cardiff, Peninsula

Medicine appeals to me as a career choice because of experiences I have already had, as related below, the challenges it will provide both academically and personally, and how it uses ever-developing science and technology to improve people's lives.

My family situation has provided me with direct experience as a carer. My mum was diagnosed with Multiple Sclerosis (MS), and she also suffered acute depression. I have had to assist her physically on a daily basis, due to fatigue, mobility problems and occasional limb paralysis. Recently she has been prescribed a disease-modifying drug that has to be injected daily, and I have been trained to administer this by a specialist MS nurse, which I do on a regular basis. I regularly attend consultations. Regarding the depression I have learnt tact and patience so as not to aggravate situations, and have seen the impact drug regimes can have, both positive and negative.

I have had some exposure to age care as my grandmother has vascular dementia and I assisted her as she deteriorated. I also witnessed the development of Alzheimer's and emphysema in my uncle, who regrettably passed away as a result. Because of these experiences and my long-standing interest in science, I investigated a career in medicine, and after attending the Medlink conference decided to actively pursue it.

Last summer I volunteered on the stroke care unit of my local hospital, spending time with patients and assisting with their rehabilitation. I observed how nurses, doctors, physiotherapists and other healthcare professionals communicated and interacted with both patients and each other, practising patient-centred care. Further to this I have been involved in fundraising events for the MS Society, and met many MS sufferers with differing levels of disability. This highlighted the fact that some diseases have varying levels of severity and therefore the need for healthcare solutions to be structured around the individual.

Last year the opportunity arose to be the Young Person's Patient Champion Governor for the Basingstoke and North Hampshire Hospital NHS Foundation Trust. I attend quarterly meetings regarding the governance of the hospital, where we discuss management issues. In addition to this, members of staff give presentations on current issues within the hospital, the latest of which was infection control. I'm finding this experience a valuable insight into the organisation of the NHS.

For the past seven years I have been a keen horse rider, and through perseverance and determination I have become an advanced rider and have competed successfully.

I have been a member of Wessex Christian Fellowship, which has a congregation in excess of 200, for two years. Last year I joined the technical team, which manages the computer-based audio-visual system, and is integral to the running of the church. Recently I have taken over as director where my role is to ensure the effective delivery of this resource. I facilitate communication between team members and provide leadership. In this role I have learnt to understand where my boundary of knowledge lies and when to call on the support of others.

Earlier this year a new youth group for 11-14 year olds was started, where I was asked to become a youth leader. This has involved acquiring mentoring skills and empathising with those from difficult backgrounds.

With all of these activities and my academic studies I have learnt effective time management and how to prioritise. I recognise that training to be a doctor requires a lot of hard work, dedication, and adherence to professional standards. I am determined to continue my successful education via a medical degree and, as a doctor, make a difference to people's lives.

11.20 Personal statement 20 (A level)

Personal statement successful for: Bristol, Newcastle, Nottingham, Sheffield

Scientific knowledge, complex skills, creativity and personal relationships are all aspects of medicine. For me they are also essential aspects of my education and personal outlook. Medicine's daily challenge will be academically stimulating and I hope that my intellectual ability and warm-hearted, compassionate nature will make me a stable and dependable doctor. I have been inspired by many people with whom I have worked and I noticed that the ability to make even the smallest difference to a life is precious. The range of specialities makes the career path exciting and unpredictable. From a young age I have questioned everything to do with medicine, keen to learn as much as possible.

This summer, I worked for two weeks on a research study in Boston, USA, investigating the effects of nutrition and drug abuse on people with HIV within the Hispanic community. I worked on determining causes of death of participants, and analysing this data. Surprisingly, liver disease and violence were as common as AIDS as a cause of death. This has resulted in my interest in medical research and epidemiology. I have shadowed doctors in several departments at my local hospital, including observing an aneurysm operation, which resulted in a splenectomy due to complications. Whilst working in a GP surgery in London for a week I learned the importance of teamwork, communication and leadership in a health centre. The diversity of the work interests me, as I saw that patients varied from having minor injuries to being recovering drug addicts. I also visited a local nursing home, where flu vaccinations were given. The possibility to build up relationships with families and follow them through life is appealing. The Medlink conference that I attended taught me that being a doctor is not just about patients but being a teacher and innovator too.

Coaching young children in tennis for the last three years has enabled me to develop my teaching skills, using initiative and improvisation. I teach violin and find that perseverance, creativity and determination are crucial to maintaining attention. In school I am a year 8 mentor, maths mentor and Junior Sports Leader and am currently senior prefect and music prefect. This means I have responsibility for younger pupils: developing skills such as organisation that will be useful in a medical career. My very rewarding work in a nursery and in a school for children with special needs showed me that there are many ways to communicate with children and that patience is essential. I learned to appreciate the complexities of teaching when physical and mental needs are so varied, including the devastating effects that meningitis can have. Each child is working to achieve as normal a lifestyle as possible; small challenges to some can seem like mountains to others.

I have passed my grade 8 violin and I also play the oboe and piano to grade 7 standard. This requires devotion, commitment and reliability. I am a member of the Wirral Youth Orchestra, Liverpool Philharmonic Youth Orchestra, and two string quartets. Music and medicine require teamwork and integration of mind with body, intellect with emotion and communication ability with commitment. I hope that I can use these skills learned from music in medicine. In addition to my music I play tennis regularly for my local club and was junior captain in 2005. I am a keen kayaker and have competed regularly for many years for my trampolining club. These sports require trusting others and teamwork, skills important in medicine.

I would like to take a gap year and teach children in South America. It would allow me to live in another culture, and to further my experience of medicine in another environment. This decision has been fuelled both by a love of languages, I speak French and German, and a love of travelling. The opportunities I have had so far have increased my curiosity and desire to study medicine and I relish the challenge of a demanding medical career.

11.21 Personal statement 21 (A level)

Personal statement successful for: Brighton, Bristol, Cambridge, Edinburgh, Imperial College, St Andrews

(Note: the candidate received 6 invitations to interview due to confusion at medical schools following substitutions)

Since early childhood, I was surrounded by doctors both in the family and in hospital, where I spent much time as a patient. Having had many opportunities for observing doctors' work, I was able to see their professionalism, knowledge and efficiency in caring for what I deem the most precious possession: health. This made me aim for the vocation of a doctor, which I began seeing as my mission in life. Furthermore, on a less emotional level, medicine seems to me to be the ideal discipline as it combines my passion for science with my love of social contact. Moreover, it promises to quench my thirst for learning new things as medicine is ever-developing, requiring lifelong study.

My passion for medicine led me to volunteer at a ward for terminally ill people in a local hospital. The insights I gain from weekly contact with these, mainly elderly, people enable me to see how people cope with illness, which I consider fundamental in effecting recovery. I also find that these conversations develop my listening skills, which I deem vital for a future doctor because, without listening to and understanding the patient, it is impossible to identify their needs and consequently to help them get better. Listening belongs to the sphere of communication skills, which I have been able to develop greatly throughout my life, where I had to change school five times due to my family's moving house, twice abroad. I was required to learn English, French and some German besides my native Czech and to socialise with people of different backgrounds, nationalities and religions, increasing my adaptability. Perhaps because of this, I enjoy working with people and learning from my experiences, which has led me to participate as a counsellor at a camp for mentally disabled people, helping to raise my awareness of mental disorders. I consider this important for a future doctor as it is common that mental problems accompany physical ones and vice versa.

Changing school five times increased both my social and academic flexibility. What's more, over the past five years, I have been a scholarship student at my current school, compelling me to maintain high standards both in and outside the classroom. I believe my learning to cope with pressure will come in use both at university, and in my chosen career, where critical situations are common. I also find that my logic and critical thinking enable me to achieve high standards in mathematics and science. I chose to explore the latter beyond the curriculum, chiefly in the medical field, by subscribing to the Medscape medical newsletter, which keeps me up to date with events in the medical circles, and also by deciding to write my Extended Essay on biochemistry, focusing on the effects of paracetamol and aspirin on living organisms.

In my free time, I engage in many other activities. Last year, I was elected to represent my class in the Student Council, comprising elected representatives of all classes between Years 7 and 13, aiming to improve the school for the students. This year I was chosen to be Vice President of the Grammar School, making me responsible for the Student Council. I also enjoy debating and was picked for the school Senior Debate, where I defended the winning motion that children under 15 should be monitored while on the Internet. For several years, I have been learning to play the flute, which allowed me to participate at last year's Maribor Spring Festival, where we explored the theme 'Diversity in Unity' with students from all over Europe through the media of music, dance and art. To keep fit I do cross-country running, and this year for the second time ran the 5km race for women in Prague. I am also working towards my Duke of Edinburgh Gold Award. I look forward to enhancing these skills further at university by actively participating in the Student Union.

11.22 Personal statement 22 (A level)

Personal statement successful for: Barts, Imperial College

Doctors play a central role in society; they have the opportunity to improve people's welfare and contribute to their well being. I realised this early, having been raised in medical campuses in various countries. I was an intensely curious child querying the simple relationships between structure and function underpinning science and I was immediately fascinated by the diverse aspects of medicine and its application in those varied countries. This early exposure allowed me to understand shifts in focuses of medicine over the years; it was also the foundation for my current dream. I've had many obstacles to overcome: I was in the gifted and talented stream of my comprehensive, yet I felt I was not challenged enough, so I applied to those sixth forms which could offer greater opportunities for development. My motivation won me scholarships to all, and I took up the Newham scholarship to the most well-rounded school.

To gain hands-on experience, I worked in Plaistow Hospital. For two weeks I provided companionship and realised that patience, compassion, and sensitivity are just as crucial as scientific skills. I also acquired wheel chair training. I volunteered in the community for four years, making language teaching materials for refugees and asylum seekers. My own acquisition of multilingualism helped me to present basic learning effectively. I enjoyed developing my interpersonal and communication skills and received a Millennium Award for 200 hours of voluntary work.

To broaden my range of experiences, I worked in a school for the disabled. My challenge was to provide the 'therapy' of everyday activities in ways that were easy, interesting, and functional. Furthermore, I found my ongoing voluntary work at the nursing home very enlightening. Sometimes improving the quality of life is all we can do. Medlink lectures, a 10-credit, Level 4 TVU course and Pre-Med programmes strengthened my career convictions. The defining moment was a week's paediatric placement at Lewisham. I learnt the simple laws of physics that underpin the use of instruments. I experienced the stress of ICU and had the opportunity to talk to support staff and patients which provided an amazingly holistic view of medicine. Empathy for stressful situations, humility and multitasking were qualities I gained from this placement.

As a Secondary School Prefect, I had to assert myself over my peers, motivate and make quick and effective decisions. In sixth form, I used my talents for fund-raising. I was the lead dancer, actor and model in TAAL 2007, which was a charity-based Asian cultural performance that raised GBP 7000 for Water Aid and other charities. Consequently, though a fresher, my organisational skills and team work got me elected onto the committee for TAAL 2008 and my House elected me to the school charity committee. This inspired me to create an awareness-raising charity. I also participate in events from competitive shooting to flying – for which I have an RAF proficiency certificate. I am passionate about history, love Sci-fi novels, write stories and poems. My poem won the Islington libraries' competition and was read on BBC. I produce music and I am currently negotiating with a record company. My performance on environmental issues was chosen to be aired on the BBC.

Medicine will be an incredibly varied, challenging and rewarding career, as it will allow me to apply theoretical knowledge, ethics and life events to improve health. It is hope, along with commitment and stamina, that has brought me to where I am. I believe medicine to be the path that leads to a better tomorrow, and I look forward to walking down that path.

11.23 Personal statement 23 (A level)

Personal statement successful for: Birmingham, Imperial College, UCL

I have always been intrigued by the trust that patients place in their doctor and I appreciate the responsibility involved in medicine, where a doctor's input can significantly influence people's lives and well-being. It is the combination of science and human interaction that I find stimulating about medicine, along with the prospect of lifelong learning. I am aware that life as a doctor can be both physically and emotionally demanding. Knowing, however, that I will be able to use my strengths in science for the benefit of others will be the greatest reward.

Shadowing doctors in several departments at Manchester Royal Infirmary for four weeks has confirmed to me that medicine is the career I wish to follow. I especially enjoyed conversing with patients both acutely and chronically unwell and became aware that attentive listening performed a crucial role in good communication. Encountering psychological illness and dementia has sparked my interest in the mental welfare of patients. I could see that it was important to give the same attention and care as is given to those with physiological ailments, but understood the greater difficulty in diagnosing patients with psychiatric conditions. The ward rounds made me realise the importance of teamwork and communication between doctors, nurses, pharmacists and physiotherapists to formulate efficient treatment plans as a multidisciplinary team. I was fortunate to experience another taster of life as a medic on MedSIM. I am also a chapel volunteer at Christie Hospital, which exposes me to the emotional distress of patients and their families, where comforting them proves to be a difficult and challenging task. I also take part in a health professions group where we discuss current ethical issues. Leading a discussion about the use of cannabis in the treatment of multiple sclerosis required research into the ethics of this controversial issue. By volunteering at a nursing home I have become a better communicator by listening to the concerns and anxieties of residents and their families.

Further to my academic pursuits, I am a Year 7 form prefect and have also been a mentor to a child from a disadvantaged background for a year. This commitment, alongside mentoring a younger girl in German, has improved my interpersonal skills and helped me to develop patience. In school, I created and managed 'GreenSoc', an environmental society formed to raise awareness and sell recycled stationery. This taught me how to motivate others and the importance of teamwork. I am an active member of Amnesty International, and organising campaigns has broadened my knowledge of current affairs and human rights issues. Working as the editor of the school newspaper has been extremely rewarding and has taught me how to manage a team and work to strict deadlines. Effective teamwork in the 'Young Analyst' Chemistry competition meant that not only did we come fifth out of twenty-eight schools, but we also won the 'Good Lab Practice' award.

As a member of St John Ambulance, I have acquired some experience and knowledge of healthcare. I am qualified in first aid and perform duties at pop concerts and football matches. I am proud of my Indian heritage, and my Indian Kathak dance certificate is a result of commitment to classes for more than two years. Both dance and sport help me to relax during times of academic pressure. For four years, I have been a member of a Hindu youth group, helping me to preserve my Indian roots through prayer and other cultural activities. As a part-time worker for a personal injury company at a call centre, I have been introduced to the responsibilities of working life and to the need for careful decision-making founded on basic medical knowledge.

I feel that, by managing demanding academic and extracurricular commitments successfully so far, I have proved that I have the ability to handle the significant pressures of a medical career.

11.24 Personal statement 24 (A level)

Personal statement successful for: Brighton

Observing an emergency Caesarean Section was intensely emotional; just fifteen minutes earlier I had been in the intensive care unit where an elderly lady was dying. My experience of these two extremes whilst shadowing a consultant anaesthetist last year illustrated to me the demands of being a doctor. An additional week with the anaesthetist this summer gave me further insight into life in the operating theatre. I was particularly impressed by the surgeon's dexterity with hip and knee replacements and laparoscopic surgery. Comparing the controlled drama of the operating theatre to the stillness of the intensive care unit highlighted the diversity of the medical profession, as did the Medlink course I attended. These contrasts and challenges attract me.

Time spent in a fracture clinic with a consultant orthopaedic surgeon and accompanying a GP on home visits accentuated the importance of trust and confidentiality between doctor and patient. For over a year I have been visiting a nursing home on a weekly basis. Talking to the patients has been a humbling and rewarding experience; it has improved my communication skills and taught me to be an empathetic listener.

Studying Biology, Chemistry and Mathematics A level has enabled me to develop my analytical skills, imperative to medicine. My enthusiasm for these disciplines is reflected in my academic aptitude; I won the Lower 6 Chemistry prize and I am a scholarship boy and holder of an academic bursary. Biology has always been my favourite subject because of its broad scope, ranging from cellular investigation to whole organisms. I would now like to learn the aetiology of diseases, understand why patients are ill and formulate methods of treatment. The study of chemistry, the composition of substances and their properties and reactions, came to life for me in the operating theatre when witnessing the immediate effect of anaesthesia on patients.

As part of my Gold Duke of Edinburgh award, word processing and IT courses have broadened my computer knowledge and a first aid course completed whilst in the school CCF has given me useful life skills. Being a school prefect it is necessary for me to take on important duties, a position I enjoy.

I would like to continue my sport at university. I play county squash for Hampshire at Under 19's level and I am the Under 19 Channel Islands champion. As captain of the Guernsey junior squad I developed my leadership skills; I looked after the juniors at national tournaments and adopted a pastoral role during their time away from home.

Over the past two years I have acquired a professional level II coaching qualification, enabling me to work as a squash coach. I now run the weekly junior league matches for up to forty children, enhancing my organisational and interpersonal skills. For my Sports Leadership award I am teaching basketball to underprivileged children and am now confident in child management.

Playing in the school cricket and football first XI's and in the Guernsey under 19 cricket team has highlighted to me the value of teamwork. This seems relevant to medicine, as I witnessed the collective participation of the surgeon and nurses in the operating theatre.

What I have experienced to date has strengthened my ambition to be a doctor; my exposure to the extensive responsibilities of an anaesthetist in pain clinics and pre-operative assessments as well as the operating theatre and the intensive care unit has inspired me to pursue a career in hospital medicine. In my role as referee at county and national squash matches, making decisions quickly and with authority is essential. I believe these skills would transfer well to higher education. My ability to balance my time between my studies, sporting commitments and other activities demonstrates my determination to succeed and gain a life-changing experience at university.

11.25 Personal statement 25 (A level)

Personal statement successful for: St Andrews

Having encountered the rites of birth, death and disease at first hand, I know the care and compassion needed as a doctor is second to none. Reflecting on my past few years in the NHS, I have seen that people's experience of health and illness is uniquely personal and influenced by the medical intervention they receive. With this in mind I am committed to entering a vocation where I will be able to make a positive impact on others' quality of life. It is this challenge, coupled with enthusiasm to understand how disease affects the body, which has made me determined to succeed in medicine.

Working with the Learning Disabilities Network in Lancaster, my goal was to empower the clients to integrate with the community. Being ultimately responsible for clients in crises honed my ability to listen, give reassurance and lend emotional support in times of distress. I developed techniques in interpersonal communication whilst gaining the trust of the clients and the multidisciplinary team. Making decisions to benefit the client was an evolving skill which required autonomy and delicate reasoning and could often expose ethical dilemmas.

Whilst studying for the Access course I worked part-time as an auxiliary nurse. Nursing allowed me to talk closely with patients about their feelings and experiences of illness and I saw the difference that both a good and bad bedside manner can make. I recognised the need to quickly prioritise tasks, often in pressured circumstances, and learned that it is vital to function as a team and manage time effectively. It opened my eyes to the reality of working on a ward and I felt closer to my goals as a result.

In 2005 I was asked by a friend to be her birthing partner. It was an inspirational yet daunting time, from the early months through to cutting the cord, which was based on her trust and confidence that I could support her through the pregnancy and labour. I realised how vital it is for doctors to respect the beliefs of the mother, her preferences for treatment and her need for encouragement and explanation.

More recently I provided respite care for my Grandfather who had Parkinson's disease. I hold no illusions of how devastating and debilitating chronic disease can be for both patient and family. I recognise the importance of the doctor's role in diagnosing and treating Grandpa's condition, helping him to live independently and with dignity. As a family member I can reflect on how important the medical team's sensitive and empathic approach was in meeting our family's concerns and expectations about the future.

I know that new situations give an excellent framework for learning and my enthusiasm to broaden my understanding and skills has been continuous. Deciding to work as a clinical coder allowed me to enhance my medical knowledge whilst integrating with a variety of hospital staff. I maximised opportunities to get involved with medical teams by shadowing doctors in orthopaedic surgery, anaesthetics, A&E and general practice, where my ambition was fully encouraged.

Having taught myself to play several musical instruments I have led 3 major bands and produced 6 recordings, one of which was on sale commercially. Between playing Ultimate Frisbee and cycling, I captain the BioMed football team, organising matches twice a week, and take pleasure in the competitive edge it brings. Being a captain makes me feel proud and able to conduct the players with confidence. I have volunteered for Homeless Action and over the last year for St John Ambulance, developing skills in first aid and helping at community and sporting events.

Achieving highly in the Access to Medicine course and continuing on to biomedicine provides an excellent academic basis from which to approach a pure medical course which offers both science and humanity. My diverse work experience has equipped me with a realistic concept of modern medical practice and its pressures, and I remain determined to become one of tomorrow's doctors.

11.26 Personal statement 26 (A level)

Personal statement successful for: Aberdeen, Dundee, Keele

When I learned that my Uncle was suffering from bowel cancer, I was forced to realise the full effects of cancer upon both the sufferer and their relatives and how important a role the state of mind plays in helping to influence the outcome of a disease. The influence of the mind on recovery was highlighted again during my work experience at Leeds University Oncology Department in July 2007 where I saw cancer patients' different attitudes to their diagnoses and prognoses. Some were in denial, some were fearful and some faced their disease with determined optimism. The professionalism of the staff in dealing and sympathising with these differing attitudes reinforced my decision to choose medicine as a career and I was further inspired during work experience at a local primary school, where I helped disabled children undertake their everyday tasks successfully.

I spent a week at a GP Practice in June 2007 where I was allowed to perform some simple procedures and attend house visits, discovering the importance of bedside manner. I have also spent a day at the Douglas Macmillan Hospice as a listener. For five months in 2007 I listened weekly to primary school children reading and my time at the two primary schools helped to improve my ability to communicate with children. I shadowed senior psychiatrists at Harplands Hospital in August 2008 and this increased my understanding of mental illnesses. I attended Medlink in December 2007 and a course at Keele University Medical School in March 2008, both of which reinforced my motivation to pursue a medical career as I realised just how varied it is as a profession. I have also attended a number of Medical School Open Days to discover the methods which best suit my way of learning and to investigate fully what is involved in taking a medical degree. I read the Biological Science Review and medical reports in the daily newspapers to help increase my understanding and provide information on topics outside my biology course. In 2008 I wrote an extended Biology essay on the effects of smoking on the body and also investigated the synthesis and analysis of aspirin, which taught me about the structure of the drug.

Travel to Cambodia and Laos allowed me to see the conditions which many people in developing countries have to endure and I would like to eventually spend some time working with an organisation like 'Médecins sans Frontières' to put my medical knowledge into practice in a Third World situation. Having taken French at AS level, I wish to use my knowledge of and interest in French to its full potential in my medical career.

In July 2008 I won a School Prize for 'Scholarship and Initiative' and I am a Senior Prefect. I have played hockey for school throughout my school life, am in the 1st XI and coach younger players to improve their skills and teamwork. I play in the school orchestra, wind band and flute group, accompany drama productions, participate in concerts inside and outside school and this year I was a judge for Junior House Music. I hold Full Colours in Music and Half Colours in Hockey and have been in the CCF for four years. My Young Enterprise Group, where I was part of the operations and sales teams, won the Local Finals and three prizes at the County Finals. I am self-motivated and determined to succeed and work to the best of my abilities.

Outside school I am Head Chorister at our church where I am responsible for the Junior Choir and where I occasionally play hymns on the organ during services. I take piano, flute and organ lessons. I have achieved Grade 7 on piano and flute and will be taking the Grade 8 flute examination in July 2009. I have also achieved Grade 3 on the violin. My intellectual interests include reading fiction and playing and listening to music of all genres. I enjoy watching films which feature different cultures and languages. I have travelled extensively, and enjoy walking, cycling and spending time with my friends.

11.27 Personal statement 27 (A level)

Personal statement successful for: Leeds, Manchester, Sheffield

Medicine appeals to me as I have a strong interest and aptitude for sciences and I get a great deal of satisfaction when helping people. I am interested in the practical application of knowledge and am particularly excited by the prospect of applying ongoing genetic research to helping people with a wide range of illnesses. My enthusiasm for medicine has been confirmed and heightened by my work experience and conversations with practising doctors.

I attended the 'Hospex' course in Derby Hospital and shadowed a variety of medical staff. I enjoyed the course as I experienced real practical cases and was able to ask questions and discuss details with the doctors and patients. I noted the doctors' excellent communication skills even with non-English-speaking patients. In surgery I witnessed an appendectomy, keyhole surgery for gall bladder removal and a blood clot removed from a man's abdomen. It was my first experience in an operating theatre and although initially nervous I felt at ease watching the operations once the initial feelings had subsided. The teamwork was impressive and allowed procedures to run very smoothly. I accompanied consultants on ward rounds and the many conversations I had have given me great insight. Time management was important as I had a busy schedule to keep around the hospital.

I have attended many medical talks in school and universities; I have spoken with doctors during work experience and had long conversations with a consultant radiologist and a consultant vascular surgeon. Reading medical articles and listening to radio programmes such as 'Case Notes' has improved my knowledge of a wide spectrum of topics. This information has strengthened my ambition to be a doctor.

I work four hours a week as a voluntary carer at a local nursing home. This involves feeding, moving, and helping people to the toilet and to bed. I am enjoying getting to know the patients and find helping out very fulfilling. My caring and practical skills are improving and I feel competent to help. Communication in the home can be a challenge as many of the staff have limited English and some patients are physically unable to speak. I am learning a lot about patient care and respect, and find that working as part of a team has many benefits; I can ask members of the team for support when I lack experience of the task in hand.

In year 12 I was part of a team of twenty Millennium Volunteers; we designed and produced a charity calendar with comical pictures of senior teachers. I took responsibility for generating ideas and collecting props; team work was important to ensure a successful outcome. Also in year 12 I helped a year 7 maths class once a fortnight. I especially enjoyed helping two boys who were struggling most; I got satisfaction from passing on some of my maths skills.

I have taken weekly lessons in trumpet and piano since I was 5, passed grade 6 in both and play in both school bands. I attend tennis coaching weekly and enjoy football, snooker and cycling. I organise summertime canoe/camping trips in the Norfolk Broads with my friends which have made me more independent and built my confidence. I also like reading books, especially autobiographies and novels.

I have an RLSS lifeguard qualification with first aid training and work as a lifeguard at my local pool. Working for several hours a week, the role requires me to be alert whilst observing the pool and identifying weak swimmers and hazards; I enjoy the feeling of responsibility. My shifts vary each week so I must manage my time well to keep this, my other interests, and schoolwork in the right balance.

Work experience and talking with doctors has given me real insight and a commitment to the medical profession. I am eager to learn, have good personal skills, am responsible and hardworking and have a strong desire to help people. I am ambitious, have a strong record of commitment and success and am confident I have the capabilities to be a capable, caring doctor.

11.28 Personal statement 28 (A level)

Personal statement successful for: King's College, Leicester, Nottingham, UCL

It wasn't just in a single spark of inspiration that I decided I would like to pursue medicine as a career. Rather, it was my enthusiasm for science from an early age, which nurtured and instilled my love for human biology, with all its complexities and intricacies.

Recently, I was able to explore areas of advanced science independently while completing the Open University degree on 'Molecules, Medicines and Drugs'. In particular, the action of non-steroidal anti-inflammatory drugs captivated my interest. I learnt that aspirin is a selective inhibitor of the enzyme cyclooxygenase which prevents the synthesis of the pain sensitising prostaglandins. It has been fascinating to deepen my knowledge of the interaction between various chemicals and the human body.

My interest in medicine was fuelled too by weekly visits to a local residential home for the partially blind. Over the last three years I learnt how to empathise with a diverse group of people while playing board games, organising competitions and reading to them. Not only has this improved my communication skills and given me a sense of responsibility, but I have since developed an interest in the functioning of the human eye and read about the causes and preventative measures of blindness.

Work placements at two university hospitals allowed me to comprehend the demands of a medical career as I talked to consultants and junior doctors. I witnessed the importance of teamwork skills and the understanding between the surgeon, anaesthetist and nursing staff during a cardiac bypass operation. Observing the workings of an orthopaedic clinic, ward rounds and the ICU gave me an insight into the breadth of healthcare provided by the NHS. I then arranged a week's placement in the department of radiology at Coventry where the importance of the Breast Screening Service in diagnosing early cancer was highlighted. Here I watched as one of the doctors broke bad news of cancer to an elderly patient with care and compassion. This emphasised the significance of the holistic approach that doctors take when caring for their patients. I had the opportunity to compare the health service in this country with India when I completed a project on amputees at a regional limb centre in

Lucknow. I noticed that the success of proper rehabilitation of amputees is directly related to the type of accident, injury, the creation of stump and the selection of prosthesis which suited the lifestyle of the amputee. It was the 'Mukti' limb prosthesis which was the most economical and best suited for the Indian conditions.

My organisational and leadership skills developed further during the Duke of Edinburgh expedition, as I took responsibility for planning the route to be taken with my team mates. Taking an active part in the school debating society allows me to discuss and address the arguments surrounding ethical issues such as euthanasia. At lunchtimes, I listen to Year 3 children read at a local primary school, helping them improve their skills. This has made me aware of the different approaches required when interacting with the young and the use of encouragement whilst correcting their mistakes.

I am well aware that the ability to cope with pressures of student life is essential and so I enjoy playing badminton on a weekly basis and train in Indian classical dance, both of which help me to relax and keep fit. Through this I am also able to maintain my multilingual skills as the 'Kathak' dance is primarily taught in Hindi. I have also enjoyed learning the Spanish composition 'Mi Palomita Blanca' while working towards my Grade 5 singing. My experiences have affirmed that medicine is a career path I would like to follow and the demands of lifelong learning and dedication have only deepened my desire to become a doctor.

11.29 Personal statement 29 (A level)

Personal statement successful for: Cardiff, Edinburgh, UCL

A week at a GP surgery was an eye-opening experience. Observing patient consultations and clinics to accompanying district nurses' visits gave me a taste of the challenges and rewards that medicine can offer with its unique combination of scientific investigation, patient interaction and the ability to contribute positively to a community. Medicine, I decided, was to be my future.

Pursuing my interest, a week with a Urological consultant at King's College Hospital offered an insight into the evolving field of laparoscopic surgery, the dedication and skills of surgeons and the impact of doctor-patient communication. Time on a geriatric ward at Kent & Sussex Hospital highlighted the complex clinical and social needs of our increasingly elderly population, in particular the interdisciplinary coordination between diverse services such as physiotherapy, occupational therapy and social services. Shadowing an FY1 doctor revealed the sheer hard work and dedication that medicine requires. My commitment to helping weekly at a school for the disabled has been a most rewarding experience. The pleasure of building a rapport with the children has been especially fulfilling and developed my communication skills with vulnerable patients. Attending Medlink demonstrated the opportunities of working in a constantly developing scientific environment and further inspired my career choice.

Arguably medicine is both an art and a science and the IB has enabled me to pursue both disciplines. I have the sound scientific base required for medicine, balanced by the arts skills of logic, analysis of evidence and communication – all vitally important for a medical career. My interest in biology was deepened by my IB extended essay on the feeding behaviour of barnacles – excellent preparation for the independent research of an undergraduate degree. The problem-solving and analytical aspects of chemistry are ones I especially enjoy. I have expanded my intellectual curiosity through the IB Theory of Knowledge, and my essay on the relationship between knowledge gained from science and the arts was particularly thought-provoking. Reading the New Scientist and contemporary science literature has deepened my awareness of critical issues.

One of my passions is drama. Both acting and supporting backstage have developed my commitment and teamwork, both of which were tested on a tour of Germany with a school production of 'Oedipus' and 'Antigone'. I am an avid theatre-goer and value the camaraderie of singing with school and local choirs. I keep fit with swimming and badminton; relish the thrills of skiing; and have taken great satisfaction from mastering the technicalities of ballroom dancing. I am keen to continue these activities at university, as opportunities for reinforcing my perseverance, coordination and stamina.

Having lived abroad, I enjoy travelling and the challenge of new destinations. A recent biology expedition to Ecuador and the Galapagos was physically demanding but rewarding, teaching me that I am adaptable, resourceful and resilient. My determination to participate in this project tested my ingenuity as I funded the trip myself through organising fundraising activities and working as a waitress at a local NT property.

Completing my Gold DofE Award has been a great challenge, in physical and organisational terms. This success confirms my maturity and determination. I am a calm and committed individual and these qualities, together with my excellent communication skills, have been recognised by my school. Chosen to be a Prefect, I was also selected as a Classroom Assistant on their summer science course for Gifted and Talented primary school children. I immensely enjoyed contributing to this stimulating week.

A caring and focused individual with an independence of mind and a lively intelligence, I am confident and excited to face the demands, challenges and intellectual stimulus that a vocational career in medicine offers.

11.30 Personal statement 30 (A level)

Personal statement successful for: Leeds, Liverpool, Manchester

My desire to pursue a career in medicine is based on my interest in science, aptitude for problem solving along with good communication and leadership skills.

In July 2007 I did a week of work experience in the John Radcliffe Hospital, Oxford. I spent time in several departments including radiology, surgery and pathology. I especially enjoyed shadowing an F1 doctor on the acute surgical admission ward. I spent one day with a surgical manager and a morning with the UNISON representative. This gave me an insight into managerial issues and some health service employment problems.

Since September 2007 I have been working as a volunteer on a female geriatric ward in the local hospital. Although it was initially distressing to see confused elderly patients, I have enjoyed getting to know individual patients and have gained an appreciation of some of the problems of long-term care for the elderly. I sensed that simply talking to some of these patients had a positive impact on their quality of life. This has shown me a much less glamorous side to hospital life. I also spent a week shadowing a local GP. This included a day with a drug rehabilitation clinic. This experience illustrated the importance of continuity of care and good communication skills. In January 2008 I organised further work experience in the genetics department. I was given several examples of ethical and clinical dilemmas related to genetic diseases. This stimulated my interest in both ethics and genetics. I have subsequently read several books on these topics such as 'Introduction to Medical Ethics' by A. Hope and 'The Language of Genes' by S. Jones.

During this summer I worked as a Nanny, looking after three boys aged 2, 5 and 7 years. This challenged my patience and organisational skills.

Since August 2009 I have been working for a medical research company, Colonix. The project involves taking samples of mucus from the inside of the lower bowel with a balloon. The DNA content of the mucus is measured. The concept is that raised DNA levels may be indicative of upstream bowel pathology. The ultimate aim is to screen for colon cancer with less need for invasive expensive procedures such as colonoscopy. My role is to ensure accurate data collection and correct transport to the laboratory. I have observed and progressively assisted in the processing of samples in the laboratory. This has already improved my understanding of the scientific basis of modern medical practice.

In October 2009 I am going to spend a month as an observer in a hospital in Manali in Northern India. Having never been to India before, I am both excited and anxious about the vast difference in culture that I am going to experience. I am looking forward to seeing how healthcare is delivered in a very different environment to the UK. I have also organised two weeks' work experience in a university hospital in Singapore in January 2010.

I was a member of my school 1st XI Hockey team together with representing the school in tennis and athletics. I was also a sports leader. This involved taking sports lessons and organising sporting events for younger pupils. My favourite sport, however, is cross-country skiing. I am currently training to do the Engadin ski marathon in March 2010. My training involves keeping fit and also roller skiing as there is no snow here in Oxford. At school I was a founder member of a film club. With three friends, we acted in, directed and produced two films. This required team work, good communication skills and lots of problem solving.

My work and voluntary experience has illustrated the demands of a medical career, the variety of types of careers within medicine and some of the challenges to the healthcare system. I hope that my gap year opportunities will enhance my understanding of medical research and healthcare systems in different parts of the world. My exposure to different aspects of medicine has strengthened my desire to pursue a career in this profession.

11.31 Personal statement 31 (A level)

Personal statement successful for: Brighton, Nottingham, Peninsula

Having always enjoyed and been fascinated by science, my interest in studying Medicine began three years ago when I experienced life as a patient first-hand. Whilst I was in hospital with a broken arm I became intrigued by the diagnostic and curative process of medicine and the care, sensitivity and understanding shown to me by hospital staff made a significant impression on me.

I began to realise that the attributes of a doctor necessitate not only a scientific and intelligent mind but encompass qualities such as logical thinking, compassion and effective communication – traits I believe I possess and could develop should I be successful in achieving my goal to study medicine.

My enthusiasm for becoming a doctor became more profound following work experience in two local hospitals. I had the opportunity to attend placements in a variety of areas from Radiology to Elderly Medicine but I particularly enjoyed the time I spent in the Accident and Emergency department. I was able to observe the efficient interactions of the multidisciplinary team in achieving effective patient care in often pressured and demanding situations. This, I am sure, is a challenge that I would relish being part of in the future.

My A level subjects reflect my passion for science and have taught me to look at the world with a thoughtful and analytical approach. I have enjoyed reading around and beyond the subjects we have studied at school and I have become an avid reader of various scientific journals. I have also been introduced to the Student BMJ, which has given me an insight into life as a medical student and some of the issues they face on a daily basis. The accounts of student's electives I have found particularly stimulating. I see this period of training as a potential opportunity to practise and develop my linguistic skills in both French and Spanish, as well as a great chance to travel to a different part of the world.

In addition to my academic studies I have taken on various extracurricular activities in School. I was recently selected as Captain of my School House – a role that has allowed me to develop my communication, organisational and leadership skills. I have also been involved in the pastoral care of younger pupils, an undertaking that I have not only found rewarding but one that encourages unity and cohesiveness in school life.

I have always recognised the importance of having interests and hobbies outside academia, to provide both a balance to and outlet from the pressures of studying. I am an enthusiastic sportsman and have represented my school in Athletics, Water polo and Fives – a sport in which I reached the National Championship semi-finals.

Over the last year I have been working towards my Duke of Edinburgh Gold Award, a goal I aim to achieve before I leave school. I have a keen interest in modern music and have played the drums for various school and other bands over the last four years, a hobby I am eager to continue whilst at university.

During the last two years I have worked regularly as a baby sitter for a family friend with a young child. In the school holidays I play an important part in the care of my younger brother as my mother is in full-time employment. I feel that these active caring roles have contributed greatly to my character building.

I believe that the attributes I have mentioned previously and the enjoyment I receive from meeting new people and finding out more about them make me an ideal candidate. Should I be given the opportunity to study, I believe my determination and enthusiasm will allow me to succeed in the challenge that is a career in Medicine

11.32 Personal statement 32 (A level)

Personal statement successful for: Cambridge, Imperial College, King's College, UCL

My desire to pursue a career in medicine started at the age of twelve when my aunt gave birth to a baby girl at 24 weeks. I was awe-struck as I watched the paediatric team miraculously nurture a tiny speck of life, no bigger than my hand with such care and capability so that she is now healthy and thriving at six years of age. My aspiration was refuelled when I was confined to hospital earlier this year following a road traffic accident. In that time I witnessed and absorbed first-hand a very full range of hospital experiences: staff anxiety about my injuries; the application of a wide range of medical practices and expertise; the extreme demands on medical staff time as well as the satisfaction gained by the hospital team as they led me to a full recovery.

I have tried to expand my understanding of medicine by attending Med-link and by gaining experience in a number of medical areas including Medical Research at Imperial College. A week spent at a local General Medical Practice has given me an insight into the rapport established between doctor and patient. I have undertaken hospital-based work experience on the Rheumatology Ward at Northwick Park Hospital where I was intrigued by maggot therapy and on the Paediatrics Ward at Ealing Hospital. I was able to shadow the Senior House Officer who cared for me during my stay at St Mark's Hospital which was an extremely unique experience and allowed me to observe a range of procedures including colonoscopies. All the above facets have given me a sound overview of the responsibilities and dedication required by a medical team towards the recovery of their patients.

Voluntary work on the HIV and AIDS Ward at University College Hospital every week over the past school year has proved very satisfying as it has enabled me to help people from many walks of life. Similarly, entertaining the elderly and disabled at John Grooms Home and assisting in the care of Reception Class at school has taught me to adapt to the needs of different age groups and varying backgrounds. I have spent considerable time nursing at my father's dental surgery and this has confirmed my passion for inter-acting with people.

The value of diplomatic leadership and rewarding teamwork were apparent to me while holding the post of Marketing Director of a highly successful Young Enterprise Company which won numerous awards. I am a member of the Publicity team of an active Science Society, responsible for producing a fortnightly newsletter and I am thoroughly enjoying the research and exploration involved in this project. In addition, being appointed Secretary of the Asian Society has taught me to be self-reliant and cultivate my organisational and time management skills.

My extracurricular activities include playing the piano to Grade 8 and the guitar to Grade 7. Achieving these grades has increased my manual dexterity and has required high levels of discipline and perseverance. I enjoy playing badminton, have represented the school in lacrosse and hold a Bronze Medallion in Lifesaving. In July 2002, I participated in a strenuous charity cycle run of 200km across Holland. Involvement in the Duke of Edinburgh Scheme has enhanced my interpersonal and teamwork skills and, to my immense satisfaction, I achieved the Gold Award this summer.

Coming from a family of people with medical backgrounds, it is clear that the depth of medical understanding has increased enormously over the years and continues to grow. I desire intensely to be at the forefront of this dynamic and challenging career which promises even further exciting innovations and advances. Given my personal and work experiences, I believe I am aptly suited to the combination of application of scientific knowledge, dedication and enthusiasm needed to pursue a medical profession successfully.

11.33 Personal statement 33 (A level)

Personal statement successful for: Cardiff, King's College, Sheffield, UCL

Medicine is the career in which I believe I could best use my abilities, providing personal fulfilment and benefit to others. My empathy and concern for other people has especially contributed to this aspiration.

My A level subjects were an easy choice for me. They are the subjects I find most rewarding and feel I am good at. Biology is particularly fascinating, especially aspects of human biology. In chemistry I enjoy experimental work where you can apply knowledge learnt in a more practical way. Maths is very satisfying, especially when a problem is solved as a product of hard work. Studying German has allowed me to pursue my interest in languages and enhance my frequent trips to Germany.

Work experience at my local hospital confirmed and strengthened my desire for a career in Medicine. Through shadowing members of staff on a short stay surgical ward I was able to experience many aspects of hospital work. The opportunity to interact with current medical students reinforced my enthusiasm for the subject. Recently I helped at the hospital as a weekly volunteer, spending most of my time chatting with patients on the ward and making sure they had everything they needed. This gave me a totally different perspective, from the view of a patient. From my experiences in a hospital I feel I have gained a realistic view of a career in Medicine.

As a member of the Medical Society in college and the local NHS Trust, I attend lectures on a variety of health issues. Alongside my A levels, I am taking an Open University course in 'Human Genetics and Health Issues': broadening my knowledge in a more specific and often controversial field. The course provides greater insight into many issues in the A level syllabus and the media, whilst also developing important independent study skills.

I have worked as a volunteer with a swimming club for disabled children since 2004. My inspiration came after close contact with a young boy with severe disabilities. I help with structured lessons for children of all ages and disabilities. I now know many of the children well and it is extremely rewarding to see them steadily improve while enjoying themselves. During the holidays I was asked to work with a disabled child in a wheelchair on a one-to-one basis as part of a play scheme. Although this requires much patience and is often challenging, I enjoy the work. Last year, I completed the 'National Pool Lifeguard Qualification' and now work at a local pool – dealing with the public, administering first aid and ensuring pool safety. Teamwork is essential, and I have gained much through working with colleagues and the general public.

I swim with my city Swimming Club. Having previously competed at county level, I now swim three times a week for fitness. Since completing two exchange visits to Germany, including a week working in a primary school, my confidence in speaking German has grown. Socially I enjoy travel, music, meeting friends and the occasional salsa class.

I believe myself to be a committed student with the vocation, determination and ability to succeed in a career in Medicine. My AS results have placed me on track to achieve the necessary academic standard. Through my work and experience I have developed excellent communication skills and the sensitivity to deal with people in varied situations. I feel strongly that I would meet the challenges and value the rewards of being a doctor.

11.34 Personal statement 34 (A level)

Personal statement successful for: Leicester, UCL

My desire to enter the medical profession is based upon a fascination with the workings of the human body, both physically and psychologically. Although I may not be able to 'cure' every patient, I believe I am a passionate person who would always strive to ensure patients receive the best quality of life possible.

During my work experience in a cardiology outpatients unit at Bedford Hospital, I had the opportunity to observe the roles of a variety of staff within the department. I was able to watch the doctor collate the available information about a patient and use his knowledge to make a diagnosis. I learnt how important it is for a doctor to be able to communicate with a multidisciplinary team who continued the care of the patient. In order to increase my knowledge of hospital life I am volunteering at a local hospital and I am currently placed on an orthopaedic ward. My duties include serving meals to patients, reception and paperwork tasks. I have built up a professional working relationship with patients, their families and staff; this allows me to improve my communication skills through working with a diverse range of people.

I have been employed part-time since February 2007 in a busy high street fashion store working closely and constantly with the general public. My experience on customer services has shown the variety of approaches that different members of society use and I now appreciate that it is very important to listen, confirm and resolve any issue as calmly as possible. The demands of a vibrant retail environment have required me to be flexible and adaptable and not to expect to leave work on time!

A level Chemistry and Biology have increased my scientific knowledge and I particularly enjoy lab-based work and the application of theory to practical situations. After dissecting a heart, I was able to perceive the variation that exists between text book and specimen. My hard work was acknowledged when I received the only subject excellence certificate in both Chemistry and Biology from my school. In Maths I have learnt to make judgements about which knowledge to best apply to different problems, a valuable and transferable skill.

As a member of the sixth form year council, I participate in weekly discussions concerning school events. This has involved me listening to ideas, developing them and reaching a final conclusion as part of a group. For the past four years I have acted as a guide for parents and students transferring to my school, which involves answering questions and giving opinions. I was given the responsibility of being a 'buddy' for a class of year 9 students; this required me to organise team building activities during their induction day. I also conducted informal discussions with the students to ensure they were settled in their new school environment. I volunteered to assist at a local Brownie Pack, helping at weekly sessions which covered areas as diverse as canoeing and a beauty pageant.

Since completing a GCSE in Textiles, I have continued to use my skills for my own pleasure and satisfaction and I am currently working on an evening dress. I read a wide variety of books, including 'Bedside Confessions of a Junior Doctor' and 'Bodies', both written by junior doctors. Both books highlighted the demand on a doctor's time and patience; however, neither deterred me from wanting to study medicine!

I appreciate that a medical degree can be emotionally, physically and academically challenging; however, I consider myself to have the determination and ambition to complete the course and continue using the knowledge I acquire. I hope my positive attitude to my studies and life provides a stimulus for my peers, which I wish to maintain throughout my professional working life. I am an enthusiastic self-motivated individual who is committed to continual learning and personal development for a rewarding and fulfilling career in Medicine.

11.35 Personal statement 35 (A level)

Personal statement successful for: Birmingham, Southampton

From having ileal atresia at birth to abdominal adhesions at seventeen, medicine has been a strong factor in my life. Growing up, I spent a great deal of time at Great Ormond Street Hospital, allowing me to observe and appreciate the role of doctors in our society, and aspire to become one myself.

The Medlink and MedSim conferences strengthened my understanding of medicine, both as a course and a career, reinforcing my desire to read it at University. The obscure mechanics of the heart intrigue me: Biology has deepened my understanding of conditions like atherosclerosis, and how it leads to myocardial infarction or peripheral arterial disease. From an article in a medical journal, I discovered how they can be reduced using anticoagulants or antiplatelet agents. Chemistry increases my practical skills, and allows me to understand everyday phenomena on a molecular level. Latin and Greek indirectly provide me with skills to read medicine. I formed a logical approach doing translations: elucidating the sentence structure and carefully assembling it. Literature produces many heated class discussions; we construct arguments, working as a team to come to a consensus when composing translations. Mathematics has improved my problem-solving and time-keeping skills, as I persevered through challenges despite the volume of work.

Working on a diabetes ward shows me the importance of communication: a patient's anxiety is often due to a fear of the unknown. My fluency in Gujarati allowed me to help a patient who did not speak English; conveying their concerns to the healthcare team was very rewarding. I explore interests that I develop there: I discovered that dual-action insulin can influence the patient in a positive manner, providing more stable blood glucose levels over the day. Volunteering here shows me the unglamorous side of medicine, but convinces me that this is where my future lies.

I spent a week shadowing doctors at Lister Hospital. Endoscopy interested me, having undergone similar procedures myself. Seeing it from the doctor's point of view was powerful as I appreciated the intricacy involved. I was fortunate enough to spend time in Cardiology watching ECGs of stroke patients as well as observing joint replacements and a fasciectomy. I realised how demanding the life of a doctor is, but conversely, when witnessing a patient being told her IVF treatment was successful, I perceived the career satisfaction.

Volunteering for Mencap enables me to work with fine role models with learning disabilities like Down's syndrome. Attending two training courses has improved my knowledge on this topic and developed my interactive skills. I play an active role in the community by volunteering at the Garden House Hospice shop four hours a week and by working closely with children and their eager parents at the Kumon Centre. The past three years here have been fulfilling and have heightened my responsibilities. Volunteering at a GP's practice has shown me the value of the administrative staff and has increased my management and organisational skills.

In school, I am a Senior Prefect and a member of the Classics Society, demonstrating my dependability and self-confidence. I am entrusted with mentoring a Year 10 student: preparing suitable materials, building her confidence, as well as gaining her trust.

In my spare time, I play the violin and piano, the latter of which I have played for ten years; I am currently about to take my Grade 8 examination. I also sing in the school choir, Vox Humana. Completing Bronze Duke of Edinburgh was an achievement as it honed my teamwork skills, requiring cooperation and leadership. In addition, I play sports such as badminton and tennis every week.

I believe that my diverse interests, both academic and extracurricular, have enhanced the skills I need to pursue a career in medicine. I am eager to study this fascinating subject at University and reinforce my skills to make me a worthy doctor in the future.

11.36 Personal statement 36 (A level)

Personal statement successful for: Birmingham, Bristol, Leeds, Nottingham

My recent two-week work experience in a Ghanaian medical centre provided me with exceptional experiences, consolidating my desire to become a doctor. Two incidents stand out as examples of extremes to be found in a medical career. The accidental death of our guide, as he took three of us on a jungle trek, and the realisation that I could do nothing to save him made me acutely aware that doctors regularly face situations in which the saving or extending of life is beyond the realm of medical skill. Conversely, the excitement of sitting in on a consultation with a patient presenting with the rare Diabetes Insipidus, a condition the doctor had not seen in 10 years' practice, was incredible. I was also privileged to stand in theatre and watch a hysterectomy and appendectomy, take and record blood pressure, weigh and check babies and advise mothers on basic baby care. An unbeatable experience which has given me a perspective on medicine I would not otherwise have had.

Shadowing medical staff at Wexham Park Hospital showed me that effective patient care is as much teamwork as individual responsibility. Tolerant junior doctors shared information with me about their 'interesting' patients; I was shown the CT scan of a cancerous tumour and could see the trauma caused to the patient by the tumour pushing aside the rest of the organs in his abdomen. I saw patients on the road to recovery but also the dead body of a man I had spoken to earlier that day and this made me aware of the conscientiousness, yet necessary objectivity, exercised by staff in the care of terminal patients.

At Hillingdon Hospital, a consultant radiologist explained to me how to interpret simple MRI and CT scans and how to detect tumours and calcification of blood vessels. I watched on screen as he injected painkiller into the spine of a patient to discover which vertebra was causing chronic pain. This enabled me to appreciate the radiologist's skill, the intricacy of the human body, the interconnectivity between systems and the genius of MRI and CT machines as diagnostic tools.

Ongoing voluntary work at the National Epilepsy Centre, helping with 'Brain Gym' for those with mental impairment, has shown me that clear communication, great patience and empathy are essential in the treatment of sufferers for whom there is no cure, only control.

As Deputy Head Girl, my responsibilities include initiating an academic mentoring system, helping students understand their learning types, public speaking, coordinating meetings between pupils and teachers and helping at school events. This role has not only furthered my sense of responsibility but enhanced crucial organisational skills. I have completed CSLA, gained Bronze D of E and am completing Silver, have competed nationally in gymnastics and cross country, at county level in athletics and at inter-school level in netball, rounders and swimming. I coach children in gymnastics, have achieved grade 5 drama and my enjoyment of Chemistry motivated me to tutor a pupil for GCSE. These activities, together with waitressing and shop work, I believe, have equipped me with the teamwork skills, time management, patience, diplomacy, determination and endurance vital in medicine. I believe, too, that my Spanish has not only given depth to my other studies but would also be useful for future medical work in Spanish-speaking countries.

At Medlink and PreMed, I learned that life as a doctor is both rewarding and demanding; that it provides ongoing education, that no two days are the same and that a doctor has a direct impact on a patient's life, for better or worse; an enormous responsibility but also hugely fulfilling. As the first person in my immediate and extended family to go to university, I would embrace this opportunity fully and, as someone who thrives on academic and physical challenge, I am eager to pursue medicine as a career.

11.37 Personal statement 37 (A level)

Personal statement successful for: Barts, Imperial College, King's College, UCL

My interest in medicine developed at an early age when I lost my grandfather to lung cancer and I did not understand why. In my quest to find out about the disease I soon found myself fascinated by the human body and how it works and, more recently, the way in which illnesses can be cured and prevented. It took me little time to realise that this was my passion and was what I wanted to study and pursue as a lifelong career due to the variety and dynamic nature of the subject.

By studying Biology at A-level I have discovered that human physiology is my strength, attaining 98% in the AS-level. With Biology and Chemistry I feel that not only have I developed my intellectual skills but I have also learnt to analyse data and research topics effectively, while Further Maths has enhanced my ability to solve problems in a logical manner. After intending to study Ethics to AS-level, my curiosity for the subject has motivated me to continue it at A2. I find that it is extremely relevant in the world of medicine today where advances in science are forever pushing the boundaries of what seems to be morally acceptable and it is only by keeping an open mind that these issues can be resolved.

To reinforce my belief that medicine is the career for me, I spent three weeks at Ashford and St Peter's hospitals both shadowing doctors and helping nurses on the wards. This taught me a great deal about how the wards are run, the administering of drugs and what being a doctor involves on a day-to-day basis, from communicating with patients to team work and interacting with a range of health professionals. I observed the pace of the work, the rigour, skills and level of competence required whilst forging confidence and trust and the responsibility placed on the doctors. After witnessing two abdominal aneurisms, both associated with smoking, I appreciate the role of preventative medicine and why the NHS campaigns to deter people from the habit. Attending a week-long course 'An Introduction to the NHS' and Medlink highlighted the role of the multidisciplinary team in the effective treatment of patients. Additionally, since December 2005 I have been volunteering at a local nursing home where I help with the meals and enjoy communicating with the residents, from whom I learn a vast amount, not only of their chronic debilitating illnesses such as arthritis but also of their invaluable life experiences. As part of the silver Duke of Edinburgh award scheme I have been volunteering in my community assisting the elderly and disabled, thereby raising my awareness of the limitations they face and the need for empathy.

In my free time I am an avid badminton player, playing regularly with my family and at school, as I find that keeping fit is an important part of achieving success in the long run. In the summer I relish the opportunity and challenge of playing cricket for the school's 3rd XI. It is our teamwork and determination which has led to the great success of the team and such qualities are equally important in the medical field.

Being both a mentor and prefect has provided me with great responsibility. However, I enjoy the opportunity to reassure and give sound advice, especially to new students who may feel out of place in an unfamiliar environment. As form representative for the school council, I liaise between staff and students and this has conveyed to me the importance of an open mind when searching for compromise. In addition to responsibilities at school, having a part-time job for over a year has challenged my time management and organisational skills whilst working in a public environment has taught me much about working under pressure and communicating with people of all ages.

With my work experience and varied interaction with people at all levels, I have learnt a lot about the challenging and demanding yet fulfilling nature of medicine and am looking forward to making a positive contribution and enjoying medicine as a lifelong profession.

11.38 Personal statement 38 (A level)

Personal statement successful for: Liverpool

For me, a career in medicine is the perfect opportunity to stimulate my mind in a fascinating field in which I am highly motivated to succeed. I eagerly anticipate the opportunity to be able to combine my caring personality with the practical aspects of the subject, and so have a major impact on people's lives. The prospect of lifelong learning in a subject for which I have such an affinity excites me.

I thoroughly enjoy studying A-level Biology and Chemistry and my intellectual curiosity ensures I stay well ahead of the syllabus. For example, I was recently intrigued by an article on developments in cancer treatment, discussing how antibodies can be engineered to bind to specific antigens on the surface of cancer cells, allowing attached drugs to be delivered directly to tumours, and was inspired to do further research.

More inspiration to choose medicine came from participating in the Access to Medicine Course at King's College London and attending lectures given by top practitioners. A lecture on Cardiac Diseases was particularly relevant as my father suffers from angina and this prompted me to do further research into the subject.

My commitment to study medicine was reinforced by a work experience placement at Princess Royal University Hospital in Orpington, which provided a valuable perspective on the challenges of the profession. As I spent time in the A&E department shadowing the doctors in minors, majors and resuscitation, I gained valuable insight into the roles of both junior doctors and senior consultants. As well as helping me to appreciate the emotional and physical stresses doctors are faced with daily, I saw the rewards of being able to have such a significant impact on patients' lives. As I witnessed consultations, I learned the importance of a good bedside manner, as well as the crucial role of empathy and good communication both with patients and other members of staff.

I currently volunteer at a social gathering for the elderly at my local church, which has been a great opportunity to serve the elderly members. Befriending them and ensuring they have a good time is very rewarding. I also regularly volunteer as part of the 'Welcome Team', where a friendly personality and good communication skills are essential when welcoming guests. Good team work is also crucial to the smooth running of the meetings.

The residential science Summer School at Imperial College was a fantastic experience. Leading a project team required me to be proactive in planning, organising and making decisions to complete our project on time. We achieved a Silver B.A. Crest award for our 'Green Power' project and I was thrilled to receive the 'Most Likely to be a Mentor Award' from the mentors.

Travelling widely in India has been a great experience of life beyond my immediate environment. I attended an international boarding school (Hebron) for 3 years, which enabled me to experience a diverse range of cultures and develop independence and responsibility. Returning to the UK halfway through Year 10 was a challenging experience, having to make friends and catch up on missed work. Hard work and determination, however, resulted in good GCSE grades and election as a prefect by students and staff.

I am a keen table tennis player and play regularly at a local club as well as with my friends and family. I organise a table tennis club for the sixth form as well as an after school club where I offer coaching to beginners. This has not only been of huge enjoyment but has also helped me develop my organisational and leadership skills. I also captained the football and hockey teams at Hebron for two years.

Essentially, I feel I have gained a realistic appreciation of the challenges, both emotional and physical, involved in pursuing a career in medicine, but believe that my experiences have given me the motivation and commitment to withstand such trials and enable me to succeed as a valuable member of the developing medical field.

11.39 Personal statement 39 (A level)

Personal statement successful for: Aberdeen, Dundee, Edinburgh, Glasgow

From a very early age I have been fascinated by science and how things work, particularly in the human body. This, combined with my desire to help people and my concern for the prevention and cure of illness, has confirmed my long-term ambition to become a doctor.

To broaden my knowledge and experience of the medical profession I spent time at Stirling and Falkirk Royal Infirmaries including Cardiology, ENT and Pathology. This gave me a wonderful opportunity to witness first-hand the everyday life of a busy hospital. At A&E the range of patients and excitement of the department showed me that medicine offers a diverse and satisfying career. I was privileged to be given the opportunity to attend several operations, including an endoscopic sinus surgery for sinusitis and nasal polyps. I saw how important good teamwork is and how everybody plays their part. I had many chances to speak to consultants, junior doctors and other staff around the hospital and was inspired by their dedication and positive feedback about their profession. Following my placements in hospitals, I have been shadowing a GP which has given me a perspective of medicine outside the hospital setting and emphasised the importance of a doctor in the community. I am currently volunteering with NHC Action for Children in Alloa which helps to look after vulnerable homeless young people from 16-21. I work at Kumon Education Centre and find it very rewarding to use my knowledge and skills to help educate younger children whilst fulfilling my vocation of working with others. I have attended a 3 month St Andrews Ambulance first aid course which gave me a taste of learning about how to deal with common accidents and medical situations.

As Head Boy and Dux of my school, I play an active part in all aspects of the school, such as organising events, representing the school at functions and communicating the views of my peers. I have completed my bronze and silver Duke of Edinburgh Awards and am now working towards gold. I thoroughly enjoy the responsibility of undertaking these awards and being part of a team in the expeditions. I also represent my school at the Stirling Student Forum and the area at the Forth Valley Young People's Conference. In fifth year, I joined the paired reading scheme which helps younger children who find reading difficult. I won the Arichi prize for science and have represented the school at Chemistry and Physics competitions which enabled me to combine my teamwork with my academic abilities. I attended a week-long Salter's Chemistry Camp in St Andrews University. Having been awarded several gold awards in the UK maths challenge I was then selected for the European mathematical Olympiad. My excellent communication skills have been shown by my achievements in public speaking and debating competitions which, along with regular appearances in our school productions, have earned me full colours. I am a keen musician and have completed grade 4 piano.

Sport plays a very important part in my life, and requires good time management to fit it in alongside all my school activities. I represent the school at rugby (captained the sevens team), football, golf and badminton. I play tennis to a national level, having represented Scotland at Internationals and reaching a ranking of 3 in the country. In order to put something back into the tennis community, I qualified as a coach and regularly assist the Scottish National coach with junior squads. Being involved in the development of people has given me great satisfaction, and I would relish the opportunity to further this in a career within medicine.

My eagerness to study medicine has been reinforced by the awareness and insight I acquired during my work experience. I believe I have the motivation, dedication and commitment to make the most of medical school and university life as a whole. My heart is set on a medical career.

11.40 Personal statement 40 (A level)

Personal statement successful for: Birmingham, Cambridge, UCL

Throughout my school life I have been fascinated by science, and my ambition now is to embark on a career that will contribute to medical knowledge. This is a challenging and competitive field, but I believe I have the dedication and academic ability to achieve great success. Studying four A levels in Maths and Science will give me the grounding I need to study Medicine. I enjoy working with people and would like a career that combines medical research and clinical practice.

I have achieved 5 As at AS level and an early entry B in Economics. I have particularly enjoyed course elements relevant to medicine. For example, the Biology course made me want to learn more about haematology and the complex role of blood, and drug production pathways was an enjoyable part of the Chemistry syllabus. As a member of the college Medical and Chemistry Societies I have attended many lectures, including one talk about rotary motion in mitochondrial enzymes. I was fascinated by the subject, and biochemistry is an area I would like to pursue further. Studying Further Mathematics has been challenging, but has improved my problem solving abilities and Statistics is useful for medicine. Physics is essential for medicine, and studying Economics is useful in a healthcare system that has many financial worries.

My career choice follows work experience in both pure and applied scientific fields. I worked for one week at Addenbrooke's hospital in the Plastic and Oral Surgery ward where interacting with staff and patients helped to improve my communication skills, and I learnt basic clinical techniques such as how to take the blood pressure and temperature of a patient. I also attended the medical induction course Medlink, which I enjoyed because I was introduced to areas of medicine such as paediatrics, psychiatry and neurology. In terms of research, I learnt a lot during a fortnight at the Cambridge Department of Plant Sciences. My role was to set up and take part in students' experiments, during which I became competent at using scientific equipment and enjoyed the discipline of research work. It helped me to achieve distinction in the Analytical Measurement Proficiency Competition.

During weekends I have volunteered at a care home, organising games and entertainment to keep residents active. I have met some wonderful personalities and enjoyed helping them with creative tasks and activities. Talking with elderly people who are suffering from long-term physical and mental illness has helped me to empathise with them and appreciate their needs. I also pursue a range of sporting, musical, outdoor and social activities. I am a Committee Member for the village tennis club and am responsible for managing the website and junior matches. I play cricket and football for the village and cycle into college, all of which helps to keep me fit. With my family I have had many active holidays in Britain and abroad and have visited all the large National Parks in the UK. I have completed the Duke of Edinburgh Bronze and Silver Awards and will soon complete Gold. The expeditions were a fantastic opportunity to lead my group maturely and successfully to the finish.

I play piano and will soon finish Grade 5. I have taught myself bass guitar and formed a rock band. We have successfully built our own website, recorded a CD, and performed at many clubs and festivals. Playing to audiences of up to 300 has given me confidence and my public speaking has also been enhanced through reaching the semi-final in the Youth Debating Competition and the final of the Young Consumer of the Year Competition. For both events I worked with my team to think quickly and present ideas.

A degree in Medicine will provide me with a wide and varied range of opportunities as a career and I would hope to make breakthroughs into new drugs and medical techniques. I want to work on diseases such as HIV/AIDS and tuberculosis which have such a devastating effect on people in developing countries.

11.41 Personal statement 41 (A level)

Personal statement successful for: King's College, Leeds, Newcastle

Medicine, as a cocktail of hard science, social interaction and pragmatic thinking, suits me more than any other discipline. The precision with which medicine explains the complex human body thrills me. Meanwhile, the ever dynamic nature of the subject, its constant progression, appeals to me greatly since it makes a medical career one of lifelong learning. Honestly, I haven't met a doctor who has not experienced great pressure intellectually, emotionally and physically in his/her professional life. But somehow, I regard the challenging nature of the occupation to be a merit, something which adds to the job satisfaction. Studying medicine creates the possibility to have an intellectual and rewarding career working with people of high expertise and thus would allow me to fulfil many of my goals for the future.

Medicine is also a discipline with which I am familiar. Three years of after-school receptionist work at Tollgate Surgery have rendered me at ease with the medical setting and patients. Observing consultants in ophthalmology and family planning, I have experienced theatre settings and seen the rewards of specialisation. Sitting-in with GPs has shown me the importance of a good patient/doctor rapport. It also highlighted that sensitivity to a patient's mental and social conditions, as well as physical, is integral to providing care. Volunteering in Northern India with a group of doctors and medical students to offer health camps for nomads also gave me insight into primary healthcare delivery in rural, underdeveloped areas. Encountering patients sceptical about modern diagnosis and treatments, and learning about the traditional Amchi practices, made me appreciate the effect cultural setting can have on care delivery. More than anything, my time there showed me that working with and learning from a team of able, driven individuals is hugely stimulating.

From a young age, I have enjoyed contributing to my community and in 2005 I received the Princess Diana Memorial Award and was nominated as Colchester Volunteer of the Year. More recently, since last October I've spent an afternoon each week in an underprivileged community helping children with homework and teaching them English. In college, I have been involved in mediation and peer listening, the principals of which have helped me enhance my interpersonal skills. And in my holidays, I was involved in a summer scheme for refugee children in South London. I particularly enjoy voluntary work which involves my own interests, therefore this term I've taken up training athletes for Special Olympics.

At 15, I won a place at the newly founded United World College Costa Rica. Seeing communication as vital, my decision was swayed by a desire to learn a new language. Being involved in building such an international community has been an invaluable experience. I have learnt how to overcome cultural differences which, in the increasingly multicultural setting of the UK, would come in useful in a medical career. I have also developed a high level of conscientiousness through living with people of 75 different nationalities which is another key quality for a doctor. Finally, while living in an intense environment and trying to meet a high academic standard, I have learnt to maintain a healthy work-life balance. Thus, I enjoy many activities here from Sign Language classes to Latin American dance.

The last two years of living away from home have taught me a great deal about independence. Faced with myriad opportunities opened by the UWC movement, I have really had to evaluate my goals, from which subject to study to in which country to do so. The fact that I am still applying to medicine is a testament to my dedication to the career. Moreover, I genuinely believe that I would contribute successfully through the medical profession.

11.42 Personal statement 42 (A level)

Personal statement successful for: Belfast, Birmingham, Cardiff, Imperial College

I have always gained a deep sense of fulfilment from striving towards the well-being of others. The opportunity to have such a tangible and direct impact on patients' lives, and to pursue my passion for human biology, is what compels me to study medicine.

To gain a greater insight into a life in medicine, I spent a week at a GP clinic, during which I was fascinated by the role of the GP as one of the 'frontlines' of the NHS. I realised the need for an approachable figure in whom people can confide, and the array of interpersonal skills needed to establish a good rapport with the patient. A week at the A&E department at the Hillingdon Hospital and talking to the staff there has taught me about how doctors deal with pressure, such as their ability to communicate effectively with their team in emergencies and to prioritise cases according to clinical need. I also arranged a three week placement at hospitals in Sri Lanka and India, which gave me the chance to compare healthcare in the subcontinent with that in the NHS. I was touched by the doctors' sensitivity to complex social issues, such as the patient's socio-economic status when deciding on the treatment. Whilst studying ECGs with a cardiologist I learnt about the analytical skills required to process data before arriving at a sound diagnosis.

My placements have highlighted to me the qualities of a good doctor, and I have actively sought to hone them in me. I spent a month in India working on an HIV counselling programme, in which I had the opportunity to work closely with sex workers to help raise their awareness on sexual health. As these issues carry with them a deep social stigma in India, I approached the project with great sensitivity and a strong determination to help. By overcoming unique barriers in developing rapport and trust, like language and confidentiality, I have greatly enhanced my communication skills. Since June 2008, I have enjoyed volunteering regularly at the Three Wings Trust, supervising children with disabilities in after-school play sessions. It is a great responsibility that involves my taking the initiative in resolving distressing situations involving difficult behaviour; I remained patient and empathetic towards the children and their parents alike. I have also been volunteering weekly at a local nursing home for the past nine months. As I care for the residents during their social sessions, I have learnt to adapt my approach according to their individual needs and personalities. My experiences here have spurred me to work as an HCA at a Dementia Care Unit, where through my use of non-verbal communication I have interacted successfully with Alzheimer's patients. Working as part of a healthcare team has impressed on me how important flexibility and upholding morale are in teamwork when delivering care to the patient. In my year as a mentor, whereby I was responsible for the pastoral care of lower school pupils, I always maintained an approachable image for anybody seeking advice. I thus balanced my role as a leader and role model with that of a friend and confidant.

Cricket is a passion of mine; I play regularly for my local team, which has developed my teamwork skills under pressure. I also swim for my local club, which is an ideal way for me to cope with stress. It has also taught me the value of perseverance in achieving my goals. As the co-founder of the school's Amnesty International Group, the last four years have developed in me proficient leadership skills. I have led and supported my fellow members as I organised logistically demanding events, such as sponsored walks and assemblies. Through delegation, I have brought out the strengths of my colleagues. As a history enthusiast, I have worked as a part of a team on a publication exploring the abhorrence of genocide, entitled 'Why Should We Remember?'

Finally, these experiences have imbued in me a strong sense of commitment to medicine; I will truly cherish the opportunity to study it.

11.43 Personal statement 43 (A level)

Personal statement successful for: St George's

In July 2008 I joined Albany House Dental Practice as Practice Manager. I was responsible for the daily running of the practice, including dealing with emergencies, Devon Doctors and visiting hygienist appointments. I was also responsible for the Human Resources of the practice: I wrote and implemented the Health and Safety policies and procedures, the company contracts and many recruitment initiatives. At Albany House I learnt to use AutoCAD architectural software and used this to design a new, more efficient practice in a nearby building with improved access. This passed planning permission and was completed in June 2009. My position at Albany House was an invaluable learning experience and I took an active interest in expanding my knowledge base for the role. I attended advanced resuscitation training, a course entitled 'Dealing with Emergencies in the Dental Surgery' and I also explored new ways to expand the practice by attending the Aesthetic Medicine Exhibition in February 2009.

In August 2009 I gained a position as a Healthcare Assistant at Hays House Nursing Home where I am currently employed. Hays House is a very well respected home with 43 residents with an emphasis on dementia and palliative care. My role includes delivering full personal care to all the residents. My responsibilities include washing and dressing, application and charting of topical medicines, feeding and fluid intake assistance, maintaining food and fluid charts, assistance with mobility and with nurses in delivering medication. This is a highly responsible role involving being alone with vulnerable patients, many of whom cannot perform basic tasks of self-care. It is my job to closely observe the resident's health on a daily basis and formally report and log any changes to their condition in order to allow their care to be constantly adapted to their changing needs.

Hays House maintains very high clinical standards with medical gloves changed between each patient and strict regulations on the use of hand rub and sterilisation between patients. Full barrier nursing has been in operation for a resident who had contracted MRSA after a recent hospital visit. Hygiene is of the utmost importance, many of our residents have stoma bags, catheters or convenes and other dressings which must be maintained to the highest possible standard. My role involves the management of any pressure sores and of turn charts for several residents. I thoroughly enjoy my role at Hays House; it has been an unparalleled experience of intense patient contact and has cemented my desire to pursue a career in Medicine. I am constantly looking for ways to improve the range of care which I can deliver. I attend regular training courses such as moving and handling, emergency procedures and in January 2010 I have registered to take the Weldmar Hospicecare Trust course on Palliative Care Skills for Healthcare Assistants.

I have been inspired to embark on a career in medicine through my work, the excitement of scientific endeavour and by the people I have known who have struggled against disability and cancer. Their unfailing personal strength and belief in the medical profession have cemented my resolve to pursue a life in medicine. My aunt who was diagnosed with Multiple Sclerosis in her early twenties has been a great inspiration to me. Watching her treatment and her daily struggle with the disease serves to show how it is not only doctors who give hope to patients, but patients who give hope and inspiration to doctors.

During my preparation for this application I have felt a powerful sense of fulfilment and purpose in my work in the medical field. I have recently been accepted on to a work experience placement at Salisbury NHS Foundation Trust where I hope to widen my patient contact experience. I am a hardworking, dedicated and enthusiastic individual and I believe that there is no better way to apply my skills than in the pursuit of excellence in the medical profession.

11.44 Personal statement 44 (A level)

Personal statement successful for: Brighton, Cardiff, Leicester

My ambition to become a doctor stems from both a fascination with science and a desire to work with people. When I first investigated Medicine as a career path, I was struck by the continuous scientific learning undertaken by even the most senior of the profession. This prospect excited me as I enjoy encountering challenges in my everyday life, and it is definitely an aspect I look forward to in a medical degree and career.

I regularly search newspapers for medical articles and have a subscription to the Student BMJ; these have provided me with more in-depth knowledge of life as a doctor and current issues in Medicine. I was given a great opportunity to increase my knowledge when I independently secured a week of work experience at my local hospital, in the orthopaedic department. There, I gained a first-hand understanding of the hospital environment, and of how a specialist works. The valuable experience of shadowing the consultants reinforced my career aspirations. I have also arranged weekly voluntary work within the wards of the hospital to expand on my understanding.

Healthcare is a broad, multifaceted industry, thus I wanted to gain a more holistic understanding of how it functions. In order to do this I visited a local clinical trials unit attached to a surgery. While there, I spoke to senior nurses about their work and observed the monitoring of patients. This involved taking ECG readings, blood tests and, more fundamentally, communication with the patient. At both placements, it struck me how often more useful information was acquired through this method than through medical tests.

For several months I volunteered at a residential home for adults with severe learning disabilities. This allowed me a great insight into patient contact in a care environment. My duties involved waking the residents and serving them breakfast. I got to know several of the residents; this further improved my communication skills – particularly my listening ability. This built on the experience I gained acting as a peer mentor. Helping to care for vulnerable people gave me a real sense of satisfaction.

A strong mental attitude is an important quality for a doctor to have, so that he/she is able to remain calm even when under immense pressure. I believe that participating in the Duke of Edinburgh Silver Award helped to develop empathy and communication skills. It takes great leadership to encourage a team to persevere, when two team members have already dropped out and those remaining are tired and cold on the second day of a three-day expedition. I was able to fill that role and we succeeded in the end.

I was afforded greater opportunity to increase my leadership and mentoring skills by captaining my football team and also coaching a youth team. I have played basketball for Swindon and given up time at school to help the year eight basketball team to practise. These roles require persistence, enthusiasm and a sense of humour, as such qualities are necessary to earn respect as a leader and a motivator.

In my spare time I work in a local supermarket taking on a variety of responsibilities, which makes it enjoyable. I am frequently tasked with a security role that also involves welcoming customers to the store; this requires both vigilance and an open, friendly manner.

While at secondary school I was Managing Director of a highly successful Young Enterprise Company; we won six awards including best U16s in the county. As House Captain I was responsible for the organisation of sports teams and for speaking in assemblies about competition results. I feel that both of these positions developed my organisational abilities and my ability to cope with responsibility.

Medicine is a profession which requires a strong mental attitude, complex scientific knowledge and excellent social adaptability. I believe I am capable of combining these skills into a lifelong medical career and look forward to having the opportunity to do so.

11.45 Personal statement 45 (A level)

Personal statement successful for: Cambridge

By becoming a doctor, I believe that I'd gain the skills to put to great effect my experience shaping health systems in developing countries and knowledge gained from studying health economics and policy. Once a doctor, I'll fulfil my desire to have a direct impact on a patient's health.

While working with ministries of health in sub-Saharan Africa has been rewarding, I want something more. I've spent months working on behalf of an international organization, but it was Michael, a homeless man, who stoked my desire to become a doctor. I got to know Michael when I was volunteering in San Francisco General Hospital's emergency department. The last time I saw him we exchanged small talk, but this time he continued to talk about his life. He paused mid-sentence and went for my hand. He told me he was tired of the pain and wanted to die. I stood silent not knowing what to say. I was frustrated that I didn't have the skills or knowledge to make his situation even just a little better.

Michael was a regular in the emergency department. He was born in the Tenderloin and lived near 6th Street — a yet-to-be-gentrified San Francisco neighbourhood infamous for single occupancy hotels frequented by drug addicts and prostitutes. The sad part is that Michael's situation was not unique. Michael's cancer and pain, like that of others who've lived in underserved areas like his, was a result of his socio-economic environment.

In the third year of undergrad at the University of California at Berkeley, I read a book by Dr. Paul Farmer that helped me cement the connection between health, society and economics. The book convinced me that I needed to be able to explain both a doctor's and a health system's behaviour in order to become effective at improving a person's health. While a chemistry major at the time, I was certain I wanted to become a doctor. But I kept feeling disconnected between what I was learning and how I could apply my scientific knowledge to improving a patient's and society's health. I immediately began to study public health.

Following college, I pursued a Master's degree at the London School of Economics in health economics and policy. My coursework focused on using economic principles to provide evidence and rationale in designing efficient and equitable health policies.

I've since applied my learning to my job at the World Bank, where I work in the Africa Human Development division on health. In striving for the Millennium Development Goals by 2015, many countries around the world, particularly in sub-Saharan Africa (SSA), realise that reducing infant mortality, maternal mortality and preventing non-communicable diseases will take an appropriate health workforce with appropriate skills to fight the tasks ahead. While many SSA countries design plans to increase the stock, types, productivity and distribution of health workers, determining the costs for such plans has been out of reach. I've helped design and implement a model that puts a price on national human resources for health (HRH) strategies and plans. In this way, I've helped health ministries in Ghana and Sierra Leone deliver healthcare in a more efficient way.

But despite all the work I've done for the World Bank, it was Michael's situation that had the biggest effect on me. It helped me realise that medicine was more than just the study of the body's biology. I've learned that medicine is the deep and intimate relationship between the body and its interaction with society: a society that is influenced by both politics and economics.

I know that many will question why I'm shifting from working as a junior health economist into medicine. While effecting change at a health system's level is crucial to a sustainable public's health, I desire something more. Because of my health system's perspective and experience, taking this next step to become a doctor will satisfy my itch to make a positive and direct impact on a person's health.

However, just as a doctor's individual connection with people, breadth and depth of knowledge are necessary to help people like Michael, so is being cognizant of the greater health system to create effective and broader health change. As a doctor, it will be my duty to not only serve as an individual service practitioner but as a public servant to the community, state and nation to which I live.

11.46 Personal statement 46 (A level)

Personal statement successful for: Cambridge, Edinburgh, Newcastle, Nottingham

For me, medicine is the most exciting subject of all. It unites my interest in human biology with my love of pure science. It is constantly evolving and will challenge and stimulate me throughout my life – I will never stop learning. My enjoyment in studying cardiovascular disease in A-level biology strengthened my attraction to medical studies. I have always been interested in medicine, but the ill health and demise of a close relative made me think of it as a vocation as well as a career. There is also a huge range of career opportunities within medicine, from community work and bedside care, to academic research and laboratory work. The difficulty would be in choosing which path to follow!

I regularly read New Scientist and The British Medical Journal, fostering my interest in, and knowledge of, medicine. In talking to a GP, I learned of our ageing population and the challenges this presents to our healthcare system. We touched on the difficulties of choosing priorities when faced with many demands on limited resources. During my school's recent biology expedition to South Africa, the camp doctor brought other aspects of medicine, such as hygiene and basic emergency procedures, to my attention. Later that summer, I witnessed medical care in a busy teaching hospital in York. While there, I attended clinics in Oncology and Gynaecology where I saw ultrasound scanning. I watched endoscopies and a thyroidectomy and was struck by the skill of the surgeons and the crucial role of every member of the team. While shadowing nurses, I admired their patience and compassion in delivering close patient care. I talked to several doctors, gaining an impression of the emotional aspects of working closely with ill people, from dealing with death to saving lives. Furthermore, I gained some insight into the tiredness and stress that is part of the job.

From my experiences, I learned that the role of a doctor is a demanding one that encompasses the science of diagnosis and the art of dealing with patients. It requires an ability to listen and communicate, and to explain technical terms and complicated problems simply. I believe that much of medical practice concerns the management of symptoms, as we don't have cures to as many diseases as is popularly believed.

I am a keen actor, having been involved in productions of 'The Fiddler on the Roof' and 'Kiss Me Kate'. I also sing in the Chamber Choir. I love sport, playing regularly in the 1st XI hockey team and running a football activity for younger students. Currently, I am leading the development of a nature trail around the school grounds with young members of the Natural History Society. My responsibility for these after-school activities involves talking to, and motivating, a wide range of people from the youngest students to members of staff. It has developed and stretched my organisational, communication and time management skills to the full!

Outside school I have been a passionate horse rider for ten years and have won my village stable management prize for three consecutive years! I am also a member of a local football team. Last year I worked as a volunteer one evening a week for 3 months in the Oxfam shop in York Hospital to gain my Duke of Edinburgh Bronze Award. I also volunteered to feed the homeless in Arclight, a local shelter. In these roles I gained extra confidence in working with a wide variety of people. Recently, I participated in The York Civic Trust's Georgian Ball, which was very educational (and enjoyable!), learning about manners, attitudes and dancing in the Georgian period.

Everything that I have read about medicine, discussed with medical professionals and experienced as a volunteer has strengthened my determination to study this fascinating subject. I know that I will encounter challenges on a daily basis as a doctor, but I am certain that I will more than meet them and thoroughly enjoy doing so. I look forward with immense excitement to studying medicine.

11.47 Personal statement 47 (A level)

Personal statement successful for: Birmingham, Cambridge, King's College, UCL

A tanker colliding with a motorbike; a poor man who couldn't afford shoes or medication; a sick grandmother's unconditional love; when I look back upon my life, these moments stand out, not only as life-changing experiences but ones that subconsciously fuelled my childhood desire for medicine. At a young age, I saw someone die in front of my eyes. Although a very traumatic experience, I learned to understand and respect the true fragility of life. I felt helpless and insignificant; I wanted to be in a position to make a difference. I didn't realise it then, but my aspirations for a career in medicine had just begun.

Medicine offers the unique opportunity to integrate my dedication to science with my natural flair for interacting with people. As I matured, my yearning for medicine only grew stronger. I undertook a four-week placement shadowing a GP, which allowed me to become familiar with the full primary care cycle. I learned to empathise with patients about their illness in their time of need and saw the progression of their health, interacting with them throughout their visits.

I arranged for another placement week at a district general hospital in order to experience the secondary care aspect of the NHS. It was a hectic week in which I observed an MRI scan, a lumbar puncture and an angioplasty. These procedures were fascinating and I was impressed by the efficiency and professional manner with which they were carried out. I was also given the opportunity to see an electron microscope and a mass spectrometer being utilised. This made me appreciate the necessity for a sound scientific basis as I saw the theory that I had learnt being applied in a hospital environment.

During the week, my self-belief and interpersonal skills improved tremendously, especially whilst conversing with terminally ill patients and senior clinicians. On an acute ward round, I bore witness to two cancer patients being told that they had less than three months to live. This was hard to come to terms with. However, I persevered and helped care for the patients when the opportunity allowed. I was able to gather my thoughts and accept that medicine consists of both curative and palliative elements.

I am fluent in English, Hindi, Urdu and Punjabi – highlighting my excellent communication skills. I have achieved grade eight in both piano and electronic keyboard and my commitment towards such a time-consuming activity shows my intense dedication. I enjoy playing cricket and have played at a club level for many years which has taught me the importance of teamwork – similar to a challenging Duke of Edinburgh expedition on an extremely hot day, which proved that, with enough determination, teamwork can achieve inspiring results.

I have attended several leadership and problem-solving courses and have over twenty hours of flying experience with the armed forces. These activities have not only helped me hone my communication and organisation skills, but have also improved my physical and mental stamina. I undertook an Open University module in 'Molecules Medicines and Drugs' to further expand my knowledge, whilst also conducting extra reading on cancer to supplement my observations during work experience. I am an avid reader of New Scientist and Student BMJ, as these allow me to keep up to date with recent findings within the profession to which I truly aspire.

My voluntary experience has made me aware that medicine is a challenging profession, which is laborious, time-consuming and one that requires an extraordinary amount of dedication. However, when I get to see the look of fulfilment on a doctor's face when they have helped a patient in their time of need, I know that there can be no better feeling, and every part of me wishes to experience it for myself later on. I believe that my love for science along with my caring and empathetic nature coupled with a passionate drive to succeed and my strong communication skills make medicine the only career for me.

11.48 Personal statement 48 (A level)

Personal statement successful for: Cambridge, Imperial College, King's College, Nottingham

My interest in Medicine is in part due to the fact that I will enjoy the problem solving involved in taking histories and making diagnoses. Medicine will allow me to treat and care for patients, whilst working in demanding situations. Additionally, the high level of clinical ability that can be attained after reading medicine is something I look forward to. Furthermore I have always had a fascination with science. For example, at the age of 15, I undertook AS level physics after school. This meant juggling my work load to maintain my scientific interest. In addition, my interest in the caring profession is due to time that I have spent assisting the staff at an elderly day care centre. I admired the patience and dedication they displayed towards the elderly and I particularly enjoyed helping and interacting with the service users.

I recently attended Mediprep, a conference for medical applicants, which improved my understanding of the course and career. In particular, I have become more aware of the challenges of Medicine such as the need to undertake continued assessment beyond graduation. Finally, I read the student BMJ to keep abreast of the latest medical news and I attend my school's medical ethics society to discuss topics such as organ donation.

To confirm my interest in Medicine, I undertook work experience at a GP's surgery shadowing a GP at Easter 2007. During this time, I reviewed and filed incoming correspondence, which helped me to appreciate the range of medical problems dealt with by GPs. I also observed how GPs communicate with and treat patients, particularly taking histories of patient illnesses and making a diagnosis. This experience impressed upon me the need for strong communication and interpersonal skills when advising patients. This experience made me appreciate that doctors can help patients even where there is no medical cure.

In summer 2007, I completed work experience at both Selly Oak and Northwick Park hospitals. At Selly Oak hospital, I spent time in a liver out-patients clinic. In contrast to the GP surgery, this experience gave me exposure as to how specialist units operate and the focused knowledge of the doctors who work in this unit.

I also participate in extracurricular activities such as the charitable work I do at a 'British Heart Foundation' shop. I am also involved in team events such as creating science news podcasts, available for download from our school website, which I undertook with several classmates. I acted as the team leader, organising meetings and being responsible for ensuring that team members completed their tasks. This role has greatly improved my leadership and organisation abilities. I am a school prefect and my duties include helping at the school's entrance exam and acting as a tour guide at the school's Open Day.

Throughout year 12, I mentored a year 7 pupil, once a week during lunch break. I helped him with his maths by explaining any problems with which he had difficulty and I tried to improve his confidence in his own ability. Last year, I obtained a Sports Leadership Award, which is the first step towards becoming a sports coach. This helped me to advance my communication and interpersonal skills when coaching groups of children, whilst at the same time obtaining a recognised qualification.

In my recreational time, I like to play football and badminton with friends. I also enjoy painting and drawing, which is why I chose to do A level Art. Art has helped to balance the intensive academic science subjects I have undertaken at A level with something more creative. As part of an Art history study, I am visiting Paris in October 2007 to view a number of paintings such as Claude Monet's 'Series' paintings.

Medicine offers a tough and strenuous path but I believe that I possess the necessary energy, enthusiasm and determination to thrive on the challenges.

11.49 Personal statement 49 (A level)

Personal statement successful for: Bristol, Cambridge, UCL

I have always had a strong interest in the sciences, especially chemistry, which first attracted me to a career in medicine. The intricate nature of synthetic and natural processes, as explained by modern science, truly intrigues me and I enjoy the methodical and analytical approach. Last year I linked my physics project to medicine by researching materials used for hip prosthetics. Through work experience placements, I have discovered many other elements of the medical profession that I find appealing. For example, I am very motivated by the human interaction, variety offered and team work needed to work effectively with colleagues and treat each patient as an individual. The continuous learning that occurs in the medical profession because of the depth and breadth of the subject also interests me greatly. The final key reason why I am inspired to study medicine is that I feel it is a very worthwhile career and something that I would be committed to spending the rest of my life doing.

To further my understanding of the medical profession I have undertaken several work experience placements over the past two years. I worked at a play centre for disabled children on a weekly basis for six months where I enjoyed interacting with the children and was also able to develop my communication skills. After half an hour, during one very rewarding session, I managed to get two girls with Down's syndrome, who fought frequently despite being friends, to understand that they should not throw sand at each other. I have been working at a children's hospice since January and through this have discovered another way in which doctors are involved in the community. In July I spent four days at the Royal Sussex County Hospital where I was shown a variety of different aspects to medicine including ward rounds, laboratory work and clinics. One of the patients being cared for by the Infectious Diseases department where I was based had bacterial meningitis. I was shown her scans as well as her cerebrospinal fluid sample and from the care of this patient I was able to see the team work involved not only within the hospital but also with community organisations. For a week in August I was based at Woking Community Hospital where I was shown a variety of different departments and witnessed the removal of a sebaceous cyst, which I found fascinating. The four days I spent at Medlink also reinforced my interest in medicine and I particularly enjoyed the A&E role play session. In order to gain some understanding of the constant developments in medicine as well as in other areas of science, I have recently started reading the New Scientist as well as visiting the BMJ website.

Outside of school I am part of a Tae Kwon Do club and I also enjoy the physical challenge and outdoors nature of windsurfing. I have completed both my Bronze and Silver Duke of Edinburgh Awards and aim to finish my Gold in February. The team element of the expeditions has been a real highlight of all three awards and in preparation for my Gold final I completed a wilderness first aid course. I also have a strong interest in music and have achieved Grade 5 piano as well as playing guitar. Within the school community I have assisted with weekly paired reading and contributed to sports day and RAG week along with prospective parent tours. On top of this, I have been working at WH Smith which has given me the opportunity to interact with many people.

In summary, it is the attractions of team work, interacting with patients and having the opportunity to make a difference, along with my fascination in the sciences and the desire to keep learning that compel me to pursue a career in medicine. I know from personal experience that the impact a medic and their team can make on someone's life is huge and would like to have such a responsibility, doing something that I have a true interest in and passion for.

11.50 Personal statement 50 (A level)

Personal statement successful for: Bristol, Cambridge, Imperial College, UCL

It has always amazed me how the human organism can be reduced to a complex soup of biological molecules, yet displays emergent properties, like consciousness, so distinctly removed from the biochemical sum of its parts. My current study of science continues to magnify my wonder in the intricate beauty of life, and my desire to study medicine is driven by the prospect of integrating a scientific perspective with the diversity of the human condition. My work experience has shown me that medicine is a mentally stimulating and constantly changing profession, with the possibility of applying biological understanding in the practical solution of globally pressing issues such as HIV/AIDS. The development of antiretroviral drugs targeting Reverse Transcriptase was a topic I investigated with Pfizer researchers on Biology Project Week. I tested the potency of candidate compounds in inhibiting this enzyme and disrupting the mechanism of retroviral replication. This opportunity contextualised theoretical biology in a medical situation, and gave me an appreciation of the pharmacological basis of medical treatment.

Shadowing a respiratory medicine team in the NHS Kent & Canterbury Hospital through ward rounds, chest clinics and bronchoscopy sessions, I found that the process of diagnosing disease exemplifies the intellectual rewards of medicine as a profession requiring rigorous problem solving. Each patient is presented as a puzzle, whose pieces represent evidence collected from a diverse range of techniques, from scans and physical examinations, to physiological symptoms and occupational background. The experience was at times humbling, especially when I observed a patient being informed that he had lung cancer; I learned thus that medicine requires both intellectual and humanistic understanding.

As a volunteer in a Psychogeriatric Day Centre for five weeks, I engaged my creativity by producing activities for use in occupational therapy, thus aiding in the rehabilitation of mentally ill patients. Through attending cognitive behavioural group therapy sessions, I developed a genuine empathy with the depressed mind and an appreciation of the motivations governing the behaviour of the elderly. The diversity of patients with their individual histories kept the experience constantly refreshing, and this insight into mental health has helped me to develop a fascination in the diseases of the brain. Neurological illnesses are so frightening because organic damage to the nervous system has a translational effect on our actions and behaviour, redefining the philosophical concept of who we are, as demonstrated by the characters in the works of Oliver Sacks. Exploring this interest in neuroscience, I independently researched and wrote an essay entitled 'There's only one way to make a brain. Discuss', which was highly commended for the Peterhouse Science prize.

Applying analytical skills, I write articles on the social and ethical implications of science for the school's online science journal: www.youngscientists.co.uk. I enjoy playing many sports, from table football to hurdling for the school's athletics team. As assistant stage manager during the house evening of entertainment, I coordinated backstage activity and designed props for use in an adaptation of Shakespeare. Every Thursday afternoon during the past year, I have helped supervise a pre-prep class, nurturing creativity through art sessions and encouraging the innate curiosity of children in their environment. This has enhanced my communication skills, and the satisfaction of caring for the children has affirmed my desire to pursue a medical career.

With diligent determination and an eagerness to understand humanity, I feel that I am ready to embark upon the lifelong commitment that is the study of medicine, and become tomorrow's doctor.

11.51 Personal statement 51 (A level)

Personal statement successful for: Cambridge, Manchester, UCL

A keen scientist from a young age, I have always been fascinated by human physiology. Whilst the structural framework of the human body is undoubtedly impressive, it is the complex array of systems, organs and cells, which keep the body functioning through chemical processes that I find particularly awe-inspiring. Fusing a deep love for the sciences with my keen desire to help and care for others, Medicine seemed a logical career route for me.

My work experience at Barnet General Hospital and Edgware Community Hospital removed any doubts about my career choice. Two moments stand out: shadowing an orthopaedic surgeon, I was moved by how he put a young girl at ease during a thorough but discreet examination, and by the trust that she clearly placed within him. Despite the subsequent diagnosis of in-toeing gait, this strong relationship meant that the parents were able to cope better with the news. Later, in the intense and energetic A&E department at Barnet Hospital, I felt the concern of the doctors dealing with an unresponsive and unconscious patient whose condition was not consistent with his statistics. Working as a team, the tension was evident as the consultants were forced to make tough decisions with limited evidence in order to revive the patient. Despite witnessing the long work hours and the administrative chores, I learnt that doctors are members of a compassionate profession and combine a firm foundation in biomedical science with emotional intelligence, empathy and clinical judgement.

My interests in the subject further developed after I attended an 'Exploring Healthcare' spring school and a recent Medsim conference. From lectures to laboratory work, and from clinical practice to participation in PBL, I found the course an invaluable learning experience. I especially enjoyed wearing surgical scrubs and putting my manual dexterity to the test whilst performing a simulation of keyhole surgery. Although I was initially apprehensive about being observed by practitioners during this procedure, this challenging clinical task gave me a sense of the pressures encountered by surgeons on a daily basis.

My school achievements include a contribution of 200 hours' worth of voluntary service for the Millennium Volunteers scheme. Although volunteering weekly at Marie Foster Centre was an overwhelming and difficult experience at first, caring for patients who suffer from Multiple Sclerosis has been intrinsically rewarding and satisfying. I established the awareness that doctors need regarding the social and psychological dimensions to the lives of their patients. I also contributed to a mentoring programme for students aged 12 and 13, supporting them in particular fields of maths and science. My ability to communicate with consideration and to respond to children effectively has improved a great deal. I successfully completed the expedition required for the Silver Duke of Edinburgh award: a challenge reinforcing the importance of teamwork. Outside school, my work in Waitrose enables me to engage with a variety of people and has taught me to handle stressful situations using effective communication skills combined with self-confidence. Playing badminton with my friends at the local sports centre has become a part of my weekly timetable, in addition to regular table tennis and swimming. My interaction with diverse people on a regular basis has encouraged me to travel annually, learning about various cultures and backgrounds.

My experiences to date have allowed me to appreciate the vast boundaries of medicine. I am looking forward, however, to a lifetime of learning and a long journey towards possessing the expertise necessary to be of valuable service to society. I have always pursued my studies and all other goals in my life with rigour and conviction and I will continue to do so at university and beyond.

11.52 Personal statement 52 (A level)

Personal statement successful for: Bristol, Cambridge, Imperial College, King's College

A day may come when our practice of Medicine is so advanced that we no longer fear illness, and, to reach that ideal, students who are committed to giving their best to the subject are needed. I believe I am one of those students. A career in Medicine will involve challenges and pressures, but will ultimately be rewarding to society and personally fulfilling. I am enthused by the research and development of new and increasingly sophisticated treatments, medication and technology, but also with the caring aspects of the doctor-patient relationship, and I know this will involve a lifetime of learning and applying knowledge and skills.

Recently, I arranged a three-week work experience placement in the Gastroenterology and Ophthalmology departments at the Royal Liverpool Hospital. After speaking to both junior doctors and consultants, I gained insights into their work, noted the importance of asking the right questions of a patient, of listening skills in searching for clues, and of making patients feel at ease. I also witnessed procedures including colonoscopies, the insertion of drains, vitrectomies and artificial lens insertions in theatre. I saw how doctors and patients forged bonds with each other, and this led me to join the Red Cross as a qualified First Aid Volunteer. I have since been on many duties where I have been thrilled to provide assistance to people in need. As a compassionate person, I have developed my listening skills and the ability to keep myself and others calm in a situation.

Last summer, after winning a scholarship, I attended the Medical Future Leaders Summit in Los Angeles as part of the prestigious International People-to-People Programme. This enabled me to investigate recent research into stem cells, to argue a real-life case study for a patient to receive a liver transplant and to develop my leadership skills. These have already helped me in my appointment as Head Boy at my school. I am continually growing as a confident public speaker and team leader, and I hope that these skills serve me well in the future so that one day I may become a top expert in a field of Medicine and travel to many venues to give lectures and train future doctors. To experience medical research, I secured a four-week Nuffield Bursary research placement where I studied why social attitudes have affected public perception of sex education and the sexual health of Britain's youth. My involvement with NAGTY summer schools has allowed me to attend many enriching courses (such as Anthropology and Robotics), which have helped develop my character.

Competitively, I have captained my school's Chemistry team to victory in the this year's National RSC Top of the Bench competition. I feel that I was an effective leader for the team, as I was able to coordinate our efforts to complete the range of challenges as well as maintaining morale. These are important attributes of a doctor that apply directly to hospital life. Whilst Chemistry has given me a solid basis for understanding areas of Medicine, such as the mechanisms of drug action, Physics and Maths have helped me develop my logic and problem-solving abilities, which are indispensable in a diagnostic medical career. In Physics, I achieved my school's highest ever Gold Award in the Physics Challenge, whilst in Biology I scored 100% at AS level along with a 97% average module score in all subjects.

I enjoy playing all manner of sports. I hold a Black Belt in the Korean martial art Kuk Sool and two years ago I won the coveted UK Junior Grand Champion Title. In addition, I have completed the Duke of Edinburgh Bronze Award, and represented my school in Basketball where we came fourth nationally, both of which required teamwork, cooperation, handling pressure and resourcefulness.

Medicine is not just a career; it is a challenging vocation and one in which I feel I can succeed using the skills and achievements that I have already acquired, and those that I will work hard to gain at Medical School.

11.53 Personal statement 53 (A level)

Personal statement successful for: Bristol, Cambridge, Cardiff, Newcastle

My lifelong ambition to study medicine perfectly combines the people and problem solving skills I am developing and my very keen interest in science. I also find the medical field exciting and dynamic, such as the recent article I have read about the use of aerosol sprays containing cultivated skin cells as an alternative to skin grafting. Medicine is more than relating symptoms to treatments. I feel that I can make a positive impact on people's lives and have the ability to gain the patients' trust.

Work Experience at the Severn Hospice has shown me the importance of the more emotionally demanding side of medicine, palliative care, so people with life-threatening illnesses can enjoy more comfortable and dignified lives. Whilst helping to feed patients on my weekly visits to the Midlands Centre for Spinal Injuries, I have become a more sympathetic listener and interact better with patients. This led to my interest in the use of embryonic stem cells to grow back parts of the spinal cord as a possible treatment for paraplegics and quadriplegics. For two years I visited a Nursing Home, where I carried out basic care tasks with the patients. I attended the Medlink conference and an Open Day at the Royal Shrewsbury Hospital. As well as gaining excellent factual information, these provided opportunities to exchange experiences with others. I also helped to film a teaching video, made by a local surgeon, showing a procedure for removing facial skin cancers using skin flaps. This was fascinating, and I was allowed to practise techniques on pig's skin. Work experience in a GP's surgery gave me an understanding of primary health care, a more holistic approach to medicine. I found the continuity that the GP has with the patients appealing as it enables the doctor-patient relationship to grow stronger. I witnessed secondary healthcare in the Royal Shrewsbury Hospital; spending time with a surgeon and consultants in endocrinology, radiology and paediatrics gave me a broad view of the hospital. I sat in on clinics including oncology, diabetes and vascular surgery. On the ward rounds I saw some interesting rare cases such as the genetic condition, Williams syndrome. I would relish opportunities for lifelong learning in a medical career. I come from a medical background and am aware of the physical and emotional pressures of being doctor. Nevertheless I feel that I have the stamina, motivation and commitment to rise to these challenges.

Two years ago I was part of an Ecuadorian Highlands Reforestation Project and went on to provide local children with equipment to start up a school; interacting with children from a different culture was gratifying. Last year I spent time at a Romanian orphanage, helping the orphans, some of whom were blind, to learn English through activities and conversation. Teaching in an unfamiliar environment presented daily challenges, but the work was very rewarding. I feel this is similar to medicine, where not all patients are cooperative and grateful, but they are still worthy of our best efforts.

Gap Year: I intend to carry out a formally organised but self-funded 6 month teaching and care project with disadvantaged children in Ecuador.

Interests/Achievements: As Deputy Head Girl and Captain of the 1st XI Hockey team, I am learning leadership skills, enabling me to motivate and support others more effectively. I have represented Shropshire for hockey and cross-country, and play for Shrewsbury Hockey Club and the school lacrosse team. I have broadened my interests and gained valuable skills in time management and teamwork through gaining the Duke of Edinburgh's scheme awards at all three levels. I passed the English Speaking Board examination at advanced level, giving a presentation about the use of stem cells in medicine. This improved my communication skills and confidence still further. I understand that the medical course is demanding, but I have the determination, positive attitude and sense of humour needed to become a dedicated doctor.

11.54 Personal statement 54 (A level)

Personal statement successful for: Cambridge, Edinburgh, Imperial College, Nottingham

When I was about seven years old, I was fortunate to receive a CD-ROM about the human body with my family's first computer. I spent hours viewing the structures integral in creating such a fascinating organism, although with very little understanding of their functions; I wanted to know more. It is this curiosity that attracts me to a constantly changing profession. The combination of scientific understanding and new advances in treatments and diagnosis creates a profession which I aspire to join.

After my initial encounter with the human body, I developed an interest in the eye, as a topic drawing upon concepts covered in my A-level subjects. I enjoyed studying the areas of A-level physics, fundamental in diagnostic techniques, from using the Doppler Effect to calculate the rate of blood flow to how X-rays and ultrasound produce such individual and specialised images. I found the genetics and cell structure topics in the biology syllabus particularly interesting, researching specific diseases such as retinoblastoma and BSE to further my understanding. Chemistry showed me how certain mechanisms are used in drug manufacture, allowing me to produce aspirin through a series of reactions; practical work in these subjects, where accuracy is essential, has greatly improved my manual dexterity.

My early interest in bone structure was intensified by work experience at a local hospital, where analysing X-rays before and after surgery enabled me to evaluate the aim of surgery in each case. I was able to see how different techniques are used to analyse the cause and extent of specific ailments, essential in giving the most effective pathway of treatment. Witnessing the care provided after surgery showed me the importance of teamwork and the roles played by professionals in providing the best possible service to the patient. A year of working in a pharmacy has given an insight into the treatment of certain ailments using over the counter medicines. I enrolled in a pharmacy assistant course, where I learned how the law controls the sale of certain drugs and the role of a pharmacist in protecting members of the community. These skills were essential when confronted by a patient with a codeine addiction. I referred the patient to the pharmacist who convinced them to see a doctor, demonstrating the importance of good communication skills. In order to improve my understanding of medicine, I spent a week at a remote practice in Gt. Eccleston, where I witnessed how the doctors were able to gain the trust of patients. Establishing a comforting atmosphere is imperative in building a successful relationship, helping to provide an accurate diagnosis through extracting essential information.

Two years ago I began weightlifting; I hope to excel in the forthcoming British Junior championships, as my understanding of the science behind this sport has been supplemented by commitment and hard work. Over the summer, I conducted an experiment to see the effect of supplementation with creatine ethyl ether over a series of repetition ranges, aiming to compare the improvements within the glycolytic, phosphocreatine and aerobic stores of the muscle tissue. My other extracurricular interests include football and chess, representing the school's first teams with both winning district competitions this season. Chess has improved my logical thinking skills and ability to solve problems quickly and effectively.

It is impossible to predict exactly what new technological and scientific advances will be made within my lifetime; I want to be part of medicine as new treatments are discovered. After independent scientific reading and working amongst healthcare professionals, I believe that I can contribute to the future of medicine.

11.55 Personal statement 55 (A level)

Personal statement successful for: Cambridge, Imperial College, UCL

For the past four or five years I have been committed to a career in medicine. As well as the belief I have a true vocation, I am also drawn to medicine by a fascination with human anatomy and physiology. I am keen to follow a course with a strong scientific foundation, and, though not taking Physics A level, I have studied Astronomy to GCSE and hope to take an AS in Further Maths next year to develop my knowledge of mechanics. I am attending extension courses in Biology, Chemistry and Physics in addition to my A2 courses. Studying Latin has helped me to hone my analytical skills and learn to think with precision and clarity, whereas the interpersonal and collaborative qualities inherent to Music were especially useful in voluntary work at the Leeds General Infirmary school, where I composed an interactive 'soundboard' for their multi-sensory room as part of my AS coursework.

During work experience at the LGI I met children suffering from various cancers, sparking an interest in oncology. I wanted to understand the treatment pathways involved, from diagnosis to palliative care, and so I obtained work experience at the Haematology and Oncology Day Unit at Airedale NHS Trust as part of a week of mixed work experience that also covered Respiratory Medicine, A&E and General Practice. I observed various patients at differing stages in their disease, some during chemotherapy and one on the Liverpool Care Pathway. I am gaining experience of palliative care as a volunteer in the in-patient unit of a local hospice, where I assist nursing staff with feeding. This has exposed me to some of the more emotionally challenging aspects of medicine, but also provided many opportunities to speak to patients and relatives in trying to cater for their differing needs: something I have found very rewarding.

My time at Airedale illustrated the importance of research in the diagnosis and treatment of cancer. To gain further experience in this aspect of medicine, I gained a bursary from the Nuffield Foundation to research the role of the helicase hPif1 in cancer pathogenesis, by comparing its sequence in cancer cell lines to a wild-type in immortalised non-cancerous cells. I performed this research during a month's placement at the Institute of Cancer Research at Sheffield University. As well as providing lab experience, this required extensive background reading, including Robert Weinberg's 'The Biology of

Cancer', relevant chapters of 'The Molecular Biology of the Cell' and the research papers so far published on the gene, as well as the periodicals 'Cell' and 'Nature', culminating in a report of my results, 'A Comparative Study of Human Pif1 Helicase cDNA Sequences in MRC5VA and HCT116 Cells'.

Whilst on a cadet leadership course last summer with the OTC I gained experience of managing simulated combat injuries and learnt the importance of triage as well as some basic field medicine and casualty evacuation, often with little sleep and under significant pressure. This supplemented practical experience of anaesthesia and surgical asepsis which I gained during a week at a dental surgery and, I hope, will prove excellent preparation for the stresses of medical training! In addition to running the new cadets' training programme, my responsibilities include acting as a form warden, organising lectures for the school's science society and, most recently, head of house. As a keen musician, I play percussion for the Leeds and Yorkshire Youth Orchestras and sing with the Leeds Youth Opera. I am employed as a music tutor, and acted this year as the managing director of a Young Enterprise company.

I am a motivated and determined individual with a passion for science and human interaction, and, though aware of the challenges of a medical career, I believe that I have the intellectual, emotional and social qualities to succeed in this ambition.

11.56 Personal statement 56 (A level)

Personal statement successful for: Cambridge, Edinburgh, Imperial College, King's College

My motivation to be a doctor came from my father. Multiple infarcts in the brain have progressively reduced my grandmother from a vivacious and successful businesswoman to a patient with senile dementia, incapable of tending to her basic personal needs. One day at the dinner table, my father who has been caring for my grandmother the past eight years, told the family pensively that we should let him go if he ever became like that. That remark shook me to the core. It was then that I knew I wanted to study medicine, not only for my ageing parents, but also for patients who have to suffer personal indignities from these debilitating geriatric diseases.

The thoughts of pursuing a medical career have probably had a long gestation in my subconscious. Ever since primary school, I have been drawn to the science subjects, especially biology and chemistry. I find the rigour of scientific methods and their explaining power both stimulating and emotionally satisfying. In addition, I have taken a special interest in the human anatomy. The human body, an intricate machine, never ceases to amaze me by its ability to conform to one's needs during extreme circumstances. Despite the current rapid advancement in technology, there are still many mysteries pertaining to the operation of body mechanisms and it is this existing enigma that compels me to desire more knowledge relating to the human mind and its influence on physical functions in the body.

Yet, apart from sciences, humanities such as history, German and Chinese also inspire me, as knowledge of these subjects can be useful when integrated into medicine, since doctors are required to strike a balance between people-oriented patient care as well as the rigorous application of scientific knowledge and techniques.

To gain a broader insight into the work of the medical profession, I spent two weeks last summer break working at the integrative Community Health Centre managed by HK Polytechnic University's School of Nursing. The Centre offers health monitoring, advice and healthcare to those in public housing estates. The experience impressed upon me the importance of public education and the need for preventive medicine especially for the socially disadvantaged.

Last summer, I had the rare opportunity to shadow a cardiologist for two weeks in his clinic while staying with his family. During this period, I was able to observe first-hand the work and life of a medical professional. I fully appreciate the demand for discipline, commitment and sacrifices from a doctor and his family, especially when emergency situations arise during dinnertime and in the middle of the night. However, I too shared the same joyful sparkle in his eyes when a life had been saved. Yet, following the death of one of his patients, an elderly woman with a thoracic aortic aneurysm, I understand that medicine is not foolproof and the perfect treatment does not always exist. As a doctor, all one can do is to work to one's best ability and this, I am willing to do.

Since the start of last school year, I have devoted each Saturday morning to voluntary services in a semi-government institution for the mentally handicapped, the Fu Hong Society. From this exposure, I have realised how lucky I am to be healthy and independent. This is my way of giving back to the community for my good fortune.

I am active in many extracurricular activities, acting as School Prefect and Captain of the school's Inline Hockey Team. Moreover, I have taken part in the Silver Hong Kong Award for Young People, am an active member of the school debating team as well as the Energy Conservation team, which won the Student Environmental Protection Ambassador Award for promoting environmental education in school.

I am firmly committed to a career in medicine and prepared for the sacrifices and difficulties that lie ahead. Thus, I sincerely hope to obtain the opportunity to realise my dream.

11.57 Personal statement 57 (A level)

Personal statement successful for: Cambridge, Glasgow, Manchester, St Andrews

Medicine, for me, is not only about tackling diseases, but more fundamentally about the relationship between doctor and patient. I believe dignity and trust play an enormous part in building a relationship in which a patient feels sufficiently comfortable to disclose their problem, enabling a diagnosis to be made. In applying to study Medicine, I believe I have the qualities necessary to form such a relationship.

In December, I attended Liverpool University's 'So you want to be a doctor?' course and subsequently was fortunate to gain a work placement on the Intromed course at Arrowe Park Hospital for a week in June. I found that I was fascinated by practical applications of medical knowledge and particularly by cardiology, after observing a cardiologist in clinic. My Biology course had given me a command of the scientific facts necessary to understand what was happening, which made the experience of seeing theory in action very interesting. Time in the Operating Theatre, viewing gynaecological keyhole surgery, enabled me to witness an exciting application of modern science.

Visiting residents in a nursing home for three years has given me an insight into the care of the elderly, and my recent work experience there enabled me to appreciate some of the difficulties that I may face in a career in medicine, relating to the elderly, due to Britain's ageing population. It also led me to enjoy a range of books including 'The Man Who Mistook His Wife for a Hat' and 'The Invisible Enemy'. Through my Chemistry course I have completed work on 'What's in a medicine' and I am looking forward to the 'Medicines by Design' module.

Within my school community, my role as a Prefect has given me a great sense of responsibility via the running of the Eco-Committee and Fair Trade stalls. I have received the School Overall Achievement Award in Years 8, 9, 10 and 11 and several Bronze and Silver Awards in Maths Challenges. Partaking in the Chemistry Young Analysts' competition at Liverpool University was a great stimulus, introducing topics I was yet to cover and utilising my problem-solving skills.

In the wider community, my part-time job of three years in a local library has been immensely enjoyable due to interaction with the public. Via activities that have tested my teamwork skills and determination, such as the Duke of Edinburgh Awards, I found I enjoy both leading a group and trusting someone else to lead me. To date, I have completed the Bronze and Silver Awards and am near completion of the Gold Award. However, there is fun to be found in helping others to achieve. I have trained participants of the D of E Award and accompanied leaders during expeditions, and have organised Maths and Reading clubs. These experiences have taught me the importance of body language, empathy and patience.

I love playing the piano and have recently passed Grade 6. I have also passed Grade 3 flute. I play in an orchestra of all abilities which I find is a good outlet for my music. I play several sports including volleyball, kickboxing and running, and have broken the school record for 1,500m running. As a member of a Christian Youth Group, I am stimulated by the discussions and challenging issues raised, especially since, through my Theology course, I have explored such issues as IVF, euthanasia and abortion. This has helped me appreciate various views held on medical ethical dilemmas.

New advances in technology, such as the first beating heart transplant, place medicine at the forefront of scientific implementation, and the paths of career progression and specialisation mean there is a vast range of choices both in the UK and abroad. I look forward to studying a medical degree as the first and most important step along this path. Medicine, I feel, is a vocation in the word's truest sense and it is the combination of contact with people and science which excites me about this career.

11.58 Personal statement 58 (A level)

Personal statement successful for: Cambridge, Liverpool, Manchester, Newcastle

For several years I have been totally committed to training for, and ultimately pursuing, a career in medicine. My aspirations for the future include doing voluntary work in a developing country, and perhaps working in a lively A&E department back in the UK. By these or other means, I hope that my training will not only be personally fulfilling, but hopefully also benefit others, and particularly help those whose needs are greatest.

Science has been a longstanding fascination for me, but it has become increasingly clear that my academic interests and strengths lie in the medical field. I believe myself to be a confident and clear thinking scientist who can work consistently and accurately. Studying Health and Disease in Biology prompted me to consider some of the moral issues that have a bearing on the treatment of patients, and thus I explored Tony Hope's 'Medical Ethics'. The mental agility that I have developed from Mathematics has particularly helped my learning in Biology and Chemistry, especially in tackling practical problems. Chemistry has proven to be a particularly enjoyable choice, and the understanding of more advanced chemical principles should prove crucial at degree level. I also chose AS level French as a means of widening my horizons and, hopefully, of opening up opportunities for me later in life.

The work experience I have undertaken has also helped to confirm my decision. Working with the scientists at GSK for four days was fascinating, and, whilst recognising the importance of their work in the medical field, I still found the hectic week's work I completed in the A&E department of Lewisham Hospital far more stimulating. Here I experienced many situations which required an ability to work effectively under pressure, which I feel is a quality of mine. In all, I remain certain that the medical profession is one which I shall find challenging, varied and rewarding. I'm also currently volunteering for the National Blood Service, by helping raise awareness of donor sessions, a cause for which I feel strongly.

This summer, my World Challenge expedition to Honduras presented me with an opportunity to work both as part of a team and to nurture my leadership qualities as team leader. Being completely immersed in another culture for over a month was a fantastic experience. However, it also opened my eyes to the conditions, and more specifically the medical conditions, that people in these regions are subjected to. In the recent BBC1 series 'SuperDoctors', I was inspired by Dr Steve Mannion's selfless work in Malawi. He has a remarkable impact on such a large number of people, and as such has inspired me to one day work where I can have the greatest impact.

I like to get involved in school life and am an active member of the Medic's Society and the football squad. I am also a form prefect and a maths buddy. These two jobs allow me to care for and act as a role model for the younger members of the school. I believe I am suited to my role as prefect, as I have good social skills, meaning I don't find talking to new people too much of a challenge, and I am able to empathise with others.

In my free time, I like to keep myself busy. I both teach and play guitar. I am also a member of a tennis club, and like to play at least once a week. Most Sundays I referee youth football, which has enabled me to be able to more efficiently and more effectively deal with difficult situations – of which there are inevitably many. Furthermore, I maintain a keen interest in film and music. Despite my many interests, I have never had trouble juggling academic work with other activities, as displayed by my consistently outstanding performances in public examinations and my very high attendance.

To conclude, my academic ability and drive, along with my personality, make me an ideal candidate to read Medicine at university. I believe myself to be equipped to deal with the intellectual and mental challenges which this degree will undoubtedly pose.

11.59 Personal statement 59 (A level)

Personal statement successful for: Birmingham, Cambridge, Imperial College, UCL

He was shaking unceasingly on the floor, unable to control his body movements, unaware and non-responsive to the world around him; I was in a powerless and frightening position. I lacked the knowledge, skills and experience to be able to provide help for my cousin who was going through an epileptic seizure. Since that humbling day, I have discovered that there are different types of seizures and treatments used to control this debilitating condition. This experience has highlighted for me the importance of improving one's mind by reading, to facilitate the understanding of the world in us and around us.

For the past two years, I have been a volunteer at The Royal Brompton Harefield Hospital heart and lung transplant ward. During this time, I have had the pleasure to help the medical staff and to improve patient welfare by performing services such as changing bed covers, assisting in the use of diagnostic tools such as the ECG and talking to transplant patients. Furthermore, this year, I have had the opportunity to discover some of the ambitions and thoughts of a mentally handicapped young man through house visits. These experiences have helped me to actively exercise patience and have taught me the importance of showing compassion when dealing with people.

Last year, by shadowing a physician in an ophthalmology clinic, I gained new understanding into some commonly used diagnostic procedures, such as the retinal laser scanner. Moreover, my knowledge of medical imaging techniques such as the MRI, EEG and the novel MEG has grown considerably through a fascinating guided tour of the UCL Functional Imaging Lab. This summer I spent 8 weeks at an electrophysiology lab at UCL studying the effects of a new drug on the functioning of hippocampal CA1 Pyramidal neurons. This experience has granted me valuable insight into the life of a scientist and has equipped me with new skills, including dissection, microscopy and single cell recording.

I feel that it is important to have a balance between academic work and leisure. One of my great interests is playing the cello and I am a member of the Harrow Young Musicians Philharmonic Orchestra. I particularly enjoyed our orchestral performance in front of a full house at the Royal Albert Hall. My musical experiences have helped me to rise above my fear of performing in front of a large crowd and have helped me to build up my confidence. I also take pleasure in long-distance running. At the age of 19, I was the youngest person to finish the New Forest Marathon. The time I spent training and running the race taught me the importance of planning and perseverance, which are required for success.

From an early age, I found Science fascinating and comprehensible. Through my A level studies and my 2 years in university I have attained 'A' and first-class grades in all my subjects and have been nominated for academic awards in both my school and university. Even so, through the insights I have gained by volunteering and working as a scientist, I can confidently declare that I wish to dedicate my life to no other profession but Medicine.

Through my achievements and extracurricular activities, I feel that I have demonstrated that I am an able and committed student who is determined to dedicate the necessary time and effort to becoming a successful medical student. I believe a medical career, whilst being demanding and at times stressful, will give me the opportunity to fulfil my scientific aspirations and intellectual curiosity as well as my supreme desire to promote the health and welfare of human society.

Another pursuit of mine is travelling. I grew up in Hungary then at the age of 12 moved to South Africa before coming to live in the United Kingdom 5 years ago. This mobile lifestyle has granted me the special privilege to meet people from a wide variety of backgrounds, which I feel would be beneficial for a future career in Medicine.

11.60 Personal statement 60 (A level)

Personal statement successful for: Birmingham, Cambridge, Nottingham, UCL

I would like to study medicine because it combines an evolving base of knowledge with the need for logic and manual skill, all with the aim of helping a patient. My experience of life as a patient, however, has shaped and clarified my interest. After suffering an injury while playing rugby for my School, I developed a back condition which led to my seeing a large number and variety of healthcare professionals over the course of a year. During that time I saw first-hand how an aloof or distant bedside manner can have a negative impact, but equally how much difference the alternative can make, even when the news itself is disappointing. I also feel I better understand the limits of modern medicine.

A week of work experience in a hospital helped me identify the qualities a good doctor needs: the competence to solve problems; the compassion to look beyond the problems; the ability to deal with stress; and the ability to work in a team with other professionals. I also organised a volunteer stint on a geriatric ward for two hours a week for eight months. This opened my eyes to the realities of medicine, gave me experience of dealing with the vulnerable and confirmed my desire to study medicine. Furthermore, it showed me how rewarding that kind of work can be, and consequently in the current academic year I am working for a charity which helps children with learning disabilities. I am especially interested in neurology, as although the brain is the most powerful organ in the body it seems relatively little is known about its function. I have become a frequent reader of the Student BMJ which has given me a good introduction into medical ethics and the important role they play. For example, one article criticised Richard Dawkins' view that consciousness can be explained by atom collision as overly simplistic, a view I agree with as, when applied to medicine, it emphasises the problem over the patient; and I believe in a holistic, patient-orientated approach.

I believe one of my greatest strengths is my academic work where I combine a certain level of natural aptitude with a strong work ethic. I am constantly of the belief that no matter how well I have done, I can always improve and learn something. My AS subject choices have suited me well. Biology has intrigued me throughout the course, while Chemistry and Maths have allowed me to develop a more analytical way of thinking. Spanish meanwhile has given me a way to stretch myself in a more creative direction, as has helping to edit my School's magazine.

I feel my personality is another of my strengths, and it has been shaped in a large way by my extracurricular activities. I used to represent my School and club at rugby, and since being forced to stop I have begun to referee matches as a way of staying in touch with the game. This has taught me about the value of staying committed to something that you love, and has also improved my decision making under pressure: an invaluable asset for any doctor. My status as a Senior Prefect has allowed me to develop communication skills both with staff and junior pupils, as well as demonstrating my reliability and leadership. I have made the most of my organisational skills as Operations Director of my Young Enterprise company, and as a member of the School's charity committee. As a way of relieving stress I have begun to teach myself to play the steel pan which has been challenging but enjoyable. Above all I am a person who delights in helping a team to success as I tend to flourish in more team-based activities such as rugby, Young Enterprise and Duke of Edinburgh's Gold Award.

I look forward to the beginning of a career in medicine and feel it is one I am well suited to, through my academic qualities, my personal qualities, and the knowledge that even subtle actions can make a big difference to the life of a patient.

11.61 Personal statement 61 (A level)

Personal statement successful for: Bristol, Cambridge, Cardiff, Southampton

At the age of ten, I was taken along to a first aid course at my sailing club. I started as an onlooker but ended the course as a certified first aider. My interest in medicine started there. I maintain my certification and find it remarkable how much a CPR method can change in three years demonstrating the necessity of continued improvement in order to refine methods of treatment. My enthusiasm and enquiring mind encouraged me to study science at A level, where my interest in how the core principles are incorporated into the human body developed further. I discovered the importance of technology in medicine during a project I undertook at Lancaster University. As a small group we researched the use of nanotechnology in medicine, discovering essential progressions made in diagnosis, cancer treatments and drug delivery. Further reading has led me to 'Biomedicine and the Human Condition' by Michael Sargent who cites Jacques Monod in describing the human genome: a 'tone-deaf conservatory where the noise is preserved along with the music'. On reading this I wondered what the noise and the music represent but as I read on, the relation of noise interfering with music causing changes and evolution interfering with our DNA doing the same became clear. This highlights both the social and academic aspects of medicine by relating music, a common ground that joins people but exists in different forms, with the genome, possessed by all but unique to each individual.

During continued voluntary work in a nursing home I have illustrated that my commitment to medicine will not be deterred by the most gruelling tasks or responsibilities, taking pride in all that I do. A three-day work experience in Westmorland General Hospital helped me to learn more about the routine care of the patients by assisting with the nurses' duties. I learnt a great deal about the hospital, watching people from all different areas of medicine coming together as a perfectly balanced team.

I have recently embarked on a World Challenge expedition to Madagascar during which we spent a week in an orphanage doing building work and improving ecological schemes. My eyes were opened to the consequences of poverty especially concerning the lack of healthcare that we are so used to receiving in our western lives. Being in an underdeveloped country meant leadership, teamwork and organisation were essential in order to function as a group. As part of the medical team my first aid skills were needed as injury and illness were met daily in our foreign surroundings. Throughout the expedition I grew in confidence, became more independent and am now more socially aware than I was previously. In order to fund my expedition I have worked as a waitress for the past two years; this has enabled me to improve my teamwork and social skills.

My participation in Duke of Edinburgh bronze, silver and gold awards shows my ability to work as part of a team and my determination to see through all that I partake in. It has encouraged me to be active in my local community where I have been a young leader for my local Brownies for the past three years. I have also developed skills and found enjoyment in many activities as part of the awards such as playing the violin to Grade 5 and in the school orchestra, singing in my school's choir, horse riding for the past seven years and sailing for my county youth squad. Within my school community, I have always taken an active role including my position as a prefect, being a tutor to two GCSE Chemistry students and running a netball club. I recently represented the school in the Institute of Biology Quiz as part of a team of four; we finished first to win a microscope for our school.

I know I have the ability and commitment to join this lifelong learning profession, which connects my natural interest in science with a desire for social interaction. I am eager to have the opportunity to direct all my energy into medicine as both a subject and a career.

11.62 Personal statement 62 (A level)

Personal statement successful for: Oxford, UCL

Last month I had the opportunity to observe and assist in the delivery of a baby. It stands out as one of the most exciting, exhilarating and moving experiences in my time as a hospital volunteer. I have had the privilege of serving patients in many different areas such as endoscopy, day surgery, long-term care and maternity. Each area has offered difficult challenges as well as joyful events and recoveries. I have gained an appreciation for the work of medical staff and have an understanding of the importance of clear communication, constant support and superior patient care. My respect for doctors and my desire to enter the medical profession has been fuelled by the time I have spent volunteering. The time that I have spent speaking with doctors, asking questions, discussing their specialties and the route they took to get there has further confirmed my aspiration to become a medical doctor, an aspiration which was ignited in my early teens and inspired by my school work experience at Victoria Hospital, Cape Town.

My friends describe me as committed, disciplined, focused, hardworking, adventurous and caring. I have developed strong communication skills through my experience in the corporate world and through the leadership roles I have been offered.

I enjoy being active in the community through my volunteer work, church and sporting activities: I play on a USTA women's tennis team and we are currently top of our league. I cycle regularly and just completed a weekend cycling trip to Washington D.C, covering more than 100 miles. I have also been known to play team sports such as dodge ball and softball. Throughout my school career I enjoyed playing 1st team tennis, netball and swimming as well as participating on the athletics team.

I have held many responsibilities within my church such as leading the hospitality team, where I oversaw the catering requirements for church services as well as monthly meals for over 120 people. I recently undertook the responsibility for the feeding of over 500 cast and crewmembers at a Christmas Production in December 2007 during the many performances over two weekends. I have been active organising women's events and looking after infants in the crèche. I also lead a weekly women's bible study. Through these roles and leadership positions, I have not only learnt how to delegate, motivate and manage but I have learned how to communicate and serve well.

At the age of 25 I realise that I am classed as a mature student. I also realise that I will graduate when I am in my early thirties. However, I believe that there is great benefit in having studied at the prestigious London School of Economics, having worked hard in a commercial environment, having lived independently in an international setting and having had the experience of dealing with stress and personal challenge as well as meeting people from many different walks of life and many socio-economic classes.

These experiences have afforded me the opportunity to discover my strengths and desires. They have helped shape my dreams and create the determination and drive that I feel are essential in embarking on a medical degree. I believe that my character and the skills that I have developed will help me become an outstanding medical doctor.

11.63 Personal statement 63 (A level)

Personal statement successful for: Brighton, Cambridge, UCL

Medicine is a subject in which puzzles abound. Some challenges presented are as simple as communicating with a patient, others require greater skill, yet each patient warrants a new approach, and this is why I want to study medicine – I want to be constantly tested. The continuous learning inherent in all areas of medical study is one such test of my skills, particularly attractive to me as it will help prevent me from becoming stagnant at a certain level.

My work experience has also aided me in my decision to study medicine. Most recently, I spent a week shadowing doctors on an infectious diseases ward, learning in the process about infection control procedures such as use of negative air pressure rooms to prevent the spread of infectious disease on the ward. During this period I also made time to talk to tuberculosis patients, and in doing so learnt a great deal about the management of this disease, including the use of many drugs together to combat antibiotic resistance. In June of this year, I travelled to Aachen in Germany where I undertook a week of work experience in a paediatrician's surgery. I learnt about the range of differences between paediatric and adult medicine, from the fairly mundane alterations to dosage to the more subtle changes in behaviour and tone of voice that the doctor adopts. The trip also allowed me to hone my communication skills, needing to address both children and adults in a foreign language and to use medical terminology not normally encountered in A-level study of the language. I am also volunteering at a care centre for Multiple Sclerosis sufferers for an afternoon each week. There is one visitor to the centre who I have particularly bonded with, who has the primary progressive form of the disease. She is unable to speak, instead only mouthing words. Whilst, at first, communication was extraordinarily tough and left me wondering whether I was frustrating her, I eventually began to become accustomed to her way of communicating, and we play Scrabble each week with minimal trouble. Finally, my continuing work with St John Ambulance has trained me in first aid and given me an introduction to providing medical care.

Studying chemistry has helped me to think clearly about key scientific principles, whilst following the biology course has given me a good knowledge of, for example, the structure and function of many areas of the body. I have built on this knowledge by reading 'Mutants' by Armand Marie Leroi, a fascinating book which, by exploring deviation from normal embryological development, attempts to explain genetic disorders. I also read 'Right Hand, Left Hand' by Chris McManus, which researches the origins of handedness and puts forward a theory on why the use of the right hand is universally dominant before more widely questioning the presence of asymmetry in nature. Mathematics has enhanced my logic skills, whilst by studying German I have become proficient in the language. It has also given me a chance to constantly test myself in a non-scientific setting.

Outside of my A-level studies, I have taken an Open University short course in Molecules, Medicines and Drugs which I passed in June 2008. I was also a finalist in a nationwide essay writing competition run by the Royal College of Science Union. Furthermore, I am proud to have been a member of a Young Enterprise company which reached the London finals; as the team's Human Resources Director and Deputy Managing Director, I was responsible for the wellbeing of team members and for ensuring effective team communication. At school, I am a senior prefect in charge of the management of a number of charity events throughout the year. This has allowed me to practise my communication and leadership skills.

Whilst I am aware that medicine is an extremely demanding profession, the experiences I have had of the field so far have appealed greatly to me, and I would relish the opportunity to study this subject further.

11.64 Personal statement 64 (A level)

Personal statement successful for: Brighton, Cambridge, Nottingham, UCL

Some people say they have always wanted to be doctors, but I have discovered my ambition more gradually. I became passionate about science when I was 14 and science at school became more interesting and challenging. I thought about a career in medical research but, after my work experience, I realised that by becoming a doctor I could combine my interest in science with my love of working with people and I could help patients first-hand.

As I am inquisitive, in Biology and Chemistry I love doing practical investigations as well as learning the theory. I read New Scientist to keep up with scientific developments and I am particularly interested in genetics, especially stem cell research and its use in regenerative medicine with the possibility of curing diseases such as Parkinson's. I am also interested in the psychological side of how genes affect personality which I learnt about by reading 'Nature via Nurture' by Matt Ridley. I enjoy Maths and the satisfaction of solving problems so I think I will enjoy the diagnostic aspect of medicine. The combination of art with these scientific subjects has developed practical skills such as manual dexterity and time management. Critical Thinking helped me understand the structure of arguments and this is useful in my A-level subjects and other reading.

Work experience at a unit of the John Radcliffe Hospital exposed me to departments which research cures for conditions such as cystic fibrosis and motor neurone disease. It was interesting to see the latest research and it taught me how important it is in medicine to work as a team and share ideas. Working there also raised ethical issues about vivisection. This inspired me to set up a medical ethics discussion group at school. I attended a Medlink conference in Nottingham and another medical conference at UCL, which gave me an insight into what it would be like to be a doctor and the sort of commitment needed. Last summer I shadowed a GP in Bath and an orthopaedic surgeon at the John Radcliffe Hospital. At the GP surgery I sat in on consultations which showed me how varied the work is. I saw a hernia and skin cancer as well as minor ailments. I worked with the nurses and receptionists, and attended a Practice Meeting, which showed me how the surgery operates as a whole. In the hospital I saw a variety of patients mainly with spinal problems. I particularly enjoyed working in paediatrics with children born with scoliosis, and talking to patients in the wards. I have also participated in an experiment into psychosis involving a brain scan and psychological tests.

I find working with children very rewarding and I teach swimming at a primary school and babysit regularly. Last Christmas I helped paint decorations for the Banbury Children's Hospital. In summer 2005 I went on a World Challenge expedition to Bolivia for a month which improved my teamwork and leadership skills. This included a week working in an orphanage which was rewarding and made me more aware of how much I take for granted. I raised over GBP 3000 for this trip by working for the Cambridge School Classics Project, and organising events such as a piano recital and a barn dance. I am grade 8 standard at the piano and also enjoy accompanying. I sing in the school choir and have performed in Mozart's Requiem and Handel's Messiah. I row at the City Of Oxford rowing club and I am working towards my gold Duke of Edinburgh award.

I know medicine would be the ideal career for me. I appreciate it will be very hard work, but I would love a stimulating and challenging job where I face new problems every day, and where I could use my knowledge to improve people's lives.

11.65 Personal statement 65 (A level)

Personal statement successful for: Bristol, Cambridge, Leeds, Newcastle

Science helps me to rationalise and understand the world: it orientates the way I view and approach problems. Pure sciences have always excited me, but their application to the complex and diverse study of human health and illness offers my intellectual curiosity the greatest stimulation and compels me to pursue the study of medicine.

Work experience in a GP surgery earlier this year offered me insight into the doctor-patient relationship and the psychology of the sick. Hospital work experience has broadened my knowledge of the complexity of practising medicine whilst balancing treatment to meet patients' needs. I am attracted not by the routine, but the unpredictability, the uncertainty and the constantly developing nature of the profession. A summer job doing clerical work in a GP surgery taught me about the interactions between primary and secondary care, and made me aware of the behind-the-scenes working of general practice. I work regularly as a volunteer in an elderly care home, and this has opened my eyes to the needs of the many, highly dependent people in geriatric care. Developing personal relationships with many of them has made the impact of chronic disease on their lives evident. It made me realise that there are people whose medical needs cannot be met by science, but whose lives can be made easier by care and compassion.

Academically I have enjoyed considerable success. I am always keen to go beyond the confines of the syllabus and take a broad interest in topics relating to medicine. The New Scientist keeps me abreast of developments and news in the world of science, and the media focus on healthcare feeds my interest in the world of medicine.

My commitment to St Leonard's is not confined to the classroom. Elected Head Boy by my peers and teachers, I am relied upon to make important decisions when representing the school community, chairing the school council and ensuring the student voice is heard. Our peer support teams and various interest groups are all valued and highly effective. Through prioritisation and delegation I am able to effect change and broaden the life of our Sixth Form. Last year, I achieved a Gold Award for Creativity in Science and Technology. Under the supervision of a consulting engineer, our team conducted basic research, wrote a detailed report, and gave a presentation on the construction of a dual carriageway bypass.

Outside school, I enjoy playing a lot of sport. I have played club rugby and cricket for many years, and have captained my Durham City RUFC team for the past three seasons. I am now on the Durham County side. My adventures with the Duke of Edinburgh award scheme have developed my initiative, independence and motivation.

I have been selected by the charity, Project Trust, to go to Uganda for 12 months to teach underprivileged children. Whilst this will be a tough year, I am thoroughly looking forward to the challenge. I hope that the experience will broaden my perspective, and that I will enter university with a more mature outlook.

I relish the prospect of lifelong learning which the study and practice of medicine will bring. I would value the privilege of working with people during the highs and lows of their lives. With my rigorous grasp of science, combined with my interest in people, and a desire to help them, I feel well suited to medicine as a career.

11.66 Personal statement 66 (A level)

Personal statement successful for: Cambridge, Imperial College, Leeds, Southampton

I have always been curious about the functioning and failure of the human body. During the recent years of my education I have become increasingly absorbed by the links between biochemistry and physiology, for instance the Krebs cycle, involved in providing ATP, to sustain basic life processes. It was this interest that led me to my first work experience placement at the Imperial College Hospital's Haematology department. I worked for three days alongside a senior consultant, shadowing, sitting in on a board meeting, and observing the extraction of two separate bone marrow samples for biopsy to test for Chronic Myelogenous Leukaemia (CML). Whilst this helped to satisfy my desire for more depth than the AS level course provided, what really captivated me were the ward rounds. These allowed me to talk to the patients, and understand how their conditions affected their lives. It also allowed me to observe both the bedside manner of the doctors and to see how the patients listened, or in some cases still thought that they new better. It was this that led me to the realisation that my true vocation was to become a doctor.

In order to understand some of the other roles of a doctor I spent two days working within my local surgery, shadowing two GPs and sitting in on a learning disability seminar. What really intrigued me was the extensive role of a GP within a community and the variety of issues they deal with. I also worked at Imperial College Hospital IVF unit for four days, observing theatre, including the reversal of a sterilisation, and also fertilisation by ICSI. I was also keen to gain first-hand experience of palliative care, and so currently I am working as a volunteer at Sobell House Hospice Day Centre with patients suffering from a variety of terminal illnesses. This is a truly humbling experience and I am inspired by the positive attitude of both the patients and the staff. I have learned to appreciate that in medicine sometimes you cannot save a life, and that it is then important to really consider how you can give them the best quality of life possible, for however short it may be.

I also gained a placement in the Weatherall Institute of Molecular Medicine, conducting my own Real-Time PCR; this helped me understand the role of laboratories in medical care. This summer I spent four weeks working in virology at Oxford Brookes University, infecting cells with viruses, transfecting with plasmids, before staining and viewing them on a confocal microscope, on which I have written a short thesis. I also enjoy reading for personal development. I subscribe to the New Scientist, and am currently reading James Le Fanu's 'The Rise and Fall of Modern Medicine'. I was also particularly enthralled by Richard Dawkins' genomic portrayal of natural selection in 'The Selfish Gene'.

Having been involved with school CCF for two and a half years, I have now been promoted to a rank of Warrant Officer, as a senior NCO. This has opened up many experiences for me from leading sections of cadets on exercise, to mountaineering in the Swiss Alps, both of which I thoroughly enjoyed. In addition I am Deputy Head Boy at MCS. These roles both require me to demonstrate leadership, diplomacy and be a good team player. I am also working for my Duke of Edinburgh Gold Award. I am a keen sportsman, representing the school in cricket, hockey, rowing and rugby. I am training for my karate black belt, and have recently competed in the Boston rowing marathon, which at 52km is the longest and toughest rowing race in Britain.

I am a highly motivated and determined scientist and I am confident I have the qualities it takes to both succeed in medical studies and become an excellent doctor.

11.67 Personal statement 67 (A level)

Personal statement successful for: Bristol, Cambridge, Imperial College, King's College

The more I learn about the human body, the more I am amazed by the beauty and faults that lie within it, how it operates in health and in sickness, and the extraordinary ways that it adapts and responds to the world. It is this fascination with the ever-developing field of medicine, and its significant interpersonal element, that compels me to study medicine and embark upon a lifetime of learning.

To gain an insight into the duties of a doctor, I arranged work experience placements in several branches of medicine. I spent a week shadowing a consultant of respiratory medicine at St Mary's, London and Ealing Hospital. I witnessed many clinical consultations covering a wide range of respiratory and allergic disorders. I shadowed a palliative care team at Mount Vernon Hospital, observing their MDT meeting, new admissions and ward rounds, which enabled me to see a very different aspect of medicine. I also attended medical lectures, practicals and emergency simulations at MedLink and MedSim courses held at Nottingham University.

These experiences enabled me to appreciate the importance of teamwork within healthcare. They also made me acutely aware of the realities of medicine and the necessity for empathy and compassion within the profession, particularly when attending to the needs of terminally ill patients and their families. I have arranged a work-shadowing placement to experience primary care in a GP's surgery.

Through the Aim Higher Summer School Scheme I spent a week at The School of Pharmacy investigating 'The Science of Medicines', which included a visit to the pharmacy at Guy's and St Thomas' Hospital to see the production of chemotherapy drugs. This helped me understand the complexity of the treatment undergone by some of the cancer patients I see in my voluntary work. I also attended the 'Image your heart' conference at Imperial College, which increased my understanding of medical imaging. I am trained in First Aid and Infection Control.

I enjoy serving my community as a member of the Hillingdon Youth Council. My involvement has helped my decision-making skills and heightened my awareness of public responsibility. I volunteer at my local palliative care centre where I enjoy talking to the patients and staff. I am also fully involved in my school community. I mentored two Year Eleven students through their GCSEs and am currently producing and directing a school musical. Through my job as a waitress serving the general public, I have enhanced my interpersonal and communication skills and, as a consequence, have confidence when meeting new people.

I believe the balance between academic work and leisure is crucial. I have been playing the violin and singing for nine years and find it an excellent source of relaxation. I am a member of Hillingdon Youth Choir and Symphony Orchestra, which bring the benefits of leadership qualities and a natural sense of teamwork. Next year we embark on a tour of Northern Spain and I hope to continue my musical interests at university. I am also a keen skier and enjoy reading horror novels.

I believe my future is in medicine, the intellectual challenge, the team spirit, the caring ethos; the knowledge that every action I take is with the sole purpose of improving the health of others. I see it as a journey that at its end will leave me certain that my life has been worthwhile.

12 Personal statements from successful graduate entrants

12.1 Personal statement 1 (Graduate)

Personal statement successful for: King's College, Leicester

My interest with science was sparked at the age of seven with full marks in a science test. As I became older, my fascination grew and I was drawn towards a career in medicine yet I was acutely aware from my father, a neurosurgeon, the dedication, commitment and motivation required to succeed. He has also given me an insight into the gratifying rewards and job satisfaction of practising medicine. I know it is my vocation.

I have overcome a number of obstacles in my life to grow into an emotionally mature adult. The sudden loss of both my aunt and grandmother during my 1st year at university was devastating. I was distraught because I was unable to fly back to the Philippines in the middle of term to attend their funeral. Although it was difficult to continue, I focused on the positive impact being a doctor would have on other granddaughters/nieces. This difficult time made me more determined and motivated to succeed in pursuing my lifelong ambition.

My degree has confirmed my interest in medicine and enhanced my knowledge whilst developing my skills in problem solving and interpretation of data. I've learnt to rationally consider the pharmacological actions of drugs and predict possible side effects. From the Psychology elements of my degree, I recognise human behaviour as integral to treating the whole person. I now also have excellent time management, written and verbal communication skills which are imperative for success.

Work experience has given me valuable insight into the medical field. I have shadowed 2 GPs and 1 SHO for a few days each and was delighted to see theories applied to real life. During my placements, I attended Doctors' meetings and witnessed an A&E trauma case, where consultants, nurses, radiologists and physiotherapists worked efficiently and cohesively together as an impressive team. These placements gave me a realistic perspective on hospital life which, although physically and emotionally challenging at times, confirmed beyond any doubt that this is where my future lies. I now understand the importance of compassion, effective communication and empathy for building effective relationships with patients and their families, a perspective further confirmed as a member of the Community Service Unit (CSU) for a year. Here I cared for people ranging from the elderly in nursing homes to young infants in a day nursery. Last year, I visited a local nursing home weekly. Although I found the standard of care disappointing I appreciated the importance of palliative care. Brightening up their day and promoting the wellness of others was incredibly rewarding. I am also fortunate to distinguish the different perspective of hospitals in the Philippines compared to developed countries. Although the hospitals were busier with more physicians, their facilities are not as advanced. I feel my knowledge and appreciation of different cultures will enable me to treat patients from diverse backgrounds with the same level of understanding.

I balance academic studies with extracurricular activities by volunteering. In the 'Philippines Health Programme' based in Manila, I was privileged to help care for street children and teach them English. I assisted in giving out free vaccinations and raised awareness of the environment and health. Similarly, volunteering weekly at Oxfam this year has been another worthwhile venture. I have also used my organisation skills to contribute to the King's College Christmas Charity and Fashion Show. To relax, I enjoy playing the piano and reading novels and medical literature. I am also a member of SIFE, Brentwood Badminton Club and the church choir, where I have organised charity events and have helped raise £200 for MS.

I look forward to studying Medicine as I believe I possess the skills and the determination to meet the demands of this course and to enjoy the challenges it offers.

12.2 Personal statement 2 (Graduate)

Personal statement successful for: Brighton, Bristol (undergraduate), Leeds

It has always been my desire to become a doctor, and, although my A level grades prevented me from immediate entry to medical school, the ambition remained with me. I decided to undertake a degree in Chemistry and have since graduated with First Class Honours, which I believe demonstrates that I am well equipped for the academic rigours of Medicine. During my time at university I have undergone a diverse range of experiences at home and abroad, and now I have the insight to understand why I have always been inclined to contribute to society through the practice of Medicine.

My interest in medicine was actively stimulated through a voluntary research project I carried out during my third year of study at the prestigious University of Wollongong, Australia, 'Developing Novel Dual Action Anti-malarial Agents'; two of the agents I designed and synthesised were sent to a biomedical laboratory in Bangkok, for their in vitro anti-malarial potency against a chloroquine resistant parasite to be tested for. My interest, not only in people but the psycho-social impact of disease and illness on their lives, was manifested when I spent three weeks teaching orphans whose lives had been devastated by the AIDS virus, as well as Maasai tribesmen, during a voluntary project in Tanzania.

Through shadowing Doctors in four specialities at a Sheffield Hospital, and two GPs, I developed an awareness of the realities of being a Doctor in the modern NHS: I considered a patient's distress when their condition could not be treated and a Doctor's frustration when he was unable to help his patient to be amongst the difficulties of the job. However, I feel that the excitement of taking on the challenge of a diagnosis using essential problem-solving and decision-making skills, coupled with the immense feeling of reward that comes by making a positive difference to people's lives, far outweighs these cons.

Throughout my degree and particularly during the year-long research project I carried out as part of my Master's year, I have developed and applied skills of critical appraisal and have been trained to make decisions based upon scientific evidence: both of which have fundamental importance in evidence-based medicine. During my final year of study, I volunteered weekly at Darnell Dementia Group and carried out ward relief volunteer work at St Luke's Hospice, Sheffield for three months, which I am currently continuing with weekly at Bolton Hospice. This gave me first-hand experience in understanding the way in which disease affects individuals differently and its impact on people who are indirectly affected, such as carers and family members.

As a Relief Residential Social Care Worker for the Together Trust, and an employee of Bolton PCT Health Care Assistant Bank, I intend to further explore the healthcare profession during my gap year. Gaining practice of taking a patient-centred approach to situations and acquiring an understanding of the NHS are just some of the ways in which my gap year work will equip me well for medical school.

I have always endeavoured to be a part of the community, from my position as Head of Year Council throughout secondary school, to my responsibility of Orientation Week Leader during my study year abroad, through to being a committed member of the Sheffield University Cheerleading Squad; I have gained essential leadership and teamwork skills along the way. Activities such as boxing and running, which has helped me raise money for Cancer Research UK, help me to gain a balance between work and play, which is essential for coping with the demands and challenges of becoming a Doctor. My ambitious nature and appreciation of diversity resulted in my backpacking around Australia independently, and spontaneously extending my travel to New Zealand and Thailand.

I believe these skills and qualities that I have developed over recent years will ease my transition from science graduate into one of 'Tomorrow's Doctors'.

12.3 Personal statement 3 (Graduate)

Personal statement successful for: Warwick

I never did catch the name of the man I moved to and from radiology, but the satisfaction of doing my part in the hospital, coupled with his smile, embodies my drive towards medicine. My motivation in applying is derived from a series of experiences, both academic and extracurricular. These have stimulated my enthusiasm to become a doctor who would apply values and skills to bring advances in fundamental science to human care.

The first experience that influenced my career path was when I volunteered at my local hospital. I was able to share the view of medical care from the patient perspective and appreciate the hopes and anxieties involved in these encounters. I also interacted with many healthcare providers to gain an understanding of their roles. A high-school placement in general practice and a physiotherapy clinic further expanded my knowledge in this area.

Following this, during my first summer of university, I worked at Camp Kodiak; a wilderness boarding programme for children suffering immense physical and mental challenges. Working as a counsellor I was directly responsible for the individual wellbeing of my campers 24 hours a day, including their ability to work with others, learning from their counsellors as well as attending to their medical needs. Mornings were often spent administering the medicines required to manage an extensive variety of conditions. The intimate level of involvement in each of these campers' daily routines gave me a deeper level of patience and understanding, in helping others negotiate immense challenges. In working directly with healthcare providers I gained valuable insight into the pharmacological and psychological elements of treatment. Personally, nothing that summer could compare to the satisfaction of knowing that I'd helped my campers through days of sports, life skills and fun that would translate into future achievement in their daily lives.

Taking a different approach to the same principle of assisting the ill, I worked for two summers as a research student with the University of Toronto. My research looked at the signalling pathways implicated in pre-eclamptic placental cells in a clinical molecular-biology laboratory. I employed genetic isolation and analysis as well as advanced microscopy techniques for cell culture. This gave me invaluable hands-on experience with genetic medicine and the scientific process. Studying with professional geneticists in their lab setting exposed me to the rigours and rewards of their career. This brought the invaluable opportunity of experiencing the application of molecular genetics to clinical medicine.

My initial courses at university were in biomedical computing; however, I found that my own personal interests and strengths were in the biological sciences. This is reflected, I believe, in my university results in subsequent years. In the final year of my honours degree I was encouraged to undertake my Masters of Science. My research seeks to enhance the growth of farmed fish tissue to support human populations, with exciting first and third-world application. In addition to my lab work I took on the role of teaching undergraduate students through complex animal dissections and anatomy. I thrived on the interaction of peer-directed learning and collaborative environments, recognising that learning is a mutual process. Working both in leadership and teamwork roles has given me strong insight into the dynamics of the group learning environment. I was privileged to receive the University Award for Excellence in Teaching.

I am excited by the opportunities of a patient-focused career in medicine and new developments in healthcare based on the application of fundamental research. My time in the community, the classroom, the hospital and the research laboratory have, I believe, equipped me with the skill set to contribute to medical school, my peers and ultimately in the improvement of human health.

12.4 Personal statement 4 (Graduate)

Personal statement successful for: UEA, Warwick

From as early as I can remember I have had a passion for medicine and the effect of medicine on society. This was almost unavoidable as my father is senior partner of a GP practice in Bootle and my mother is a nurse. Bootle is one of the most deprived areas in the UK, with very high levels of chronic disease and poverty, and I have seen at first hand the difference that a compassionate and caring doctor and nurse can make.

I decided to take a gap year before entering university and I worked at my father's general practice where I organised and ran my own respiratory clinic, seeing COPD and asthma patients on a one-to-one basis to test their lung function. Following every clinic, I would discuss the results I had obtained with the practice's respiratory disease coordinator, and decisions on diagnosis and treatment would be made. I enjoyed this work very much, especially working with the patients. I also undertook a number of interesting audits for the practice and the local PCT. One such audit was carried out in conjunction with Aintree Hospital and attempted to find patients who may be unknowingly diabetic. The majority of my work experience has been in the primary care setting, where I shadowed two GPs in their respective surgeries. I have also shadowed the match doctors at Everton and Liverpool football clubs, giving me an insight into emergency medicine. This has been continued with my long-term commitment to St. John's Ambulance.

Although my urge to study medicine was very strong, I decided to apply to study Pharmacology since I was interested in the fundamental science behind medicine. I wanted to understand the mechanisms of action of drugs working in the body, and their effects on patients. I was and continue to be intrigued by the placebo and nocebo effects of drugs, and the psychology and physiology behind their effects.

I finished in the top five of my year of fifty-five students and gained a first class honours degree. Furthermore, I was the only student in the year to have my dissertation nominated for the Science, Engineering and Technology Awards 2008. Besides much else my degree in Pharmacology taught me that I would really like to work in Medicine and with people. It was not surprising that I found that the most interesting areas of my university course were when the science interlinked with humanity. It is for this main reason that I am applying to study medicine so that I can become a GP.

I currently work for Assura Medical in Liverpool auditing dermatology data. The cause and epidemiology of many of the dermatological problems I have encountered are difficult to establish, and it is this diversity that I find interesting. At the same time, I am also reading for an MSc in Medical Physics from the Open University. I am eager to learn more about the human application of diagnostic imaging and radiotherapy. I have come into contact with some imaging techniques and also studied an advanced cancer module in my degree. However, I think that gaining a greater understanding in topics such as MRI and Positron Emission Topography and in so doing developing the ability to interpret complex diagnostic results is important for a modern doctor, as is a sound understanding of the physics of radiotherapy.

While I was at school, I gained an Edmund Rice 6th Form Scholarship, was appointed deputy head boy and senior prefect, and completed my Duke of Edinburgh Gold Award. I am currently volunteering at my school, helping pupils who are participating in the Duke of Edinburgh Award. At university, I was a member of the Student Community Action volunteering service, and I enjoy playing tennis and badminton. I love to read, laugh and discuss issues with friends, and I have a passion for music – I am a grade 8 pianoforte student.

From the above it can be seen that I really want to work in medicine and help people as a GP, as well as continuing to develop my understanding of why we administer drugs and how they work.

12.5 Personal statement 5 (Graduate)

Personal statement successful for: Glasgow, Newcastle

Medicine is a career that I wish to pursue because of my enthusiasm for science, my interest in the study of the human body and my desire to help others.

After completing my master's in Physics with Astrophysics with First Class Honours, I travelled in South America and Eastern Europe for seven months. Coping with unfamiliar situations has provided me with confidence and the ability to communicate effectively with a wide variety of people. I spent time observing medical practice on a ward in Peru and witnessed how doctors significantly improved their patients' lives despite limited technology. This helped strengthen my resolve to become a doctor.

During my undergraduate years I have learnt to prioritise and manage my time effectively, in order to meet deadlines and achieve success. I also believe that the numeric, problem solving and computer literacy skills gained from Physics will be an asset in a medical career. For my research project I critically appraised journal articles, delivered presentations and communicated well with fellow scientists. Along with my mature and reflective approach to independent learning, these skills will prove invaluable as a medical student.

To gain an insight into medical practice I undertook work experience with a general practitioner, consultant physician and general surgeon. This increased my understanding of how vital communication and multidisciplinary teamwork is in optimising healthcare. Direct observation of doctor-patient relationships showed me the importance of empathy and effective communication in medical practice. The work experience also made me aware that, whilst medicine is an exciting and challenging profession, it can be extremely demanding and at times emotionally draining. I observed surgical procedures and following one of these I witnessed the compassionate and empathetic breaking of bad news to the patient. These experiences have reinforced my belief that a career in medicine is for me and I have now arranged for further experience shadowing in a local hospital, to continue gaining more insight into different areas of the medical profession.

I have also worked voluntarily at a nursing home looking after an elderly relative suffering from Alzheimer's disease. Here, I helped her with the activities of daily living and was also able to keep her in good spirits by reading, chatting and listening to her. I learnt to be patient and compassionate and found the experience very rewarding. By leading a local summer Play Scheme, I further developed my interpersonal skills, leadership and communication skills, especially in difficult and delicate situations which I learned to handle with sensitivity and consideration. These life experiences have laid foundations for some of the skills I will need in a career in medicine.

My hobbies and interests allow me to keep a balanced life. I am a keen musician, playing the violin, piano and guitar, gaining grade eight and seven in violin and piano respectively. I was also leader of the second violins in the North Wales Youth Orchestra and I continue to play. I like to play cricket and competitive football once a week and enjoy being part of a team as I work well in this setting. I also enjoy climbing and, last year, my father and I scaled Mount Kilimanjaro in Tanzania. The challenging five-day hike required co-operation with each other and determination with a shared sense of achievement at the end.

I am now certain that I want to be a doctor. I understand some of the difficult challenges, academic, physical and emotional, I will face in the coming years, but am confident that I have the enthusiasm, determination, good physical health and the academic ability to succeed.

12.6 Personal statement 6 (Graduate)

Personal statement successful for: Barts, Sheffield, Warwick

Before coming to university I didn't realise just how much I wanted to become a doctor. To help me confirm whether dedicating the rest of my own life to the lives of other people was the right decision, I undertook three long-term volunteering placements. Between October 2007 and January 2008 I worked as a Ward Befriender on one of the renal wards at the Royal London Hospital. On a weekly basis I visited the patients at their bedside, engaging them in conversation and taking the time to listen to their concerns. While at times it was an incredibly difficult experience to see people in pain or deteriorating week-on-week, I endeavoured not to let this affect my work and remained a friendly face to help take their mind away from their treatment. This experience gave me a newfound respect for nurses and an insight into the practical workings of an NHS healthcare team. From January until the exam term I moved to the Reception to work as Hospital Welcomer. This required a thorough knowledge of all the hospital wards and departments, and I soon learned to connect with patients and their relatives at the hospital's front line.

Over the course of the last 12 months as a volunteer for St. John Ambulance I have treated many patients at a variety of public events. I've been fortunate enough to attend training courses and formally certify my skills with four first aid qualifications, which I have already used to make a difference both at work and out in the community, cementing my desire to specialise in emergency medicine.

My degree in Medical Engineering has taken me from foundation engineering principles to increasingly specialist modules like Urology and Clinical Ethics. Teaching methods ranged from self-study, group and PBL exercises to working with cells under the microscope in the laboratory. Our fourth year group project centres on manipulating a proprietary bone substitute material called 'Actifuse' so that it can be surgically implanted in spinal fusion procedures. While challenging, the opportunity to be involved in a real-life clinical solution has encouraged me to further my interest in medicine by reading around the subject.

I have worked in a team of Residential Stewards in the halls of residence where I was responsible for the pastoral care of the students, as well as reacting to emergency situations like fire alarms. My role was later extended to managing that team as Senior Steward. I was able to refer to my experiences here when working towards the Leadership and Management Award.

In today's NHS, at a time when doctors are increasingly seen as team leaders, the management skills I have gained first-hand will no doubt be invaluable.

I am a firm believer that there is more to the university experience than study. I learned to snowboard through my participation in the University of London Ski and Snowboard Club and I'm looking forward to my fourth trip to the French Alps – as always it will be an excellent opportunity to wind down after the hard work of the preceding semester. I also made many friends through the College's Engineering Society. My other hobbies include music – I play keyboard at grade 3 – and I relax between study sessions by regularly attending my local gym.

The development of my preferred study styles using the 'Insights' model will help me to cope with the considerable workload of a medical degree, and my NCFE in Equality and Diversity has helped me adapt to work more effectively with a wider variety of people. I believe my engineering perspective and varied experiences both in study and at work offer clear advantages over traditional applicants as well as graduates from other degree programmes.

12.7 Personal statement 7 (Graduate)

Personal statement successful for: Southampton

Who would have thought that, as a teenager, I would have been assisting physicians with technical procedures such as colonoscopies and venepunctures during long hospital stays with my Mother. Also I had the responsibility of assisting my mother to the toilet when suffering from rectal bleeding and then reporting back to nurse. These were just one of the many things which made me yearn to study medicine. Being focused under pressure, I aspire to the challenges of diagnosing by implementation of scientific knowledge and assisting patients to recover physically and emotionally.

The realities of a medical career unfolded during my 3 months' work at Vicarage Medical Surgery where I carried out a variety of tasks from writing letters and updating patient's medical details to observing doctors during consultations. The ability to speak four different languages alongside my current studies in Arabic and British Sign Language aided me to communicate effectively to those patients I met during my work placement at the GPs and those I met while being a member of St John Ambulance for over 8 months. Here, I was also given the chance to develop my skills of working with patients, providing me with an excellent opportunity to develop first aid skills and meet new people by joining duties at public events.

Volunteering at the Royal London Hospital and Whipps Cross Hospital as a ward befriender made me share experiences and learn from junior doctors about life as a medical student. Not only did I make a contribution to patients' healthcare, but also got the opportunity to observe doctors taking medical history, performing physical examination and offering diagnosis & treatment. While at hospital I have also attended an Interdisciplinary meeting which taught me how teamwork, organisation and communication skills directly affect the quality of patient care provided.

Experience of learning about different aspects of disability and also being able to be part of a highly skilled team of physiotherapists, paediatric nurses and wheelchair trainers during a placement with Whizz Kidz over this summer was very rewarding, seeing children gain independence. I was given the responsibility of encouraging children to gain independence using wheelchairs by planning diverse activities. My love for children led me into committing myself to a year-long internship as a project leader with READ International. My responsibilities are diverse from recruiting, managing and motivating volunteers to planning workshops at secondary schools, raising funds and travelling to Tanzania in summer 2010 to distribute books: experiences that have matured me into a responsible leader. I have gained and further improved my counselling and problem-solving skills by working as a mentor for undergraduates. As a passionate learner and teacher, I would love to continue working as an undergraduate mentor at a medical school.

In response to the Kashmir earthquake in 2005, I volunteered and travelled to the affected area where I was involved with hospital fund-raising, counselling and emotional support for a month. The experience helped me to comprehend the various traumas people can experience.

Having learnt time management skills during my degree helped me manage my job as a customer assistant while working as an A-level tutor, together with time for improving my sketching and playing badminton at advanced level at my local clubs. I also have an inquisitive mind that has led me into keeping up to date with scientific and medical advancements through reading various journals such as the BMJ. Recently the scientific articles on the topic 'Varenicline and suicidal behaviour' have been the main focus of my readings. Mahatma Gandhi once said, 'Be the change you want to see in the world.' It is my ambition to continue to serve the community with my dedication, hard work and patience. These invaluable experiences have just fuelled my ambition of becoming Tomorrow's Doctor.

12.8 Personal statement 8 (Graduate)

Personal statement successful for: Cambridge, Imperial College, UCL

Studying the science of life makes the journey through your own life more fascinating. Being able to apply the knowledge gained makes your life more meaningful. This is what I have learned during summer holidays spent at an IVF clinic in Athens. There, apart from being the first point of contact with the patients as a receptionist, I shadowed my uncle who is an obstetrician-gynaecologist and his colleagues. I was fascinated by the solutions provided to couples facing infertility problems, solutions not even dreamt of a couple of decades ago. Having the opportunity to talk to patients on a daily basis and seeing the stress experienced during their treatment, I realised how important it is for a doctor to have communicative skills, be calm and pay attention to the psychological well-being of his patients. At the same time I was working for a company specialising in the isolation and storage of stem cells, which has led me to the decision to undertake a project on stem cells and heart repair in my third year of studies at UCL in order to deepen my knowledge in this most promising field.

I am sure my decision to study Biomedical Sciences as a first degree and then apply to medical school was correct. Although I felt medicine and particularly oncology was my true calling, coming from Greece at the age of 18 I knew I was not ready to gain entrance to study medicine at a prestigious UK institution. Today I feel very confident to do it and my second year results can prove it. The subjects I have studied have provided me with a thorough grounding in the sciences underlying medicine. I particularly enjoyed Cancer Biology which included an extended second year project about oestrogens and breast cancer as well as a lab project for my final year.

My conviction to become a doctor was reinforced last summer, when I spent one month at the Hammersmith Hospital. There I came in contact with various health professionals, including house officers, nurses and consultants, and had the opportunity to discuss with them. I understood that the demanding job of a doctor is often frustrating but ultimately fulfilling as it combines science with a willingness and ability to help. The most important lesson I have learned at the echocardiography department is that it is essential for a doctor not only to be responsible and conscientious but also to have an enquiring mind which helps to analyse and update the knowledge he already has.

While in high school I have had responsibilities as a student council representative as well as a member of both the health and environmental education groups which taught me the skills of teamwork and decision making. From my outdoor activities during summer camp such as hiking and rafting I learned to be ready to face a range of challenges in tough conditions. In my part time job as a bookshop assistant, I had the opportunity to communicate with children. However, these activities did not prevent me from ranking first among all students in the nationwide entrance examinations and therefore being awarded the National Scholarship Foundation Award as well as the University of Patras (Greece) Award for entering first in the university. But having always been a perfectionist and seeking the best for myself I had already decided that the United Kingdom would be the best place for me to live and study, having a unique worldwide reputation for quality higher education.

In my spare time I enjoy swimming, going to the gym, reading novels, learning foreign languages and traveling abroad. Apart from English and Greek, I speak French fluently and I am now learning Italian through a self-teaching method with a view to expand my communication skills. As the old saying says, when the student is ready the teacher will appear. Given the opportunity I know I am equal to the challenge of what must be a testing, fascinating, often frustrating but ultimately satisfying career as a doctor.

12.9 Personal statement 9 (Graduate)

Personal statement successful for: Imperial College, Warwick

Losing my brother to SCID at the age of 5 was a traumatic event, and my first experience of genetics and medicine. Some years later that experience developed into an interest in a Medical career. I discussed my options with my Grandfather, a GP, and several other doctors I met working as a Medical Team Secretary. I concluded it would be advantageous to gain a broad foundation on which to build a future in medicine, providing perspective and appreciation of the wider environment. I was still fascinated by medicine and genetics and therefore decided on a Human Genetics degree, combining both interests and specifically choosing medically related modules such as developmental biology.

Following university, I determined it was right for me to gain further skills in a non-medical background using my degree specialty. As a forensic examiner I enhanced my professional communication, problem solving and teamworking skills, through the pressures felt on time critical cases, learning the importance of confidentiality and professional integrity. Nevertheless, I maintained a contact with medicine, interpreting medical reports for some cases and relating these to my own examinations. Discovering some of the less pleasant aspects of the medical profession has not deterred my commitment to Medicine.

My particular affinity with people led me to work with Nottingham Access Centre, helping separated families interact in a neutral environment. This provided a huge learning source in mediation, adapting quickly to situations and spending time with all ages in a highly pressured atmosphere. Most rewarding was my involvement with Literacy Volunteers, helping children develop and improve their reading skills. Spending time with the children challenged my communication styles, but, by adapting a method dependent on the nature of the child, I quickly established trust and confidence with the children, their parents and teachers. Seeing remarkable progress so swiftly when given a listening environment was stunning!

I gained an insight into hospital laboratories and Radiology at Kingsmill Hospital, where interaction with patients was developed further as a volunteer at Queen's Medical Centre: seeing doctors and nurses working first-hand and helping with daily errands on the ward. Through this experience I was able to talk to patients about their experiences of the hospital and staff, gaining an appreciation of the relationships between doctors, patients and the NHS. I was privileged to spend time with a consultant physician in Sherwood Day Hospital where I saw several medical cases, including a TILT test and how a hospital deals with MRSA patients. I was able to interact with many of the patients including those with speech difficulties and Parkinson's disease. Here, I learnt many challenging but valuable lessons in being a caring and sympathetic listener, as well as the importance of excellent communication and compassionate skills to alleviate patients' and families' worries.

I have many interests including sports, travel and reading. Having lived abroad, I am interested in different cultures and spent time travelling the world. This greatly increased my interest in people and traditions, whilst developing interpersonal skills. I recently rediscovered my enjoyment in playing badminton and joined the company team. We are relatively new, so I am organising competitions between local companies to improve our skills and encourage interaction. I have organised several charity events over the past 2 years and I enjoy the challenge required to make these successful. I recently completed a sponsored skydive for the SCID-related Bubble Foundation.

I believe a medical degree will combine my love of challenges and people with a proven interest in science and the human body. I am thoroughly committed to succeeding in a medical profession, believing that I could make a positive contribution due to my enthusiasm, dedication and intellectual ability.

12.10 Personal statement 10 (Graduate)

Personal statement successful for: Barts, St George's, Southampton,

My appointment as a Management Consultant for the NHS CfH Project, one of Deloitte's most prestigious engagements, sparked my interest in the health service. I excelled and thrived, knowing my work was helping to improve healthcare delivery. From this I realised that my future career would have a people focus instead of a financial focus, therefore, on completion of the task, I left Deloitte to broaden my experience by working within a caring and emotionally rewarding setting. Wanting to combine my desire to work within the NHS with my academic ability and interest in the sciences, I aimed to enter the medical profession; however, to ensure I was perfectly suited, I took the massive step to end my business career to gain hands-on experience of patient care.

Working enthusiastically as a Healthcare Assistant on a surgical ward, I enjoyed patient interaction and the provision of care, expanded my understanding of hospital procedures and also recognised the importance of interdisciplinary communication. Doctors explained their past experiences, current challenges and future aspirations whilst some offered periods of doctor shadowing, on both surgical and orthopaedic wards, providing a valuable introduction to the experiences and challenges of consultants and also helping to consolidate my aims. My time was rewarding as I was able to perform patient care duties and also observe additional procedures in my own time, including cannulation, phlebotomy, catheterisation, NG intubation, Hickman line insertion and a lap appendix. These experiences, together with the positive outcome of my voluntary work in the mental health sector, were defining factors in my decision to proceed into medicine and, although the salary was a third of my former position, my first paid role in healthcare was infinitely more satisfying.

Aiming for broader experience, I currently work in an NHS Day Centre for adults with complex needs and learning disabilities, coordinating activity groups and assisting with personal care. As a keyworker, responsible for assessing and documenting wellbeing, I actively liaise with relevant parties to ensure care plans are appropriate and provide choice. This challenging, yet enjoyable, role has also allowed observation of review meetings with psychiatrists. I supplement this work with bank shifts as a Senior Healthcare

Assistant, allowing me to extend my experience from the surgical ward to medical, orthopaedic and accident & emergency wards. For my continuing development, I arrange and undertake additional doctor shadowing and in 2009 I plan to experience a different healthcare system by working in Canada.

Alongside full-time work, I taught myself AS Chemistry in 3 months. I found this an engaging subject which I could relate to my work in the hospital and everyday life. I am now studying AS Biology, but do understand the need for breaks from work and study. To relax, I play the guitar, trumpet and piano to grade 8, have recorded 3 albums and organised many gigs for charity. With a passion for snowboarding and hiking, I regularly take trips abroad to indoor slopes and National Parks.

Since my decision to change career, I have researched a variety of sources from the internet to the Student BMJ, experienced diverse patient care settings, learnt from professionals and performed independent academic learning to ensure my time at university and wider career will be a success. These positive steps have strengthened my desire to become a doctor and fuelled my ambition further. I now have a focused direction, about which I am passionate, and a career aim that will complement my academic ability and existing skills. I am fully committed and determined to achieve, as illustrated by my paid, voluntary and academic work. With my relevant life experience, I believe I am the perfect age to embark on my studies as I have maturity and the advantage of having many years to commit to medicine.

12.11 Personal statement 11 (Graduate)

Personal statement successful for: Nottingham, St George's

From the age of 15, when I arranged work experience in my local hospital, I have always been drawn to medicine. At that time the pure academic challenge drove me to achieve a Physics Master's at Oxford. But as a natural people person this did not satisfy my need to be part of a team. I am drawn to a profession where I can work and interact with a broad spectrum of society and experience this diversity on a daily basis. Since graduation I have reassessed my priorities and now know what I want. Medicine is everything I am looking for in a career.

I have shadowed a stroke consultant, a GP and a leading neuro-oncologist, experiencing 3 very different sides of the profession. I glimpsed the ultimate buzz of giving a patient hope and saw the patient's bitterness on receiving bad news. I feed residents in a local nursing home, have volunteered on an outpatient tea-trolley, have attended NHS volunteer training courses and am undertaking a geriatric feeding course weekly at St George's, giving me hands-on experience of caring for patients in the NHS as well as in a private care home.

What spurs me on is the challenge to understand and relate to different people as individuals. I discovered this in my weekly nursing home volunteering. Patience is essential; working with each person as a whole, seeing not just their ailment and listening out for things unsaid, is also vital. Building trust and understanding their eating and behavioural habits is extremely satisfying and the personal reward when I successfully get someone to eat a full meal or to have a conversation – no matter how brief – is enormous.

Despite the variety of my experiences so far, I know that I have only scratched the surface. Shadowing Dr Cloud in the Stroke Unit at St George's has fuelled my ambition to go further. Such a normal day for him filled me with so much enthusiasm and excitement. That is when I knew unequivocally that I had to become a doctor.

I have not taken my decision lightly. I have quizzed consultants, junior doctors, residents and students and have built a picture of common hopes, frustrations and realities. I realise that the path to becoming a doctor and specialising afterwards is a long and arduous one. But I saw in them the same underlying motivation and determination that I recognise in myself. I realised that, despite their complaints, they would not change their job for the world. That is why I have worked so hard to get to this point, and will not give up until I can say the same.

I am an extremely driven person, shown both in my academic and extracurricular achievements, a natural team player and a leader. I have always sung in choirs and was a member of the University 1st netball team for 3 years. I was awarded an Oxford Blue and was elected OUNC President in my 3rd year and social secretary in my second year. I coordinated and led a committee, fought for fairer Blues legislation and improved the squad attitude and vision. I also founded the Netball Outreach Scheme, sending netballers into primary schools to coach after-school sessions. My hunger for challenge, stamina and willingness to take on responsibility led me to achieve all this in tandem with my academic studies. This tenacity drives me every day, and will push me harder in my commitment to becoming a doctor.

I am aware that being a doctor isn't always a success story. I too have had my fair share of success and failure, but have always retained my innate desire to succeed. If anything, the failures I have had have led me to fight harder, and to relish even more the opportunity to face a challenge head-on.

12.12 Personal statement 12 (Graduate)

Personal statement successful for: UCL

Medicine has always struck me as an exciting profession, positioned as it is at the very human interface between science and society. I am attracted to the need for lifelong learning, and the wide range of specialisations open to medics. It is a long-term interest of mine, which was originally sparked during my sixth form years by time spent volunteering at a school for children with learning difficulties. With a challenging six months spent teaching English in China as well as three years of university behind me, I find myself in a carefully considered position, excited at feeling ready to enter such an intellectually and emotionally challenging field.

I of course undertook a number of work experience placements to find out more about the realities of being a doctor. The first of these was in a GP practice. I observed clinics with the doctors, and spent time with the practice nurse, the health visitor, and the reception team. This helped me to appreciate the importance of utilising and valuing the particular skills each member brings to a healthcare team. Whilst I found the detective-like nature of diagnosis appealing, what I enjoyed most was seeing the fine-tuning involved in managing the medication of patients with several chronic conditions.

I later observed a psychiatrist at work in a Drug and Alcohol Service, largely catering for heroin addicts on methadone maintenance programmes. I liked the social element to this work, and saw the importance of taking a holistic approach to patient care. It also helped me to appreciate that the aims of healthcare are often centred on improving quality of life and harm minimisation, rather than curing a patient.

I also spent time shadowing an F2 doctor on a psychiatric in-patient ward. This gave me some insight into the potential difficulties of dealing with psychotic patients, as well as highlighting the importance of meticulously kept patient notes. These proved invaluable in recognising patterns of behaviour, and seeing what had (or had not) worked in the past. It also became apparent that, as a junior doctor, honesty when assessing personal abilities is essential.

I try to contribute to my immediate community through my involvement with the college welfare team. As a 'Peer Supporter' I completed training in supportive listening, and have gained an appreciation of the importance of trust and confidentiality, as well as experience of dealing with sensitive issues in a non-judgemental manner. My wish to be more involved in the wider community has recently led me to start volunteering in a homeless centre, serving food and chatting with the visitors. As well as challenging my ideas about the causes of homelessness, this has deepened my conviction that working with vulnerable and sometimes chaotic people can be both challenging and rewarding.

Last summer I returned to China to work on an English language camp. Here the teaching team were also in charge of coordinating evening activities for the 400 attendees, a task which required great organisational efforts and endless enthusiasm. I feel that my experiences of living in China have helped broaden my cultural awareness, and have made me more flexible and willing to ask for assistance.

I understand that time management, and the ability to prioritise and balance various demands, will be an important skill. This juggling act is something I am used to; during my time at university I have managed to play for the women's football team, the college badminton and table tennis teams, and coxed the Men's Novice B rowing team alongside my studies. These activities have reinforced the importance of motivation, commitment, and strong leadership in creating a smoothly functioning team. I have played the violin and piano since I was six, and continue to find great joy in playing orchestrally, and in informal groups.

Since arriving in Oxford, I have relished studying in a demanding academic environment, and feel well equipped to deal with the rigours of an intense medical degree. In my first year I gained a distinction in my exams, and was awarded a scholarship for my achievement. The practical side of chemistry has required a degree of dexterity and accuracy that should stand me in good stead for studying practical procedures. In the coming year I will be undertaking an independent year-long laboratory project that should improve my problem solving capabilities, and prepare me further for independent study.

12.13 Personal statement 13 (Graduate)

Personal statement successful for: Leicester

Being an identical twin, genetics and heritability is of great interest to me, so I chose to study genetics in my higher education. As an undergraduate I carried out laboratory-based research and it was this experience which indicated to me that my career preferences lay elsewhere. During my studies I have particularly enjoyed researching dominant and recessive gene disorders including Sickle Cell Anaemia, PKU and Fragile X syndrome and became interested in how certain families can be particularly susceptible to various conditions. I subsequently read 'Is it in your genes?' by Philip Reilly which summarises family disease heritage. I would love the opportunity to continue studying and to develop my scientific knowledge, particularly in the areas of heritage, and to better understand the physiological implications of disease.

Since graduating I have concluded that a career in medicine would provide me with the intellectual and personal challenges I am seeking. This decision was also confirmed by attending a lecture given by a clinical geneticist. Her knowledge and experiences made me realise that the opportunity to work alongside many individuals in a scientific but caring capacity made medicine the career choice for me. I have also been inspired by my cousin, a surgeon who operated during my tonsillectomy. Through this experience and also shadowing doctors at Leicester Royal Infirmary, I have observed how rewarding it can be both personally and professionally to make a career from caring for and improving the lives of others. I am prepared to put in the same time and effort that they have demonstrated.

Whilst at university I volunteered to teach school children how to become more enterprising. This experience lead me to my current volunteering with Barnardos CareFree, where I help young carers deal with the demands that caring for those with physical and mental illness has on them as individuals. This has taught me a great deal about patience, tolerance and how to listen more effectively, especially when dealing with the mentally ill. To gain a greater understanding of how we can be affected by our circumstances and the workings of the brain I decided to read 'Nature via Nurture' by Matt Ridley which gave me insight into this whole debate. I found the theories on schizophrenia particularly interesting and have recently read in the New Scientist about how rare gene duplications and deletions have been associated with this illness. Shadowing doctors provided insight into the team dynamics necessary for the efficient running of a hospital. I also spoke with patients and observed, with interest, the importance of positive, interactive relationships between patient and doctor, particularly when preparing a patient for theatre, which I myself understand through personal experience.

I believe I have many personal qualities necessary to become a good doctor in terms of enjoying academic study and also having sound interpersonal skills around emotional challenges, which frequently arise in this profession. I have often been told I am a compassionate, responsible and an approachable person, qualities demonstrated by my previous roles as a school prefect and captain of my college basketball and volleyball team, where we won a national gold volleyball medal. I still play basketball and have previously held the responsible position of Treasurer on the committee. Currently I am enjoying work as a full-time PA and part-time bar tender. I am actively looking for work experience as a healthcare assistant whilst saving in order to travel next Summer. In the next year I have 2 trips abroad planned, and aim to pass my driving test very soon. I believe this demonstrates that I am a well-rounded individual, and most importantly that I am capable of balancing the demands of a medical profession and future studies alongside personal interest.

12.14 Personal statement 14 (Graduate)

Personal statement successful for: Barts, Brighton

My greatest desire is to become a doctor. Medicine is a career in which I expect to be constantly learning and challenging myself and through this be motivated to work harder. To be able to use my knowledge and skills to make a difference to people's lives is to be in a position of great responsibility and one that I believe will satisfy my desire to resolve problems. I am intrigued by the human body and the way in which we function and how this relates to disease when processes begin to break down. I don't expect it to be an easy journey to becoming a doctor but I am certain the rewards will be worth all the hard work.

To ensure medicine is the career path for me I have undertaken work experience in several areas of the medical field. I organised two months shadowing a vascular surgeon and during that time I had the opportunity of going into theatre and even saw such major operations as a leg amputation. I also attended ward rounds, where I could see the importance of good communication both with patients and between doctors. In my time at the hospital I managed to speak to 5th-year medical students about their experiences and even practised skills such as taking blood.

I was eager to see the primary care side of medicine and arranged placements at two surgeries. I had the opportunity to see all the different aspects of a working practice, including going out on visits and attending a monthly meeting to discuss arising issues. Seeing doctors put their sometimes hesitant patients at ease I saw the need to be patient and understanding.

I am a volunteer in several capacities; through this work, I have put to the test many of the attributes I feel are essential in a doctor. Helping at a postnatal well-being group, I am a listening ear, aiming not to judge but to reassure and encourage the overwhelmed mothers. At a hospice I do a Sunday tea time duty: serving dinners and taking the opportunity to chat with patients. Although at times I find this work heartrending, I also see how much difference this social interaction can make to their day. As a member of the Red Cross I am learning about life-saving and enjoy functioning as part of a team.

Through university I was able to participate in a placement at an inner city school, helping teenagers to aim higher. This was a challenging task but one I threw myself into and the reward of getting through to some of the pupils made it worthwhile. I also spent time at a primary school, where teaching 5-year-olds basics such as subtraction proved more difficult than I anticipated. I felt frustrated at first but this role taught me a lot about having patience and being supportive. Seeing the progress, albeit slowly, of many of the children was extremely satisfying. At present I help lead my local cub scouts, where I enjoy being a role model to the children.

Whilst at university I wanted to try something new and started salsa lessons; although daunting at first I found it was a fun way to meet new people and a great way to exercise. I was also a committed member of an intermural netball team; I enjoyed the sense of team spirit both in victory and defeat! I am a keen traveller and spent my gap year exploring solo throughout Asia and Africa; this experience taught me self-reliance and boosted my confidence. In February 2008 I intend to travel in South America and teach scuba diving for five months.

I am a mature and self-motivated person, who having already been to university is prepared to immerse myself in my studies and to make the most of all the experiences on offer. I feel I am fully aware of the demands of medicine both as a degree and a profession. I am expecting it to be a challenge but one that I am determined to succeed at.

12.15 Personal statement 15 (Graduate)

Personal statement successful for: UCL

I am not your usual medical student candidate, I have a particular history. My goal in life is to make a difference in this world and, in the many ways one can go about doing so, I got lost in the crowd of possibilities. My International Baccalaureate was leading me to study International Relations, but I decided to study a life science as a first degree because I believe that the best way to help this world is to better the human condition, through better health and better environment.

I chose to study biochemistry as a first degree, but through my years at university I grew to understand that my job needs to have direct impact on people, not solely on academic development. It was not until this summer while working at Cancer Research UK that I realised that basic research was not the only option after graduation. I loved the experience of lab work, but I disliked the detachment of the basic research from daily life. There was a physician in my lab training to earn her PhD. By talking to her and other medical researchers, I learned about academic doctors. I found this a brilliant career path because it is a dynamic environment where you can work directly with people, carry out research, and teach. What makes this position so much more exciting than purely research is that you can directly help people, that your skills can make a difference for a person instantly. It is such a simple and amazing concept.

When reading research articles, I often find a need to relate the research advancements to patient care. There was a very interesting article in 'Cell' this summer about the application of RNAi in attenuating the HIV infection. The article showed how important it is to be able to develop therapies at the cellular level, like RNAi, but, for the therapy to have relevance, it is necessary to understand if it would be effective in the body of a person, something a doctor would know. Because I am most interested in applying scientific discoveries to fighting illnesses in people, I understood that becoming a doctor would be the right career for me. My view of a research career before and after my work experience changed dramatically, and therefore I am now developing a more sensitive view of a doctor's role by volunteering in a hospital at Dr Devaki Nair's office.

In addition to my interests, I think that my personality makes the choice of a career as a doctor the right one for me. I am a very active individual, taking part in many activities at my university. I enjoy assuming positions of responsibility, and last year I was elected president of the UCLU Volleyball Club, one of the most educative experiences of my life. I learned how to prioritise, that it is important to be considerate of the people you work with, and to show patience with club members who asked many extravagant questions. In my high school, I was Vice President of the student body and a Prefect for my final two years. Being a Prefect, I was in charge of the wellbeing of the girls in my dormitory, making sure that they had someone to confide in, that they respected the curfew and that they were treating each other respectfully. I also founded an organisation called A.B.C. (A Brother's Care) to raise funds and awareness for the poor situation of Tibetan children. As I assumed these positions, I experienced pressure and stress on the job, but it taught me to endure, to believe in myself and to keep a positive attitude, because, after all, it was my choice to be there. I have a relatively wide range of experiences, which helps me interact with my peers and would help me interact with patients. I have been exposed to situations that required patience, determination and endurance. I enjoyed the personal challenge and the feeling of enrichment upon completion of these tasks, and that is why I believe I have qualities to become a doctor.

12.16 Personal statement 16 (Graduate)

Personal statement successful for: Newcastle

In July of this year I graduated with a BSc (Hons) in Biochemistry from Liverpool University. This course has focused my ambitions to study for a career in Medicine and I hope to use this year gaining valuable experiences to further my prospects.

As with all degrees, the course developed my essential life skills such as self-motivation, discipline, organisation and determination, as well as allowing me to hone my written and oral communication skills.

During my time at university I have found that modules dealing with the genetic basis of disease such as oncogenes and cancer, or the mutation of genes leading to diseases such as Cystic Fibrosis, have held great interest for me. I am also fascinated by the biochemistry of disease, how cells function, genome organisation and analysis. My honours research project utilised *C.elegans* nematode worms as a genetic model to study the effect of genetic mutation on neuron development and axon guidance. This study looked directly at mutations in the HSPG and how this effects neuronal development. While at university I worked part-time as a care assistant at a nursing and residential home in Liverpool. Duties of this post included assisting residents with mobility problems, toileting and general ancillary care such as changing colostomy bags. This role not only allowed me to enhance my communication skills, but also highlighted that one of the most important qualities a carer can have is patience. I was chief carer for two of the male residents and through this learnt the importance of building relationships with patients and their families.

During my A-level studies, I volunteered as a classroom assistant one afternoon a week at a local school for children with physical disabilities. Children who attended this school suffered from various conditions such as Autism, Myotonic Dystrophy and ADHD. It became obvious to me how important specialist care is within such an environment and also how resilient children can be even when faced with tremendous difficulties.

I deferred entry to university in 2004. In this gap year my outgoing personality secured me a job as a customer service officer for Lloyds TSB, from which I was able to finance a very rewarding chapter of my life. For four months I travelled around the South Pacific and South East Asia. The trip not only afforded me many valuable life experiences, but built my confidence in dealing with a wide range of social situations.

Away from my academic studies I played for Rankin halls of residence football team, for which I was also social secretary. During this term I organised two football tours including Wroclaw in Poland. I also managed to secure a sponsorship deal with a local Liverpool retailer for our team strips. This opportunity not only heightened my sense of team spirit, but also allowed me to develop my leadership qualities and organisational skills.

Another great passion of mine is music. I play the piano to a grade eight standard, and can also play the saxophone and bass guitar. From an early age I played in various bands and performed in numerous local concerts.

My educational career, extracurricular activities and work experience, both in and out of the care industry, have all enabled me to develop many skills such as patience and understanding, initiative, and the abilities to work within a team, on my own and often under pressure. These, when combined with my scientific interest, enthusiasm and ability to communicate effectively, have made me a well-rounded individual who is eager to apply these traits to a medical degree and throughout a career in medicine.

12.17 Personal statement 17 (Graduate)

Personal statement successful for: Warwick

Six years ago, fresh faced from University, I started my first graduate job working as an assay development scientist for a drug discovery company called Prolifix Ltd., at Harwell. Not long afterwards, the urge to travel took hold and I flew to Australia, where my part-time job as a synthetic chemist at Menai Organics Ltd. during university helped me gain a three-month position as a research assistant at the University of Sydney, School of Chemistry. I then volunteered at the Mareeba Wetlands in the far north of Queensland and after two months, plus an epic 1400km solo cycle ride down Cape York Peninsula, was offered the position of assistant warden, where I honed my communication skills, giving guided tours each day to unsuspecting tourists. Previously, I had won the Project Conference Prize at University for the best presentation and have a natural ability to communicate information. After more travelling and a 1200km cycle ride up the south island of New Zealand, I arrived back in the UK.

One year later, my daughter, Lydia was born and I had the privilege of cutting the umbilical cord. At the time I was working in treasury management, where I learned two things: the importance of managing my finances effectively and that accountancy was not for me. With the intention of 'testing the water' for one or two weeks, an enquiry about work experience at a local veterinary practice resulted in a permanent position as a veterinary nursing assistant. I immediately knew that a career in a healthcare setting was right for me, but soon realised that I would prefer to treat humans rather than animals. However, the experience was very rewarding and gave me the opportunity to perform anaesthesia and administer IV, IM and subcutaneous injections, practise suturing following post mortems and witness a variety of surgical procedures, from exploratory laparotomies to thyroidectomies.

In August 2007, I stopped working at the practice and used my savings to support myself whilst I volunteered full-time at the John Masefield Cheshire Home for the physically disabled, primarily assisting the physiotherapist with the resident's daily exercises, but also contributing to other events including 'fun-days' and excursions. My time there really opened my eyes to the reality of life in a care home and the difficulties faced by people suffering from conditions such as Multiple Sclerosis, Huntington's disease and Usher syndrome. In addition I began to appreciate the demands placed upon the carers and nurses who looked after them as well as the ongoing battle to treat these conditions. I developed a great rapport with the residents and staff and still help out when I can.

In order to demonstrate recent evidence of academic achievement, I enrolled at the Open University to study 'Molecules in Medicine', a postgraduate course focusing on the molecular structure of drugs and how they interact with their target. Shortly afterwards, I was offered a position at the University of Oxford, as a 'medical laboratory scientific officer' at CTSU (Clinical Trial Service Unit and Epidemiological Studies Unit). I have continued with my studies, achieving a pass with distinction for the continuous assessment and hope to achieve a distinction overall. In addition, I was able to find time to train for the Blenheim triathlon.

CTSU is a world-renowned research facility founded in 1975 by Professor Sir Richard Peto and Professor Sir Richard Doll and is funded by the MRC, Cancer Research UK and the BHF, whose work primarily involves studies of the causes and treatment of chronic diseases, including cancer, heart attack and stroke. My primary responsibility is to analyse blood and urine samples for several randomised, controlled trials. I feel privileged to be involved with such a prestigious organisation, which has truly inspired me, not only to become a practising physician but perhaps also to be involved with clinical trials of the future.

12.18 Personal statement 18 (Graduate)

Personal statement successful for: Barts, Warwick

My desire to pursue the challenging career of medicine arises from a deep scientific curiosity and an endless desire to learn about the human body, its processes and diseases.

In 2006, I graduated with a BSc in Genetics and Microbiology, achieving a '1st' in my dissertation entitled 'Avian Influenza: Myths and Realities'. This academic year (during the gap between applying for and starting a course in medicine), I also decided to undertake an MSc in Molecular Medicine. I believe this course will provide me with advanced medical knowledge and will strongly complement a medical degree and career.

I have undertaken work experience in the A&E department at Barnet Hospital, shadowing nurses, doctors and consultants. This provided me with an invaluable perspective on how challenging and rewarding the profession can be. I firmly believe my personal qualities, such as commitment, determination and empathy, are ideally suited to medicine.

I also enrolled in summer school at Luton and Dunstable Hospital, working in the Clean Surgery ward. This provided an insight into how healthcare workers come together to provide a patient-centred service. In addition to working alongside nurses to clean, dress and bathe patients, I also shadowed an SHO and observed a range of operations in the Orthopaedic Theatre. This illustrated the importance of precision and professionalism in the healthcare system.

I currently work as a regular ward volunteer and fundraiser at the North London Hospice. This has emphasised the importance of care and compassion in healthcare and highlighted the importance of providing emotional and social support to patients and their families. I enjoy all aspects of volunteering at the hospice, particularly communicating and spending time with patients.

I have also worked for two years for a clinical diagnostics company, Thermo Fisher Scientific, where my specialist role involved providing medical product support to hospitals. My role also involved working and training in the Biochemistry Laboratory at Queen Elizabeth's Hospital.

Although I was highly successful at Thermo Fisher Scientific, the overall job satisfaction paled in significance compared with the satisfaction received from working as a healthcare volunteer. This experience, combined with my studies, has affirmed my desire to pursue a career in medicine.

In my free time, I have visited over 30 countries and love to immerse myself in different cultures. I have witnessed first-hand that, particularly in developing countries, basic knowledge of hygiene is often lacking and there is often a need for both improved healthcare and improved health education. One of my proudest personal achievements was to lose 6 stone in weight in a bid to raise awareness of diabetes within the South Asian ethnic community. My story will be published in the winter 2008 edition of 'Asiana' lifestyle magazine.

My professional and personal life experiences, combined with my academic qualifications, make me highly suited to a career in medicine. I believe that my passion for caring for others, combined with my unfettered enthusiasm, will serve me well in this field. I look forward to continuing my personal and academic development, both during medical school and throughout my future career.

12.19 Personal statement 19 (Graduate)

Personal statement successful for: Imperial College, King's College, Newcastle, Warwick

Medicine is one of the more challenging and demanding careers, but the satisfaction and continuous learning in the field more than makes up for all the hard work. I have tried to find out as much as I can about the art and science of Medicine, and to get as much work experience as possible, so that I don't carry false impressions about the career.

I spent a week at the Royal Victoria Infirmary, Newcastle, in the Care of the Elderly ward, watching in admiration the working of the tireless multidisciplinary team, ensuring that every patient is cared for and every change carefully monitored and adjusted. It was instructive to see how the consultants and junior doctors I shadowed use their knowledge and skills to make a differential diagnosis and act as a source of hope, stability and calm confidence in that very demanding setting. I was really fortunate to be able to ask a lot of questions, while observing various procedures. Since last March I have gone on to volunteer at the Belsay Unit of the Newcastle General Hospital for Age Concern, helping patients in the wards and some outpatients carry out activities that would be hard to do themselves due to various motor disabilities. This has allowed me to talk to various patients about their experiences as well as get an outlook on continued patient care during their stay as well as after.

I also worked with St John Ambulance prior to my degree, where I was trained in First Aid and basic anatomy. I have volunteered to help out at several public duties involving large numbers of people. This has helped me appreciate working in stressful conditions where time is of the essence, and the need to be calm, confident and level-headed while being thorough at the same time.

I was able to compare the different aspects of medicine from primary care to working in hospitals, as I have also spent two weeks with a health centre and two days with a GP surgery in Newcastle. I shadowed six general practitioners, and several other specialists to see successful provision of comprehensive clinical care in primary care settings. The enthusiasm with which GPs enjoyed teaching a young student like me was infectious. I am currently coordinating a volunteer team to help out at St Oswald's Hospice by providing a day off to the dedicated members of staff there as a Project Manager at my university.

My current degree will definitely help me with graduate entry medicine as it has prepared me not only for the majority of modules from the first two years of medicine but also made me familiar with the type of commitment, hard work and personal input required in a medical degree. Modules like human anatomy and physiology, cell biology, and biology of disease greatly interest me and my third year independent project work will centre on researching cancer treatment mechanisms including the specific effects of enzymes on drug-inhibited topoisomers that regain normal cellular growth.

I take academics very seriously and have participated in Science Olympiads, Maths Olympiad and Maths Challenge (*Silver Award*). These have definitely improved my personal learning skills, and also made me very competitive. Within school I have been involved with debating, achieving a Best Debater Award (September 2003) in an interschool competition, as well as the Running Trophy. I enjoy music, and in 2004/2005 was part of the school chamber choir and also play many musical instruments. I love pursuing many extracurricular activities and am currently part of the university's spinning and mixed martial arts clubs. I am also a Skills Trainer at my current Student's Union where I deliver many skills sessions to the students to help develop their skills in areas like confidence, task management, presentation skills, leadership and teamwork skills as well as more course specific research and essay writing techniques. Teaching these sessions has invaluably increased my own understanding of interpersonal qualities that will greatly help me in a medical career.

It seems that most of my life has led me towards Medicine in many ways. I love reading and some of my favourite books include fictional and non-fictional works related to medicine. I enjoy reading the medical news in media and journals on the internet, e.g. the student BMJ. I have attended several lectures at the Centre for Life, on controversial topics, presented by world leaders, e.g. Nobel laureate James Watson. I have been to several Life Centre Genetics workshops which greatly inspired me and taught me skills like accuracy and sensitivity. Virtually every aspect of medicine fascinates me, and the amazing variation, challenges, dedication, and the journey of learning just makes it more exciting. I just cannot wait to be a part of the medical community.

12.20 Personal statement 20 (Graduate)

Personal statement successful for: Warwick

Studying Genetics has significantly advanced my scientific understanding and honed my ability to integrate and apply this knowledge. I would sincerely relish the opportunity to combine my background in science with my interpersonal instincts. University has profusely encouraged my personal development and prompted me to explore numerous activities to challenge my long-lived aspiration for a medical vocation.

A week shadowing a House Officer on the Nephrology ward at the University Heath Hospital, Cardiff, greatly developed my clinical understanding and impressed upon me the true value of team dynamics in a patient's care. The experience was most memorable for the opportunity to observe and participate in a variety of key procedures. As well as being guided through the mechanisms of dialysis and seeing first-hand the impact that ongoing treatment can have on a quality of life, I also had the chance to witness a biopsy, a practice which perfectly illustrates the tremendous levels of empathy and ability that are vital for a career in medicine. Attending both Medlink and MedWales gave me a fascinating and motivational insight into several medical specialisations.

I have taken great pleasure from devoting time to various voluntary causes over significant periods of time and as a result my confidence has blossomed. I formed a good rapport with young children in both my role as a supervisor at the local primary after-school club and from making constructive use of my otherwise spare time in the reception class. Currently I make a weekly commitment at a local rehabilitation centre for patients affected by serious head injuries. Each afternoon spent is heart-wrenching and tiring, but this is far outweighed by the immeasurable feeling of worth.

I am in the process of organising further work experience for the summer in a much less orthodox healthcare setting in Nepal. I hope to gain a mutually beneficial experience and a rewarding insight into a less affluent health service. Eventually I aspire to develop this enthusiasm and my dexterity for French, doing charity work in an African Francophone country.

Following my scientific inclinations I organised a fulfilling summer as a paid research intern studying plant genetics at the University of Missouri. It afforded me the challenging opportunity to conduct research, which has unquestionably improved my analytical technique. Whilst there I attended a wide array of scientific lectures with peers: topics ranged from Osteopenia in cyclists to controversial chemical usage in food packaging. I came away from the experience deeply committed to combining science and compassion in my future academic career.

I practise the balance of an arduous workload with a hybrid of recreational activities by keeping fit with training for middle-distance charity runs, playing in a squash club and surfing. Perhaps one of my proudest achievements to date is a gruelling 3-day cycle ride from South to North Wales. I find music to be an excellent relaxation mechanism and in the summer often volunteer with Oxfam to steward music festivals. In order to complement this role I have completed a basic course in first aid with the Red Cross. In keeping myself informed with some of the more contentious issues related to my current field of study, I have become increasingly drawn to the study of medical ethics. I hope to help promote awareness of such public-related biological issues this coming year in my role as treasurer of the University Biomolecular Society.

I am motivated by an appetite for lifelong learning combined with a passion and conviction to contribute my potential to realise a progressive and positive medical future. I consider myself to have the stamina and strength of character to accomplish my ultimate goal of taking essential medical knowledge where it is needed.

12.21 Personal statement 21 (Graduate)

Personal statement successful for: Warwick

My interest in Medicine began when, at the age of 12, I was told that my grandmother had cancer. Being naïve, I desired to cure all victims of this devastating disease like the doctors who 'magically' made my grandma well. Since then, despite realising the challenges of Medicine, my attraction has grown stronger. In my final year at school, I passed the Belgian medical entrance exam, meriting acceptance to any Belgian university. However, apprehensive that I had not fully explored the implications of pursuing a career in medicine, I decided to defer my entry and study a related subject, Biochemistry, which I knew I would enjoy.

At university, my endeavours have led me to be added to the Dean's List as well as being awarded the Sir Jack Drummond prize for outstanding academic performance in my second year. As the student with the top marks in the Life Sciences Faculty, I have also been honoured with a scholarship.

Through various work placements in the past two years, I have gained a realistic insight into what Medicine entails. My experiences at the Neurology Department in Antwerp's Middelheim Hospital, at the NHS Royal London's Radiology Department, at Neotia Hospital's pathology lab and a paediatrician's surgery in Kolkata all confirmed my commitment to Medicine.

In the Neurology Department, each day was a new experience – from witnessing the high-pressure situation of the swift handling of a stroke patient, to enjoying performing regular tasks like taking patient histories and blood pressure. From my time at Neotia and Royal London, I learnt the integral role of medical tests, both diagnostic tests and body imaging techniques, in precise and fast diagnosis.

During a summer internship with Cancer Research UK (researching the interaction between a protein called kidins220 with the microtubule motor protein dynein), I was able to work as part of a dynamic scientific team, learnt experimental techniques and further developed my practical dexterity.

As an important part of University life, I partake in diverse activities, which include the Widening Participation Scheme where, as a Student Ambassador,

I host group visits to UCL. This has taught me how to communicate effectively and impartially with people from all walks of life – a crucial skill for a doctor not only during consultations but also whilst working with medical professionals.

Patience and perseverance are virtues I continuously practise as a mentor in the Peer Assisted Learning programme, which I joined after having previously enjoyed tutoring at school. Furthermore, I was elected Student Representative for the Life Sciences Faculty, which allowed me to participate in the running of a student union thus preparing me for the bureaucratic aspect of a medical centre.

Having introduced recycling to student halls, I am a co-leader of a voluntary project 'Junk In The Trunk', juggling many responsibilities such as volunteer recruitment, promotion and finances. All these various activities have not only improved my organisational and time-management skills, but also taught me to remain calm in difficult situations: skills I am sure to need in medical practice.

As founder and president of the successful UCL Chocolate Society, I need to be a resourceful and decisive, yet approachable team leader. Always open to new ideas, I am, nonetheless, capable of making the final decision; these qualities, I believe, would stand me in good stead as a doctor.

Upholding these positions of responsibility while excelling academically demonstrates my reliability and my ability to thrive under pressure, essential to medical practice. I am convinced that my scientific background and keen interest in Medicine further kindled by my practical experiences make me an excellent candidate. With my determined yet compassionate character, I am confident, that given the opportunity to study Medicine, I would be on my way to fulfilling my ambition to make a positive difference in people's lives.

12.22 Personal statement 22 (Graduate)

Personal statement successful for: Manchester, Warwick

The idea of being a doctor had always appealed to me, yet I put it aside assuming it an idealistic wish to save lives. Still, Science was the class I looked forward to. At 15 I devised a project concerning the effects of food and sport on fitness. Using these ideas I ran the Paris Marathon in the top 10%, proving my physical and mental toughness. I chose to study Physics at university for its role in all that is fundamental and intellectual challenge. Throughout I realised I needed a more people-oriented direction. I delved into the other side of my course – business. A six-week PwC Personal Development Course sharpened skills also needed as a doctor: teamwork, adaptability, and stress-management. On reflection, I discovered that the business world did not meet my ambitions of making a positive change to my surroundings.

I started over, and after much research I chose to pursue Medicine. This was the first time I was truly excited about the projected path. Previous work experience concerned with care further pushed this drive. My first caring role, at 16, was as a football trainer for kids. I learnt the balance between being a leader and a friend. Becoming a private academic tutor, a fulfilling job, followed this. Working intensely with a student, while creating a relaxed environment, required clear communication and patience. The following year I worked as a volunteer in a retirement home. As a general carer, I would chat to, read to, and feed the residents. I had much wisdom to learn from them, but it was pleasing to know they were grateful in return. Currently, I am volunteering in a hospital. This gives me the certainty that I love caring for others. It started off with patient-transport, which was great, as my first patient-contact. From other volunteers, some with 25 years' experience, I learnt the skills necessary: compassion, listening, and comforting. When a nurse said I was naturally talented with patients, it delighted me more than any compliment could have done. I gained more responsibilities such as teaching new protocols, and shadowing doctors in areas including diagnostics, the OR, therapy, and casting. Apart from seeing the real-life procedures, I learnt most by talking to doctors. They warned me of the downsides including exhausting work hours, the huge responsibility of patient trust, and the stress this brings. However, I have not heard of a field where everyone is unanimously positive. Once, when a patient feared for her life from a gastroscopy, I used empathy combined with the knowledge of the procedure to calm her. Events in my personal life helped me gain this caring asset. My brother has autism, and needs extra care that I helped provide with his support network. My grandfather had a major stroke, and I always find it touching to watch his children care for him daily. A specific interest in medicine came from my sister's PhD research into the metastasis of prostate and breast cancer. Related is the promising drug Abiraterone – only medicine could bring such exciting developments!

Still, without having a way to unwind, a doctor can underperform with severe consequences. I stay calm and focused by playing team sports, guitar, and trying out new activities – last year being Kundalini yoga. The Manchester Leadership programme, which entailed 60 hours' volunteering in the community, and learning about the role of leaders in society, including doctors, illustrated the social responsibilities. A doctor I shadowed put this in a practical way: 'Put yourself in their shoes – if they come in with only a broken ankle, you shouldn't be bored by it, but understand that this makes a huge difference to their life.' A great doctor needs to see this bigger picture.

Overall, the problems with the MMC should not discourage students into this field, and I believe that my experiences will let me socially and medically care for a diverse range of people, while being able to handle the tough decisions needed to be made for them.

12.23 Personal statement 23 (Graduate)

Personal statement successful for: Leicester

Working as a pharmacist has been a rewarding experience to date, and while it has allowed me to develop many key skills, I would like to be challenged further through a career in Medicine. As a pharmacist I believe I contribute positively to people's lives by offering health advice, medication counselling and lifestyle checks. However, a pharmacist has limited exposure in terms of patient contact and clinical involvement. As a doctor I will have an unrivalled sense of job satisfaction, becoming far more involved and directly impacting the decision-making process of patient care: diagnosing, treating and managing long-term conditions. I look forward to building on my current understanding of patient-centred care and the opportunity to study topics such as pathology and anatomy, which I did not cover as a pharmacy student.

Work experience at Walsgrave Hospital has exposed me to a broad range of specialities. I gained an appreciation of the multidisciplinary approach within healthcare and saw how the whole team contributed to patient welfare and the clinical decision-making process. I became more aware that a doctor must be able to communicate complicated, difficult and sensitive information effectively to a diverse range of patients. Moreover, I gained insight into the consultants' regard, not only for the physical aspects of the illness, but for the social, psychological and emotional factors concerning the patient, particularly with regard to discharging the elderly. Additionally, I have travelled to Ghana on a medical volunteering programme; this gave me an appreciation of, and another perspective to, our medical and social system in Britain. As my exposure to the work of doctors has grown it has increasingly strengthened my belief that making a significant difference to the lives of others on a daily basis is the ideal career path for me.

I am proactive within my community and volunteer in various care settings. At Selly Oak Hospital, I enjoy talking to patients and offer my companionship as much as possible. I also volunteer fortnightly at Calthorpe Special Needs School. I assist in teaching, play learning and encouraging children with differing abilities. These experiences have heightened my sensitivity to conditions such as autism and Down's syndrome and how human compassion requires a degree of understanding and sensitivity to specific behavioural, physical and sensory conditions. I volunteer for Right Start

Foundation as an anti-drug facilitator, and give advice on the misuse of drugs, which requires a non-judgemental approach and an ability to understand individual circumstances. I sit on the Board of Trustees for Birmingham Citizens, a community organisation that works with local institutions for social equality. I enjoy connecting with people from all faiths, cultures and philosophies.

In my free time I enjoy cycling and annually organise a charity cyclathon. I enjoy indoor climbing and play table tennis weekly. I co-host a weekly community radio show that demonstrates my excellent presentation and communication skills. I hope to cultivate these interests further whilst at university. I have travelled extensively, including many Third World countries, and it is a keen desire of mine to assist as a medical doctor in the future in such underdeveloped areas with a medical aid organisation like Médecins Sans Frontières.

I am excited by Medicine because it is not only academically challenging and demanding, but utilises an array of skills such as empathy, communication, teamwork and prioritisation. As a graduate I feel that I am already capable of the rigours of medical school and, even though I have observed the emotionally trying, not so glamorous and at times monotonous nature of a medical career, the opportunity to make a tangible difference in the lives of others is self-evident and ever-prevailing. I feel that I have the requisite skills of an excellent doctor and am keen to excel now at medical school.

13   List of action and power words

Here is a list of over 500 power words that you can use to give more impact in your personal statement.

Abbreviated	Abolished	Abridged	Absolved
Absorbed	Accelerated	Acclimated	Accompanied
Achieved	Acquired	Acted	Activated
Actuated	Adapted	Added	Addressed
Adhered	Adjusted	Administered	Admitted
Adopted	Advanced	Advertised	Advised
Advocated	Affected	Aided	Aired
Allocated	Altered	Amended	Amplified
Analysed	Answered	Anticipated	Applied
Appointed	Appraised	Approached	Approved
Arbitrated	Arranged	Articulated	Ascertained
Asked	Assembled	Assessed	Assigned
Assisted	Assumed	Attained	Attracted
Audited	Augmented	Authored	Authorised
Awarded	Balanced	Began	Benchmarked
Benefited	Bid	Billed	Blocked
Boosted	Borrowed	Bought	Branded
Bridged	Broadened	Brought	Budgeted
Built	Calculated	Canvassed	Captured
Cared	Cast	Catalogued	Categorised
Centralised	Chaired	Challenged	Changed
Channelled	Charged	Charted	Checked
Circulated	Clarified	Classified	Cleared
Closed	Coached	Co-authored	Collaborated
Collected	Combined	Commissioned	Committed
Communicated	Compared	Compiled	Completed
Complied	Composed	Computed	Conceived
Conceptualised	Condensed	Conducted	Conserved
Consolidated	Constructed	Consulted	Contacted
Contributed	Controlled	Converted	Conveyed
Convinced	Coordinated	Copyrighted	Corrected
Corresponded	Counselled	Created	Critiqued
Cultivated	Customised	Cut	Dealt

284

Debated	Debugged	Decentralised	Decreased
Deferred	Defined	Delegated	Delivered
Demonstrated	Depreciated	Described	Designated
Designed	Detected	Determined	Developed
Devised	Diagnosed	Directed	Discovered
Dispatched	Dissembled	Distinguished	Distributed
Diversified	Divested	Documented	Doubled
Drove	Earned	Eased	Edited
Educated	Effected	Elicited	Eliminated
Emphasised	Empowered	Enabled	Encouraged
Endorsed	Enforced	Engaged	Engineered
Enhanced	Enlarged	Enlisted	Enriched
Ensured	Escalated	Established	Estimated
Evaluated	Examined	Exceeded	Exchanged
Executed	Exempted	Expanded	Expedited
Experienced	Explained	Explored	Exposed
Extended	Extracted	Fabricated	Facilitated
Fashioned	Fielded	Financed	Fired
Flagged	Focused	Forecasted	Formalised
Formatted	Formed	Formulated	Fortified
Founded	Fulfilled	Furnished	Furthered
Gained	Gathered	Gauged	Generated
Governed	Graded	Granted	Greeted
Grouped	Guided	Handled	Headed
Helped	Hired	Hosted	Identified
Ignited	Illuminated	Illustrated	Impacted
Implemented	Improved	Improvised	Inaugurated
Incorporated	Increased	Incurred	Individualised
Indoctrinated	Induced	Influenced	Initiated
Innovated	Inquired	Inspected	Inspired
Installed	Instigated	Instilled	Instituted
Instructed	Insured	Integrated	Interacted
Interpreted	Intervened	Interviewed	Introduced
Invented	Inventoried	Invested	Investigated
Invited	Involved	Isolated	Issued
Joined	Judged	Justified	Kept
Launched	Lectured	Led	Lightened
Liquidated	Litigated	Lobbied	Localised
Located	Logged	Maintained	Managed
Manufactured	Mapped	Marketed	Maximised
Measured	Mediated	Mentored	Merchandised
Merged	Minimised	Modelled	Moderated

Modernised	Modified	Monitored	Motivated
Moved	Multiplied	Named	Narrated
Navigated	Negotiated	Netted	Noticed
Nourished	Nursed	Nurtured	Observed
Obtained	Offered	Opened	Operated
Orchestrated	Ordered	Organised	Oriented
Originated	Overhauled	Oversaw	Participated
Patented	Patterned	Performed	Persuaded
Phased	Photographed	Pinpointed	Pioneered
Placed	Planned	Polled	Posted
Prepared	Presented	Preserved	Presided
Prevented	Processed	Procured	Produced
Proficient	Profiled	Programmed	Projected
Promoted	Prompted	Proposed	Prospected
Proved	Provided	Publicised	Published
Purchased	Pursued	Qualified	Quantified
Quoted	Raised	Ranked	Rated
Received	Recognised	Recommended	Reconciled
Recorded	Recovered	Recruited	Rectified
Redesigned	Reduced	Referred	Refined
Regained	Registered	Regulated	Rehabilitated
Reinforced	Reinstated	Rejected	Remedied
Remodelled	Renegotiated	Reorganised	Repaired
Replaced	Reported	Represented	Rescued
Researched	Resolved	Responded	Restored
Restructured	Resulted	Retained	Retrieved
Revamped	Revealed	Reversed	Reviewed
Revised	Revitalised	Rewarded	Safeguarded
Salvaged	Saved	Scheduled	Screened
Secured	Segmented	Selected	Separated
Served	Serviced	Settled	Shaped
Shortened	Shrank	Signed	Simplified
Simulated	Sold	Solicited	Solved
Spearheaded	Specialised	Specified	Speculated
Spoke	Spread	Stabilised	Staffed
Staged	Standardised	Steered	Stimulated
Strategised	Streamlined	Strengthened	Stressed
Structured	Studied	Submitted	Substantiated
Substituted	Suggested	Superseded	Supervised
Supplied	Supported	Surpassed	Surveyed
Synchronised	Systematised	Tabulated	Tailored
Targeted	Taught	Tested	Tightened

Took	Traced	Tracked	Traded
Trained	Transacted	Transcribed	Transferred
Transformed	Translated	Transmitted	Transported
Treated	Tripled	Troubleshot	Tutored
Uncovered	Underlined	Undertook	Unified
United	Updated	Upgraded	Urged
Used	Utilised	Validated	Valued
Verbalised	Verified	Viewed	Visited
Visualised	Voiced	Volunteered	Weathered
Weighed	Welcomed	Widened	Withstood
Witnessed	Won	Worked	Wrote
Yielded			

14   Index of personal statements by medical school

For each of the UK medical schools, you will find below the list of personal statements shown in this book. A level entry personal statements are shown first in normal font, followed by graduate entry personal statements in bold.

Medical School	Personal Statement					
Aberdeen	11.6	11.16	11.26	11.39		
Barts	11.8	11.22	11.37	**12.6**	**12.10**	**12.14**
	12.18					
Belfast	10.4	11.42				
Birmingham	10.2	10.5	11.3	11.4	11.5	11.9
	11.13	11.23	11.35	11.36	11.40	11.42
	11.47	11.59	11.60			
Brighton	10.9	10.10	11.10	11.19	11.21	11.24
	11.31	11.44	11.63	11.64	**12.2**	**12.14**
Bristol	10.7	11.4	11.7	11.20	11.21	11.36
	11.49	11.50	11.52	11.53	11.61	11.65
	11.67	**12.2**				
Cambridge	10.5	10.11	10.12	10.13	11.10	11.21
	11.32	11.40	11.45	11.46	11.47	11.48
	11.49	11.50	11.51	11.52	11.53	11.54
	11.55	11.56	11.57	11.58	11.59	11.60
	11.61	11.63	11.64	11.65	11.66	11.67
	12.8					
Cardiff	10.3	10.9	10.11	11.3	11.4	11.11
	11.19	11.29	11.33	11.42	11.44	11.53
	11.61					
Dundee	11.16	11.26	11.39			
Edinburgh	11.21	11.29	11.39	11.46	11.54	11.56
Glasgow	10.4	11.16	11.39	11.57	**12.5**	
Hull York (HYMS)	10.9	10.10	11.2			
Imperial College	10.1	10.13	11.1	11.10	11.14	11.21
	11.22	11.23	11.32	11.37	11.42	11.48
	11.50	11.52	11.54	11.55	11.56	11.59
	11.66	11.67	**10.14**	**12.8**	**12.9**	**12.19**
Keele	11.26					

King's College (GKT)	10.1	10.13	11.1	11.3	11.13	11.14
	11.28	11.32	11.33	11.37	11.41	11.47
	11.48	11.52	11.56	11.67	**10.14**	**12.1**
	12.19					
Leeds	10.2	11.2	11.5	11.9	11.15	11.17
	11.27	11.30	11.36	11.41	11.65	11.66
	12.2					
Leicester	10.3	11.11	11.17	11.28	11.34	11.44
	12.1	**12.13**	**12.23**			
Liverpool	10.4	11.5	11.9	11.17	11.30	11.38
	11.58					
Manchester	10.5	11.8	11.15	11.27	11.30	11.51
	11.57	11.58	**12.22**			
Newcastle	10.3	10.6	10.12	11.6	11.15	11.18
	11.20	11.41	11.46	11.53	11.58	11.65
	12.5	**12.16**	**12.19**			
Nottingham	10.2	10.5	11.4	11.6	11.20	11.28
	11.31	11.36	11.46	11.48	11.54	11.60
	11.64	**12.11**				
Oxford	10.6	11.13	11.62			
Peninsula	10.9	10.10	11.11	11.19	11.31	
St Andrews	11.16	11.21	11.25	11.57		
St George's	10.1	10.8	11.7	11.43	**12.10**	**12.11**
Sheffield	10.2	10.3	10.6	10.12	11.2	11.3
	11.15	11.17	11.20	11.27	11.33	**12.6**
Southampton	10.8	10.12	11.12	11.18	11.35	11.61
	11.66	**12.7**	**12.10**			
UCL	10.7	10.15	11.1	11.7	11.10	11.12
	11.13	11.14	11.18	11.23	11.28	11.29
	11.32	11.33	11.34	11.37	11.40	11.47
	11.49	11.50	11.51	11.55	11.59	11.60
	11.62	11.63	11.64	**12.8**	**12.12**	**12.15**
UEA	**12.4**					
Warwick	**10.14**	**12.3**	**12.4**	**12.6**	**12.9**	**12.17**
	12.18	**12.19**	**12.20**	**12.21**	**12.22**	

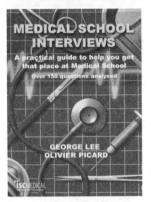
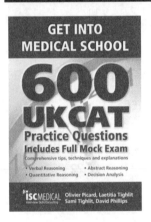